Feelin

Feelin

Creative Practice, Pleasure, and Black Feminist Thought

BETTINA JUDD

NORTHWESTERN UNIVERSITY PRESS
EVANSTON, ILLINOIS

Northwestern University Press
www.nupress.northwestern.edu

Printed in the United States of America

10 9 8 7 6 5 4 3 2 1

Library of Congress Cataloging-in-Publication Data

Names: Judd, Bettina, author.
Title: Feelin : creative practice, pleasure, and Black feminist thought / Bettina
    Judd.
Description: Evanston, Illinois : Northwestern University Press, 2023. | Includes
    bibliographical references and index.
Identifiers: LCCN 2022041756 | ISBN 9780810145320 (paperback) | ISBN
    9780810145337 (cloth) | ISBN 9780810145344 (ebook)
Subjects: LCSH: African American arts. | American literature—African American
    authors—History and criticism. | American literature—Women authors—
    History and criticism. | Emotions in art. | Emotions in literature. | Emotions in
    music. | Feminism and the arts.
Classification: LCC NX512.3.A35 J83 2023 | DDC 700.89/96073—dc23/eng/20220926
LC record available at https://lccn.loc.gov/2022041756

For Laura Ella Powell Grissom

poet, mathematician, mother of mothers.

Contents

Contents

Acknowledgments

I am grateful for the community that helped this project come into being over the course of many years and permutations. As it has been so long, please charge any forgetfulness to my head and not my heart. Many thanks to Elsa Barkley Brown, Deborah Rosenfelt, Sheri Parks, Psyche Williams-Forson, Michelle Rowley, Mary Helen Washington, A. Lynn Bolles, Seung Kyung-Kim, Bonnie Thornton-Dill, and Katie King. Warm thanks to Cliffornia Howard and Tiaria Harris.

This project and I have traveled and have thus benefitted from varied support in the form of colleagues such as Amanda Gilvin, Kevin Quashie, Christian Gunderman, Tanisha Ford, David Hernandez, Nate Therien, and the faculty and staff in the Five Colleges. Many thanks to Hermine Pinson, Jennifer Putzi, Victoria Castillo, Suzanne Raitt, and Gul Ozyegin at the College of William and Mary.

Thanks to Avery*Sunshine and Renee Cox. Thanks to the staff and librarians at the Stuart A. Rose Manuscript, Archives, and Rare Book Library. Big thank you to Micah Powell for sedulity. Thanks to Karla FC Holloway, Dorothy Roberts, and Sharan Strange. Thanks to Beverly Guy-Sheftall, M. Bahati Kuumba, Holly Smith, and the entire community at the Women's Research and Resource Center and the Archive at Spelman College. This thanks extends to the community of Sisterfire, founded by L'Erin Alta and sustained for many years in the hearts and minds of the genius weird folks at Spelman College. With Spelman in mind, I must also thank my dear Morehouse brother Joseph Barden.

I have benefitted from an amazing group of colleagues at the University of Washington, Seattle. Thanks to Kathleen Woodward at the Simpson Center for the financial support toward this project. Thanks to the Royalty Research Fund. Thank you to the WIRED collective, with special thanks to Habiba Ibrahim, Stephanie Smallwood, LaShawnDa Pittman, Rae Paris, Dian Million, and Latasha Levy. Thanks to Shirley Yee, Young Kim, Sasha Su-Ling Welland, Regina Y. Lee, Amanda Lock Swarr, Cricket Keating, Priti Ramamurthy, Michelle Habel-Pallan, Luana Ross, Nancy Kenney, and Angela Ginorio. Thank you, Kemi Adeyemi, for being a great incoming faculty sibling and friend. Huge thanks for the care and generosity of Chandan Reddy.

Thanks to the wonderful research assistants Bobbi Kindred, Fabian Romero, and Praise Idika who have helped this project and future projects at various stages. Thanks to the brilliant graduate students in my Black Feminist Creativity course who have thought along with me.

To the best cohort and first colleagues, Ana Perez, Rajani Bhatia, Mel Lewis, Safourah Norbakash, and Rachel Caidor, thank you. Many thanks to Angel Miles, Barbara Boswell, Jeanette Soon-Ludes, Lanice Avery, Wendy Thompson Taiwo, and Maria Vargas for sustained grounded extended family and intellectual community. Thanks to Savannah Shange, Ashante Reese, Ruha Benjamin, and Jessica Marie Johnson. Thanks to Tiffany Lethabo King and Izetta Autumn Mobley for the endless conversations on Black feminist pleasures, for talking me down from so many theoretical ledges, and generally for being sisters. I love you all with my whole heart.

Thanks to the community in Seattle for ushering me in and allowing me to land someplace soft: Ms. Briq House, Christa Bell, Kimberly Williams, Naa Akua, Helen K. Thomas, and Rezina Habtemariam. Huge thanks to Phillip B. Williams, Jericho Brown, Khadijah Queen, L. Lamar Wilson, Anastacia Renee, and Ashaki Jackson for poetry, for genuine love, and for huge belly laughs. Huge thanks to my sister-editor-friend Teresa Leggard, there are not enough words. Thanks to Ndelea Simama for long-lasting sisterhood.

I have had the benefit of love and mentorship from Ruby Sales and Cheryl Blankenship, and I am grateful to them as well as to pastors Christine Wiley, Dennis Wiley, and William T. Young, and the whole Covenant Baptist UCC Family. Many thanks to Aaron Myers, M.O.M. of the sacred and the secular. Deepest gratitude to Kimberly Brown, Lisa B. Thompson, and Christina Sharpe. Thank you, Jacqueline Jones Lamon, for everything. Many thanks to Janice Eteme, Thomas Young, and Charles Williams for the vocal tutelage that has sustained me through this project.

As I think about the thanks due my family, I am overwhelmed by the hard reality that this book began with so many more people who could pick this book up, read the thanks, then set the book down. They will have already known my thanks, now as I type it, think it, feel it. Thank you, Dear Ones named and unnamed here. Thank you.

Thanks to cousin Vermonja Alston for being a blueprint. Thanks to Aunt Faye and Aunt Margaret. Thank you, Aunt Katherine and Uncle Keith. Thanks to my cousins Keith II, Justin, Teyah, and Bryan. Thanks to my dad and my father Clifton Taylor and James R. Judd. Thanks to my grandfather, Bennie Grissom. Thanks to my brothers DaWayne and Anthony and my brilliant niece Angela Morris. Finally, deep thanks to my mother and matriarchal line. Thank you, Ella Juanita Taylor. Thank you, Laura P. Grissom. Thank you, Ella M. Powell. Thank you, Laura, thank you, Margaret, thank you all—for saying yes to us.

Feelin

Introduction: Feel Me

In the delirium of a felt life is the made thing and making a thing worth feeling for. I lose myself in the frenzied rapture called life, can attest to having felt, and in that heightened state of life—create. The evidence of creation means that I came out on the other side of rapture, and yet I am still in it. We now (me, you, reader, viewer, listener) are still in it, even as I may have moved on to the next thing. If I know anything, I know how to bend time this way—the pen, the flickering cursor, the soft flesh in the throat and its sound, the pastel's residue on my oily fingertips—my small bit of power the universe has given.

Living with arduous time—global pandemics, war, genocide, extinctions, and destruction of habitable lands and clean water—one could ask if artistic creation matters at all. If creative practice is frivolous, ornamental, or in poor taste in respect to our current conditions? To a question like this, I offer the poet's response in Ntozake Shange's *The Lizard Series*:

> that's why poetry is enuf/ eisa/ it brings us to our knees
> & when we look up from puddles of sweat/
> the world's still right there & the children still have bruises
> tiny white satin caskets & their mothers' weep like mary
> shlda
> there is nothing more sacred than a glimpse of power of the
> universe
> it brought james brown to his knees lil anthony too/ even
> jackie Wilson/ arrogant pretty muthafuckah he was/
> dropped/ no knee pads in the face
> of the might we have to contend with/ & sometimes yng blk
> boys bleed to death face down on asphalt cuz fallin' to our
> knees is a public admission to a great big ol' scarlet letter that
> we cain't/ don't wanna escape any feelin'/ any sensation of
> being' alive can come right down on us/ & yes
> my tears & sweat may decorate the ground like a veve in
> Haiti or a sand drawing in Melbourne/ but in the swooning/
> in the delirium/ of a felt lif
> lies a poem to be proud of/ does it matter?
>
> Can ya stand up 'chile?[1]

Well, how does it feel to live amid global disaster? What do you know of it? Disaster is here, has been here, will be here, even as we are torn up along with it. To run from feelin is to attempt to run from disaster itself—and exactly where are you going anyway? As the late Nina Simone said in a moment of grief for the very recent loss of Dr. Martin Luther King, "Folks, you better stop and think and feel again."[2] For it is not the feeling that is frivolous—but the avoidance of that feeling that orders destruction, makes it unremarkable, ordinary. And truly, even if you don't feel—feeling is likely to catch up to you, "no knee pads in the face."

This book is interested in how Black women artists take up our glimpse of power of the universe—how creativity makes its way through feeling and what we can know with the work left behind. It is interested for the same reason some of the artists' words and work direct us toward the creative process as one of self-revelation, exploration, and need. Toni Morrison has described her own impulse toward writing in terms of a need—a longing to read something not yet written: "Writing to me is an advanced and slow form of reading. If you find a book you really want to read but it hasn't been written yet, then you must write it."[3] Renée Stout describes her creative *process* as the very purpose of her art as well:

> While I can make a piece and think it's nice, I want to be on to the
> next piece, because I get everything from the process. The piece that
> I create is sort of the evidence of the process, but is also for the viewer
> to enjoy whatever it is that I was doing in my studio. But I want to be
> on to the actual act of creating the work.[4]

The work—that which is left behind—is evidence that something has happened here. We may enjoy the evidence of that experience in status—the gallery, the recording. And if we are lucky we might peek in to catch a glimpse of the universe's power in motion:

In the photograph, Edna Smith Edet's eyes are closed and her mouth is relaxed. If there is any expression here, it is inward.[5] She is in the moment of making music happen. We can tell by the blurred movement of her ring finger as she plays the upright bass. The scene is dark, but there is a hint of artificial light emanating from a square box above and to the left of Smith's head. Save for the shine from a metallic watch on her wrist, the glimmer of the tuning keys on the bass, and a soft light bouncing off her forehead, nose, and hand, the rest is darkness. We might see the silhouette of something in the background, but the light of the image is Smith herself in a moment of creative expression that we cannot touch or hear save for this remnant, for this evidence, a photo offering the only proof of this moment having taken place at all. Roy DeCarava is known for these kinds of intimate portraits, but I'd never seen one quite like this—a Black woman artist deeply in an internal space of creativity. What might strike the viewer is that it is hard to situate this photograph in time. Even the shadow of Smith Edet's clothes could be mistaken for a more recent era than 1955, when it was taken. There is nothing she is doing, no way that she is staged, no visual cue that says that she is in any other time but now.

Edna Smith Edet was a lifelong musician and music educator. In addition to playing with the International Sweethearts of Rhythm, an all-female jazz big band especially popular during World War II, she also led her own jazz trio, traveled to

Ghana and Nigeria to learn and teach Black diasporic music, and returned to New York to continue teaching music anthropology with an expertise in diasporic children's songs at Medgar Evers and Queens Colleges.[6] Her studies and recordings of Black children's songs and games are still available to us. Knowing all of that does not mean that I can glean what chord she was striking, how it felt to her, and how it felt to be in this moment of making. But I do have this photo.

And . . .

The sculpture was just an idea—a sketch of a monument that would never be cast or put on display. But for Meta Veaux Warrick Fuller it was worth keeping close in the small quarters of her attic studio. She would render more well known works from this same room where *In Memory of Mary Turner as a Silent Protest against Mob Violence* would sit—only a foot tall, unimposing in size but heavy in content—as a memorial for Mary Turner, who was brutally lynched by a mob in Valdosta, Georgia, in 1918. I wonder about this insistence on proximity. Necessary because the size of Fuller's studio was very small, but also necessary as a personal talisman—a remembrance of the stakes of living as a Black woman in America.

Figure 1. Photograph of Meta Warrick Fuller in her attic studio, 1919. Harmon Foundation Papers. Manuscript Division, Library of Congress, Washington, DC. Courtesy of John L. Fuller.

Here, Fuller is in her studio working at this sculpture (figure 1). She is in a smock, her hair only slightly disheveled. It is a drastically different photograph from the one of her in her parlor wearing the fashions of a middle-class woman in the early twentieth century. Again, though aware of the camera, and perhaps because of her smock and disheveled hair, she, like Edna Smith Edet, appears to be suspended in time—at work, without the trappings of the era, in an ever-present state.[7] The photograph is high-grain because of the technical limitations of low light photography at the time. It has not the artistic mood of the DeCarava photograph, but it appears as timeless nonetheless. The same sun emanating through two small windows, the clay forming underneath Fuller's hands—the clutter of her attic studio appearing as homely as anyone's attic.

If we are lucky, a photograph may be left behind. But what we usually have (also if we are lucky) is the art itself—the evidence of having been in the studio, the rehearsal hall, the desk. It is a gift if what we call *the work* is documented, published, recorded, or performed for an audience's pleasure. And it is work, isn't it? To develop a craft, hone it, master it, or deliberately choose not to master—to reach for something other than the craft itself. To collaborate, choose the precise color, brushstroke, lighting, chord, the most exacting word that would communicate the very thing, yes perhaps said before, but newly felt. "For there are no new ideas," as one poet said, "there are only new ways of making them felt."[8] This project is interested in that effort—in Black feminist thought made possible through art, what I call *feelin* or the affective sedulity of Black women's creative process that takes place in the studio where the work of art making, tinkering, experimenting, emoting, and sensing happens and may manifest in photographic series, collections of poetry, songs, albums, or not available to an audience at all. I am interested in the impulse to create because it was a book the writer needed to read, an image that brought the painter sinister joy to stroke through, or a note the vocalist needed to reach. This project is interested in the motivations, the will, and compulsion to make art through the weight of needing to feel, the *affective sedulity* that compels the artist to create—and most importantly, the knowledge produced in the "delirium of a felt life."

Those of us in the fields of critical theory, cultural studies, and feminist studies might have turned twice around in the so-called affective turn: the first into the complexities of emotion and emotion's relationship to knowledge and power, and the next, away from the bodies that inhabit, experience, and produce those feelings as knowledge. Patricia Ticineto Clough describes the affective turn as a transdisciplinary development that occurred "at a time when critical theory is facing the analytic challenges of ongoing war, trauma, torture, massacre, and counter/terrorism."[9] This list of terrible things to happen in the face of critical theory considered to be a developing moment specifically made legible through the works of European philosophers Gilles Deleuze, Félix Guatarri, Baruch Spinoza, and Henri Bergson is curious to me. Had not critical theory emerged in exactly these times of trauma, torture, massacre, and all of the other terrible endings of worlds? Had terrible things not preceded it? And if so, what of this gesture of a *turn* toward affect? Who does it serve now? This effort to cite a moment in which affect is an appropriate object to examine seems doubly curious to me as Clough further describes the affective turn as "[throwing] thought back to the disavowals constitutive of Western industrial capitalist societies, bringing forth ghosted bodies and the traumatized remains of erased histories."[10] Clough describes a warranted reckoning, no doubt, but I am left to wonder *who* has woken up to these atrocities and what synapses have worked to shutter or open their eyes? Had not thought long been "thrown back" to Western thought itself even as the accumulations of destruction and greed mounted for half a millennium? What forms of thought, what bodies are enabled to make such a reckoning within the discourse of this new affective turn? *Feelin: Creative Practice, Pleasure, and Black Feminist Thought* turns toward the body, indeed in the flesh of Black women by engaging discourses of emotion and affect as they already exist in lexicons of Black cultural production and Black women artists specifically. *Feelin* argues that Black women artists approach and produce knowledge as internal and complex sensation entangled with pleasure, pain, anger, and joy to name a few emotions, making artistic production itself the meaning of the work. *Feelin* intervenes in discourses in critical theory built on logics that would make terrible things a happenstance rather than endemic to the very circulations of discourse in which theory traffics. Discourses that would disembody feeling as knowledge only to put it back together pallid and disjointed. It expands notions of Black women's pleasure politics in Black feminist studies that are inclusive of the erotic, of grief and pain, of joy and shame, and the sensations and emotions that yet have no name.

Feelin as Sacred Knowledge

Feelin is interested in how Black women artists create knowledge in the studio by engaging emotion and sensation. It is curious about how Black women artists engage how racism, (hetero)sexism, and classism are felt and how those felt experiences are connected to Black feminist thought. It asks how Black women's art and artistic production negotiates, shares and acknowledges emotion as a form of knowing that, in Audre Lorde's terms, galvanizes radical thought into "more tangible action."[11] As Angela Davis notes in *Blues Legacies and Black Feminism*, "Art is special because of its ability to influence feelings as well as knowledge."[12] Feelin is a thing that I trace here through close, empathetic readings with the works of Black women artists who practice the visual, the literary, and the audile. By looking at Black women's art we are also looking at processes through which Black feminist thought engages mind, body, and spirit as knowledge or as Dian Million notes of Indigenous women scholars who "feel our histories as well as think them."[13] Here, Black women's creative production (as opposed to the products themselves) is Black feminist theorizing.

Audre Lorde greatly influences my understanding of feelin. I understand Lorde's essays "Uses of the Erotic," "Poetry Is Not a Luxury," and "Uses of Anger" to be Black feminist engagements with what is now being discussed as affect theory. Writing in 1984, Lorde cites the erotic as a source of knowledge of systemic forces, as well as knowledge of the power within us. She states: "In order to perpetuate itself, every oppression must corrupt or distort those various sources of power within the culture of the oppressed that can provide energy for change. For women, this has meant a suppression of the erotic as a considered source of power and information in our lives."[14] This book demonstrates that Black women artists willfully explore interiority.

Black feminist criticism serves as an interpretive lens, an invitation to creative thought and practice that allows me to wade through material that shares themes, motifs, and language that these artists have used in their creative meaning-making processes. I read Barbara Christian's "The Race for Theory" as a direct critique for pronouncements of theoretical turns as they plainly center the work of theorizing *as the production of critical thought*. There she states:

I have become convinced that there has been a takeover in the literary world by Western philosophers from the old literary élite, the neutral humanists. Philosophers have been able to effect such a takeover become so much of the literature of the West has become pallid, laden with despair, self-indulgent, and disconnected. The New Philosophers, eager to understand a world that is today fast escaping their political control, have redefined literature so that the distinctions implied by that term, that is, the distinctions between everything written and those things written to evoke feeling as well as to express thought, have been blurred.[15]

Christian makes the case for situating this particular "race for theory" as an intentional effort to reassert Western abstract logic as the reliable, publishable, and thus valuable form of meaning making—an effort which becomes increasingly palpable as Black women literary writers emerge on the very same scene. "For people of color have always theorized," she says, "but in forms quite different from the Western form of abstract logic. And I am inclined to say that our theorizing (and I intentionally use the verb rather than the noun) is often in narrative forms, in the stories we create, in riddles and proverbs, in the play with language, since dynamic rather than fixed ideas seem more to our liking."[16] This project takes Christian's assertion quite seriously, and offers that Black women's creative production outside of literary prose, which has long been a focus of Black literary criticism, is a valuable site of theorizing—to once again bring attention to the verb. However, this project does reach toward new ways of thinking, new frameworks for looking at and feelin Black women's creative production. As bell hooks has interjected, "Theory is not inherently healing, liberatory, or revolutionary. It fulfills this function only when we ask that it do so and direct our theorizing toward this end."[17] She describes theory's capacities for liberation as visceral, felt change that is integral for social change. In my efforts here to name the ways that racism and sexism are felt, and thus creative responses to those experiences must also be felt, I point this project in the direction of a "feminist theory, a feminist practice, a revolutionary feminist movement that can speak directly to the pain that is within folks, and offer them healing words, healing strategies, healing theory."[18] Black feminist theoretical texts serve as a companion here to the theoretical substance already endemic to Black women's art. Together with creative production, Black feminist criticism in the form of expository propositional prose assists in creating a foundation for talking about how Black women reveal the workings of our inner lives and make meaning of it in the world.

On the Holiness of Black Language
Regards to Ralph Ellison

In high school there was a white girl who stopped me in the middle of a sentence because she claimed that it was against her religion for me to say "I Am." While the Hebrew translation of אהיה אשר אהיה reads into the future "I shall be, as I shall be," perhaps it is fitting that I could say, "I Be" and not offend her by speaking myself into past, present, and future existence.

―――――

*Often translated as "I Am that I Am," the answer God gave to Moses at the burning bush when he asked for God's name in Exodus 3:14.

Black English is useful here as a way of speaking and knowing that asserts, as the above poem does, one's history and self-knowledge. You will find that I use the standard term *feeling* here to describe sensations as they are widely understood, but *feelin* is a term I use to describe holistic sensory experiences as knowledge. *Feelin* is a term rooted in diasporic Black speech. As a verb, *feelin* encompasses cognitive understanding as well as affective, bodily response to an object. It is different from "understanding" an object, in that *feelin* brings the subject into active, identity-shaping response but more aligned with the concept of overstanding, or "profound knowledge and insight, over and beyond that of mere 'understanding.'"[19] Linguistic scholar Geneva Smitherman discusses the importance of style and shifted meaning across time and its meanings for the Language across time and identity in her book *Talkin and Testifyin*. The verb "to be," for example, marks habitual or continuing conditions when the word "be" is stressed. However, the word is omitted when such conditions are not recurring.[20] In order to denote the stylistic and phonetic uses of the term, I've dropped the "g" in "feeling" to say and mean feelin. Feelin sounds this way in the mouth, and dropping the g in what would be a gerund fixes the term in the present progressive. Feelin is most always used after the verb "to be," and most often after the implied or present phrase, "I am." In the present progressive, feelin marks self-hood and time.

Feelin is the experience of knowing tinkered with in the process of creation. In the process of creation, one can explore the possibilities of being that are to one's own pleasures and needs. I am proposing that creative knowledge production is so self-centered, a kind of self-centeredness that is transcendent—beyond oneself—which would allow for the creation to exist outside of the studio and have others feel it too. Kevin Quashie offers an approach to the concept of Black female subjectivity through a one-ness that is self-centered. This oneness is not individualism, but relationality, in which being is constantly unfurling, in a state of self-creation and definition. "Oneness, " Quashie observes, "is a relation, a habitat that facilitates one's being to all that is around, beyond, within it—a capacious and transcendent inhabiting."[21] Not to be confused with two-ness, seeing oneself through the position of another, nor individualism, oneness makes possible ways of being that are both connected to a collective and audaciously self-centered.

Feelin denotes a moment of self-knowing and experience. In an instant, they who experience feelin acknowledge sensations in the body. Something touches them in a core of knowing and identity in time. The word *feelin* signifies something deeper than its corollary term, "feeling," which is defined in verb form as

9

the ability to "have a sensation, impression, perception, or emotion"; in noun form as, "senses relating to sensation or touch"; and as an adjective, "capable of sensory perception" and "conscious, sentient."[22] *Feelin* appropriates and elevates "feeling" through emphasis and context.[23] *Feelin* incorporates this "standard English" definition while giving particular emphasis to the experience as one that happens in a place beyond tactile sensation, emotion, or thought. To be feelin something is to touch, experience, be impressed upon, and sense something in all matters of being: physical, intellectual, and spiritual.

Feelin is what Claude Brown would call "soul language."[24] Its meaning is inferred in the way that it is pronounced, and that pronunciation signifies its connection to spirit and soul. The sound of *feelin* has its own pitch and cadence, which it is important to approximate in my written rendering. *Feelin* is pronounced FEEL-uhn rather than FEEL-een. This particular *utterance* of "feeling" to produce *feelin* enhances the music of the term and points to the signification of its multilayered meanings. According to Brown, "it can be asserted that spoken soul is more of a sound than a language. It generally possesses a pronounced lyrical quality, which is frequently incompatible to any music other than that ceaseless and relentlessly driving rhythm that flows from poignantly spent lives."[25] This is why it is important in my use of it here, that I do not place the apostrophe as often used to communicate a kind of broken English. An apostrophe would mark an incompletion in relation to the word "feeling." *Feelin* is related to that word but is a concept on its own, complete in its use here. Feelin is a reality, a deep-down-in-your-bones way of knowing that, like haunting, is not "cold knowledge" but "transformative recognition."[26] *To be* feelin as verb is to experience, to be open to experience, and to identify, be identified by stimuli. It is a way of being called, chosen into recognition and overstanding.

There is also the use of *feelin* in the form of a noun that signals moving inward to sort through thoughts, emotions, *and* feelings as in the phrase, "I got in my feelins." This means that one has taken something personally. To get in one's feelins is to make the decision to reflect, to acknowledge that emotions are giving one information, and to listen closely to that information. It acknowledges the interconnected aspect of knowing and sensation as it happens in the body. The body may experience lethargy, hunger, loss of appetite, bloat, sudden bursts of energy, all of which signal emotions packed with information. To get in one's feelins demands cognitive pause and reflection.

To speak of feelin is to deal with states of being across mind, body, and spirit. *Feelin* implicates all three at once. As a bodily way of knowing, it reverberates in the spirit and the mind. In order to navigate through feelin, I engage aspects of experience that cross these boundaries. It is at the site of creative production that the artists I discuss here articulate these reverberations. Therefore, in order to engage with their work, I have to engage with what M. Jacqui Alexander calls sacred subjectivity—a particular way of knowing that allows for subjugated knowledges to emerge.[27] The use of the terms *soul* and *spirit* here signify on experiences that can be described as existential—identity as it exists outside of the realm of the mind. These terms are not intended to bind the subjects in a particular understanding of religious experience or even a particular mode of understanding one's identity. Instead, they are deployed to give room to the many ways in which the artists' works explored here articulate consciousness and experience differently. Born from a language in which "I am" is articulated as "I be," the power of feelin marks time in the present while also implicating the past and the future. Alexander describes spiritual time and space in this way:

> Spirit brings knowledge from past, present, and future to a particular moment called a now. Time becomes a moment, an instant, experienced in the now, but also a space crammed with moments of wisdom about an event or series of events already having inhabited different moments, or with the intention of inhabiting them, while all occurring simultaneously in this instant, in this space, as well as in other instants and spaces of which we are not immediately aware.[28]

To be feelin—is to recognize currents of knowledge already running through an individual. However, the acknowledgement of getting in one's feelins, or feelin something marks time. One is feelin in the moment, getting in one's feelins for a moment, but even that time is not linear. The moment at which one is feelin something is also the ringing of the familiar (as in memory and the past), the experience of the present, and what may be perceived to know habitually and into the future.

As an experience through which body, mind, and spirit inform at once, feelin makes self-knowledge. One, "is" or "be" through feelin because it occurs at the core of one's self. The moment one acknowledges feelin, it is a signal to move inward—continuing a process of knowing. Something already within an individual has been struck or awakened into speaking. Alexander speaks of a similar experience through diasporic iterations of African diasporic spiritual systems like Voudon and Lucumi. To know oneself in these spiritual systems is to know the currents, Orisha, and spirits already running through the nexus of mind, body, and spirit. To know these spirits is important business for practitioners because without knowing, Alexander states, "we could indeed not address subjectivity of any kind."[29] Therefore to "know who follows you" is to truly know the self. This process of knowing is tenuous: "Knowing who walks with you and maintaining that company on the long journey is a dance of balance in which the fine lines between and among will and surrender; self-effacement and humility; doing and being; and listlessness and waiting for the Divine are being constantly drawn."[30] To know who follows you mandates what she calls "traveling to the interior," and surrendering oneself to spirit.

Spiritual self-knowledge and the processes toward introspection guide the efforts of what I call affective sedulity—the impulse, desire, and rigorous relationship toward felt knowledge. Feelin is the shorthand for affective sedulity in verb, noun, and adjective form—it is a cultural formation of the aesthetic value of felt knowledge as both common practice and particular experience. This particular focus on felt knowledge resituates the very concept of knowledge and thus its transmissions, transmutations, and forms of habit. For what would the concept of the rational human be useful, if sedulous engagement of *felt* knowledge is valued as knowledge?

As Nina Simone demanded of her audience in her performance of "Why? (The King of Love Is Dead)" at the 1968 Westbury Music Festival days after the assassination of Dr. Martin Luther King, "You better stop and think and feel again." This book shares her sentiments. Another way to state this is that this book is feelin Simone on this one. Simone's demand for thinking and feeling emerges from her mourning and rage and is also an invitation to experience the assassination of

King through rage and mourning. Her urgency is felt through her musical styling: her vocal timbre; how she edges out the lyrics by tightening the vocal chords and giving us the impression of limited breath; the improvisational function of the ad-lib as she changes the lyrics and takes us out of the expected meter and rhyme of the song; and the arresting nature of the bridge and coda where improvisation takes over and the instrumentals seem to slow and build. Her demand for the audience to think and feel undercuts the consistently methodical, restrained, and logical tactics of civil rights activism and co-signs Black folk's right to rage and mourning at the profound loss of the icon and leader. Those tactics which were efforts to humanize Black folks through respectability and peace for Simone were not effective because this country would, without remorse, react violently to even the most civil and appeasing (what would be called "logical") actions of Black folks.

I'm feelin Simone on this because it seems as though—for me, over here in this work at the nexus of Black and gender studies, efforts to be included into the order of knowledge have been unsuccessful thus far. I'm feelin Simone on this one even if I am not imbibing or even understanding her precise emotions—I can recognize the value of those emotions, their direction, and more importantly, can think and feel with her. This project, with Simone, asks that we think and feel again, not toward a mythical past of better relationships to knowledge, but again in the sense of repetition, ritual to remind ourselves that we always do feel, and thus, thinking could never be done without feelin it. And what could we learn anew if we were to recognize and honor that knowledge?

Affective sedulity invites us to dig deeper into registers of knowledge through feeling. This project takes up Black women's creative production, the work engaged in the studio, and highlights singular affective registers and engages those registers through the art itself and the conditions under which the art was made. Because creative process itself is multifaceted, this project takes up a limited number of affective registers as diving boards for deeper study: joy (and thus mourning), shame (and thus pride), Black grief, sacred sexual ecstasy, and anger. The decision to take up these particular affective registers emerged from direct engagement with the art as well as the prominence of the feeling in Black feminist study engaged with the topics and engaged by the artist whose work and creative practice is discussed here.

For example, Black grief is encountered here as a lens through which to read both Black studies and my own very personal grief while penning this book. I pause here in order to do the work of grief and ask that you feel me, mourn with me for a moment as I reflect on personal and collective loss through a catalog of Black grief. Joy emerges in Lucille Clifton's poetry because of her own insistence on joy in her life and work—yet what also emerges in sedulous study of her poetry is the complexity of joy and its relationship to mourning and sadness. Feelin her atheology of joy necessitates a depthful discussion of religious and secular humanism. Ecstasy is explored through the timbral and stylistic vocal practices of Black women singers. Ecstasy here is read through the lyrical content and stylistic quality of R&B singer and choir director Avery*Sunshine and other Black women singers who perform and experience ecstasy through vocal practice. Feelin Black women's vocality invites listeners to succumb to sacred sexual ecstasy. Shame also emerges in this book as an affective register by which images of the Black maternal figure have circulated. The specter of racial shame and images of demeaned Black motherhood coalesce at mythical images of Black maternal figures such as the mammy, the matriarch, the welfare queen, and so on. Black women artists have engaged the visual field of Black motherhood, and my reading of the photographs and multimedia sculptures of Renee Cox, Betye Saar, and Deana Lawson will explore how twentieth- and twenty-first century formations of Black maternal imagery have informed this visual field. I discuss anger, because—well—how could I not discuss Black feminist thought and emotional registers without engaging the trope of the angry Black woman or the Black feminist mandate to embrace anger as righteous fuel? These points of entry—grief, joy, ecstasy, shame, and anger invite us all to feel these artists' work and Black feminist interventions on Western humanism and its Cartesian obsessions.

Pleasure and the Black Feminist Oceanographic: Genres of Knowledge Production

Nikky Finney writes of the clitoris:

> New studies show
> The shy curl
> To be longer
> Than the penis,
> But like Africa,
> The continent,
> It is never drawn
> To size.[31]

The cartographer or the poet? One who has already mapped the effable terrains of desire, circumscribed the possibilities of fungibility, and graphed relevance by size. The cartographer is by vocation, topical. She takes up the human concerns of trafficking feet, the efficacy of building edifices, and access to much needed oxygen. But Nikky Finney, the Black and lesbian poet, directs us to the depths of pleasure by water, where "desire can rise," "refuses retreat." While there are indeed many cartographies of desire, and the fields of Black and gender studies have drawn our attention to the geographies of terror and belonging that shape Black lives, here I follow a path of desire with the poet/oceanographer who begins with the knowability of pleasure "9cm deep / in the pelvis." Likening this subjugated physiognomy to less than understood geography, Finney draws lines of epistemological grounding between that which can be understood, should be understood, and is likely to be intentionally misunderstood. What science names the female, the female pelvis, and its possibilities for climax and pleasure; what is known as the continent of Africa and its size both geographically and historically are all named and known on mis-mapped, and mis-named grounds. The poet points toward the watery otherwise knowing, to the negative space of the continents—the oceans—that in their depths provide location of the largest clitoris known to humans.

To succumb to desire, to ask these questions, is to risk drowning, but perhaps Black studies of the Atlantic have taught us that we have already drowned, that we are in the wake of that drowning. That is, as many Black theorists have taught us, Black subjectivity in the Americas is forever connected to/shaped by/in processes of becoming through what was lost through racial injury—made metaphor by the Atlantic Ocean's abyss. What do we make of ourselves in this abyss? What are our possibilities of becoming, of self-determination, as chaos in the flesh, as dwellers of no-land? It is no surprise then, that Black feminist thinkers have long been questioning and reaching for answers for the possibilities of joy, of pleasure in such conditions.

Let us consider our metaphors: Black female sexuality has been described as "black (w)holes," left unspoken of by the "culture of dissemblance," "awaiting their verb" and otherwise resistant to limited paradigms that cannot attest to the particular, queer, expansive possibilities of Black sexuality and gender.[32] All of these assertions seem to be dire descriptions of what can never be known but what they actually attest to is that what may be called Black female sexuality (even this moniker of "Black female" has critical meaning) cannot be named through the language and terms by which we understand sexuality or gender—and thus I'd argue, what we understand as pleasure.[33] Finney invites us into the waters, invites us into new and expansive ways of knowing that do not limit our bodies to land, using a Black queer lexicon of desire, by centering mammalian clitoral pleasure that exceeds the human penis in size. What now to the sexologist, the psychoanalyst is the penis in relation to the clitoris? How do logics of gender and sex upend with this knowledge? In the poet's ocean, the logics of gender and sex are exposed for what L. H. Stallings would call the "biopolitics or necropolitics of asexual cutlures."[34] Finney opts for the "unknowable and immesurable." She points toward the possibilities of knowing that are otherwise wrongly mapped. These are ways of knowing that Black queer poetry makes possible. Ways of knowing that I navigate here in attempting to analyze not just the work of Black women artists but the workings, the feelings, of our inner lives as knowledge production.

What I want to say is that Black clitoral pleasure and its position as subjugated physiognomy (even if by metaphor) has its own means of charting its own "discursive terrains."[35] These means are produced in the creative field where Black women, nonbinary, trans, and queer folks are able to use many tongues that witness to the manifold ways that Black bodies have been subject to injury, abjection, and yet, also, pleasure.

It might be of some importance to those of us dedicated to language to be precise in the uses of terms here. Pleasure is defined in the *Oxford English Dictionary* as: "The condition or sensation induced by the experience or anticipation of what is felt to be good or desirable; a feeling of happy satisfaction or enjoyment; delight, gratification. *Opposed to pain*."[36] One might immediately see why pleasure is such a fraught concept in Black feminist thought. It is in the Atlantic that Black bodies became what Hortense Spillers calls "flesh" characterized by the suffering of human bondage, bodies without the perception of sensation and simultaneously an open wound. Black flesh is ungendered and as such, it has been of particular difficulty to talk about Black sensation without also, and quite immediately, talking about the system that would deny Black people—and in particular Black women—the utterance of sensation. That utterance, according to some, has been mired by a culture of pain that, if taken into a hedonist understanding of the concepts of pleasure and pain, is antithetical to possibilities for speaking of pleasure and pain at once.

Of course, sexual practices which center pain would be otherwise proof of the fallacy of this dichotomy, and as such, the axes of power and play in matters of who can experience or inflict pain float to the surface of this messy discourse of pleasure and its multiple moving parts. But according to Amber Musser, Black women have been relegated to the underside of "the discussions of masochism."[37] Either as subjects who are the embodiment of pain, or inured to pain. Black women, in effect, are illustrative flesh upon which others' desires are projected—even the desire for pleasurable pain.

Deborah Walker King's concept of *blackpain* describes the Black body as the image of suffering in the United States. When pain on Black bodies is read, it is often devoid of the Black skin which suffers it. King states, "Blackpain has a metonymic function as a sign of social, economic, and cultural woundedness that can be co-opted by anyone suffering in a manner associated historically with black people."[38] King continues by noting the way in which white first wave feminists deployed Black pain as a mode of "reading" their own struggle for visibility. In this example, the suffrage movement in the United States activated by invoking blackpain in chattel slavery as unjust insofar as suffering is imagined to be incurred by white women who do not have the right to vote.[39]

Rebecca Wanzo's study of Black women's suffering in the media highlights Black women's particular lack of access to sentimental narrative in which our pain would be perceivable.[40] This disembodied understanding of pain in which pain and suffering exist in the social (even as currency) implicates pain's symbolic attachment to the flesh of black women. Symbolic attachment does not include the material of those bodies in pain, but further obscures the internal experiences of Black women. Black women's pain can never be *read* on the bodies of Black women because Black women are symbolically and perpetually bodies of pain.

I have previously written about the medicalization of Black bodies which differentiated medical subject from white master, and freak-show Americana from American.[41] Flesh is medicalized where the body is human, and as such, the fleshed body is without its I. It is subject to, not subject. It looks like pain but feels no pain. It pleasures but does not feel pleasure. Pleasure is a sensation equally difficult to trace and troubled for Black feminist scholars who would also give utterance to Black women's pain otherwise unsentimentalized as such. The legacy of the Atlantic, the specter of interracial rape that permeates race relations in the United States further problematizes the possibility to utter pleasure in the din of pain. There is within Black feminist thought a ritual of speaking about pleasure *in spite of* or in efforts to *break silence*, to challenge what Darlene Clark Hine calls "the culture of dissemblance," intended to protect middle-class Black women from a particular kind of pornotroping—hypersexualization in favor of a more challenging, often difficult conversation about Black women's sexuality and, within it, the possibilities of pleasure.[42] In my reading of the texts above, neither pleasure nor pain are given concepts as they relate to discourses about Black female experience.

Pleasure in its dichotomous rendering mobilizes pleasure as absence of pain save for the curious concept of sadomasochism in which pain *is* pleasure. Pleasure without pain is not possible for Black women, particularly in the visual world, and yet to describe the broad stroke of Black women's lot in pleasure seems to continually orient Black women's pleasure toward structures bent on Black women's annihilation. Jennifer Nash differentiates pleasure from ecstasy in her study of racialized pornography in order to make clear the aspects of sexual enjoyment that may not be "pleasing," but indeed center representations of Black female pleasure.[43] By reading racialized pornographic texts for signs of possibilities of pleasurable enjoyment within the racial script, Nash reveals how Black women's pleasure is possible within the pornotroping white gaze. Not in spite of it, but with the grain of it. This is one kind of charting—to describe ecstasy is to note an *otherwise* form of pleasure that belies or rather, deeply reveals, one's politics. Not in spite of racial subjugation, but deeply embedded within racial subjugation because we are raced subjects, living and learning in a racist world. I agree with Amber Musser that masochism is an important analytic with which to think about Black women's pleasure.[44] I do take it up here as masochism and sadomasochism emerge as important lenses through which to analyze the interstices of power and pleasure, particularly in chapter 4, where I discuss the image of shame and Black motherhood. However, in order to make room for otherwise possibilities of articulating sensation, I do not couch all pleasurable sensation within this framework. To do so, in my mind, would be to start at a location other than the creative moment in which pleasure is created and ever unfolding. As I said, I am interested in the creative *process* as knowledge producing, and the affective experience within creative production holds within it registers of pleasure complex and otherwise.

Diving deeper, L. H. Stallings proposes the concept of *funky erotixxx* for discussing Black female pleasure that exceeds Western patriarchy and its medicalization of Black flesh. She defines funky erotixxx as "unknowable and immeasurable, with transgenerational, affective, and psychic modalities that problematize the erotic and what it means to be human," that "can be made legible in sexual cultures rather than the biopolitics or necropolitics of asexual cultures."[45] *Funky erotixxx* demonstrates a uniquely Black transatlantic understanding of sexual pleasure that exceeds the limited boundaries of the Enlightenment's human subject by which Black folks have been defined in opposition.[46]

I am influenced here by L. H. Stallings's reframing of the meaning of sex work as inherently sacred and necessary to survive in the new world.[47] Creative production, or art *work* here presumes "art as experience." Stallings's intervention on the idea of work is key to this study in that it tags M. Jacqui Alexander's push toward a transdisciplinary approach to spirit work that centers Black women's self-knowledge through spiritual knowledge, acknowledges the erotic compulsion to engage such work with the sacred, and situates this particular way of knowing as a practice for survival. Stallings identifies the libidinal current of life in the New World mandated by logics of capitalism and post-Enlightenment thought by centering the Black aesthetic practice of funk and its sacred profane. She states, "Sacredly profane sexuality ritualizes and makes sacred what is libidinous and blasphemous in Western humanism so as to unseat and criticize the inherent imperialistic aims within its social mores and sexual morality."[48] Funky erotixxx thus challenges the bifurcation of the sexual and the sacred, exposing how Western humanism's hypocritical profiteering from social mores and sexual morality through libidinal economies is inherent to its imperialist project. Funk as an aesthetic practice that does a lot of work in all aspects of Black life runs counter and *irregardless* of hegemonic logics and "reminds us that there are aesthetics, or rather trans aesthetics, of sexuality that can aid in the creation of neoteric modes of being human."[49] As this project is invested in the erotic functions of creative practice, I understand its making, and the processes of making of the artists engaged here as erotic, err, sex work.

I am also drawn to Stallings's discussion of work and the erotic for a key point about the structure of what we call pleasure, particularly in Black feminist discourse. Western humanism's formulation of sexuality, sex, the erotic, and thus pleasure is so dependent on concepts of sexual morality and social mores that define respectability, and particularly genres of the human. It is Western humanism's formulation of sex, what Stallings calls "asexual cultures," that valuate pleasure along axes of morality and its relationship to suffering. These logics also valuate the nature of work itself. To take up sacred sexual work is to make a series of deliberate choices to be and feel in the world and approach existence itself through a different set of evaluative processes or aesthetics that make sacred and sexual work—the erotic—important and resistant to the social mores and moral structures of dominant logic. The impulse, deliberate choice, and rituals of engaging funk are what I call affective sedulity. These are the rigorous practices that value messy feelings that make way for different modes of being. What these scholars attest to is that the means of charting Black pleasure are complex and cannot begin or end with notions of sensation that are couched in the same frameworks of difference/sameness, flesh/body, human/nonhuman in humanist study. Pleasure is both individuated and relational, embodied and spiritual.

It is quite compulsory for this project to engage in a discussion of studies of affect with the guiding hand of Black feminist thought as Black feminist thought has always asked that we reorient ourselves to suppressed forms of knowledge. Patricia Hill Collins's foundational intervention on Black feminist thought describes Black feminist thought through the lens of the "social construction of knowledge." Through a feminist standpoint, feminist scholars are able to negotiate power relations in the production of knowledge and privilege the knowledge held by those who are disempowered.[50] Standpoint theory, specifically, was formulated in opposition to positivist forms of knowledge production set forth through Enlightenment-era notions of truth and rational thought.[51] Collins expands the notion of knowledge production by citing the ways in which Black women's actions and everyday experiences are instances of Black feminist knowledge production.[52] Under Collins's decree, not only are prototypical figures such as Sojourner Truth progenitors of Black feminist thought, but women otherwise unnamed in history—domestic workers, mothers, my grandmother—are producers of a particularly Black feminist way of knowing.

Black feminist thought is found in the places wherein Black women have most been able to create. According to Collins:

> An historically oppressed group, U.S. Black women have produced social thought designed to oppose oppression. Not only does the form assumed by this thought diverge from standard academic theory—it can take the form of poetry, music, essays, and the like—but the purpose of Black women's collective thought is distinctly different.[53]

The purpose of Black feminist thought extends beyond feminist actions for social or civic equality but even more deeply to affirm Black women's experiences. Black women's creative and life-affirming work also taps into the workings of our inner lives. According to Collins, "U.S. Black women intellectuals have long explored this private, hidden space of Black women's consciousness, the 'inside' ideas that allow Black women to cope with and, in many cases, transcend the confines of intersecting oppressions of race, class, gender, and sexuality."[54] In her influential call for a Black feminist criticism, Barbara Smith notes that the deep desires and lived experiences of Black women, otherwise rendered invisible in the real world, are legible in Black women's writing.[55] These interconnections indicate that feminist action and feminist thought are interwoven with "the state of Black women's literature" and that a Black feminist movement would "open up the space needed for the exploration of Black women's lives and the creation of consciously Black woman–identified art."[56] Therefore, in developing a robust body of scholarship that centers the lives of Black women and their feminist work, Black feminist thinkers have had to develop a distinctive Black feminist criticism.

When I say Black feminist thought and note its relationship to Black women's creative production I am not ascribing a particular virtue of Black feminist thinking or allegiance and identity to individual artists. Instead, I am writing in the tradition of Black feminist thinkers who draw on the everyday knowledge of Black women as distinguishing features of Black feminist thought. That is, the particular knowledge that Black women and nonbinary people hold that unfolds from the conditions of our lives to reveal a map toward otherwise possibility is feminist thought. As Daphne Brooks notes of Black women musicians on this matter,

> Black women's musical practices are, in short, revolutionary because they are inextricably linked to the matter of Black life. Their strategies of performance perpetually and inventively philosophize the prodigiousness of its scope. But also—and quite crucially—Black women's musical practices are revolutionary because of the ways in which said practices both forecast and execute the viability and potentiality of Black life.[57]

The contours of the gender and race politics of individual Black women artists may make or unmake the revolutionary potential of the work, and here is the crucial commentary for thinking with Black women artists. As Black feminist scholars may disagree deeply, as scholars in the field of Black studies might have full-on arguments with each other, the quality of creation that makes way for Black life is at the core of why we gather here. I am interested in how Black feminist thought can come to contradictory problems and tarry with them. That is, to engage in forms of curiosity, ways of thinking *with* that revel in possibilities unforeclosed and constantly emerging. Black feminist thought as improvisational and sedulous—cunning and inventive.

> *Black women have long possessed 'magical'*
> *powers and told their daughters stories.*
> —MARJORIE PRYSE[58]

The rich legacy of Black women intellectuals engaging with the literary work of Black women writers in a way that is both scholarly and familiar informs the mode of this project. By approaching Black women's art in the genres of literature, photography, and music this project engages with the concept of Black women's literary traditions while also attempting to expand the analysis through creative production and across critical disciplines.

Developing a critical lens and a familiar sensitivity is perhaps responsible for the ways in which Black feminist intellectual work has engaged familiar language otherwise taboo in academic parlance: the incorporation of pronouns such as *we* and *our*, the use of familial naming in reflections on the meaning of Black feminist writing as Farah Jasmine Griffin and Alice Walker offer, the insistence on the use of Black language in engagements with such knowledge production are but a few examples.[59] The familial relationships imagined by these scholars who are moved to read Black women's writing echo the very substance of Black feminist life-affirming work. Black feminist scholars are called to Black women's writing as Black women are called to write—affirming each other in the process. Mary Helen Washington describes this circle of affirmation in terms of a distinctly Black women's literary tradition. In *Invented Lives* she states: "Women talk to other women in this tradition, and their friendships with other women—mothers, sisters, grandmothers, friends, lovers—are vital to their growth and well being."[60] This "talking to each other" occurs in the circle of Black women readers, scholars, and writers, and within the literary work of Black women as well. As Washington observes in the work of Black women writers collected in her edited volume *Invented Lives*, "A common scene recurring in at least five of the eight fiction writers in this collection is one in which women (usually two) gather together in a small room to share intimacies that can be trusted only to a kindred female spirit. That intimacy is a tool, allowing women writers to represent women more fully."[61] This circle repeats, unbroken, within the pages of the work of Black women writers, their own lives, and the interconnected bond in which Black feminist scholars read their work.

Instructive to this project is Deborah McDowell's deployment of archival research and interviews that consider the context and the lives of Black women artists. This is a direct rejection of the behest of literary analysis (via Roland Barthes and Michel Foucault, among others) that critics set aside the author's experience as instructive to reading their work. McDowell takes up the contestation that Black women's lives are intricately interwoven in our art, and places it directly within academic discourse. According to McDowell, "Despite the power and appeal of Foucault . . . it is not yet time to toll the death knell for the 'author' or for 'literary tradition,' although we must proceed with more complicated definitions of 'tradition' and how it functions."[62] Not only is it imperative that Black women writers' lives be considered parallel to their work, but the tradition in which Black women writers write must also be reconsidered as Black cultures operate nonlinearly.

Hortense Spillers offers a mode of reading Black women writers that observes a tradition in which Black women engage literary work in a nonlinear relationship to time.[63] It is a circular tradition in which Black women writers are most freely able to engage in discourse. Any other understanding of their discourse would be simplistic. She states, "It is exactly the right not to accede to the simplifications and mystifications of a strictly historiographical timeline that now promises the greatest freedom of discourse to black people, to black women, as critics, teachers, writers, and thinkers."[64] The metaphoric circularity of discourse proposed by Spillers occurs again in Bernice Johnson Reagon's account of the spiritual song tradition carried on by Black women in which spiritual songs and freedom songs speak across and to each other.[65] This kind of circularity highlights how Black women artists, across genre, speak to each other across time and space.

Black women's speaking with each other necessitates these kinds of border crossings between the public and private, the personal and the political, the creative and the scholarly. Black women speak with each other in discourse and this book project through modes of call-and-response that affirm, disagree with, and elaborate on each other's work. In her study on Black women's caring and accountability, Marsha Houston notes that Black women's communication with each other across generations and within communities operates on a level with which truth can be found in many voices and held all at once.[66] To speak in a circle across time and space is an apt metaphor that includes the concept of non-linear literary traditions, and for the purposes of this study, the time relative to knowledge production itself and the evidence thereof.

Regarding ellipses: Entering into Tongues is like entering into something already begun. No so much as getting into a car and starting the engine, but having left a car running and returning to it for warmth. It was already there, motor humming, pistons firing. It is as if you were already speaking, and realized it. (Has that ever happened to you? You suddenly become aware of your own speaking?) Its like that. In that sense, there is no observable beginning and you begin to doubt if there is an end.

In the humanities we call this Discourse.

Figure 2. Still detail of "S.i.T.Experiment" by Bettina Judd, 2011. Hover your mobile device over the QR code to navigate to http://dr.bettinajudd.com/sit-experiment.

It is in honor of this circular tradition that I put Black women artists in conversation with each other in this project. Throughout, I pull quotes—snatches of knowing—that speak back to and in chorus with other Black women writers, scholars, and artists. These thinkers speak to each other, talk to and about each other, and signify on each other's thoughts. In a circle, everyone's face is forward and the voices and expressions of those in the circle converge at the center. It is in that center that the diverse, complicated, and sometimes contradictory shared experiences and knowledge held by Black women converge.

This project imagines a circle of knowledge. As artist-researcher (and daughter) who has been called to this project, I speak with these women through the familiar, conversing in the languages germane to our conversation. I am aware that in my speaking this conversation began even before this project started. The unbroken circle of Black feminist discourse necessitates that this project practices what it preaches—that is that I speak in the familiar and engage in our shared modes of knowledge production. Black feminist knowledge production, we know, must necessarily exist outside of academia and thus what I call the compulsory language regime of expository propositional prose. That is, the common parlance of theoretical discourse by which knowledge production is recognized in the academy: the monograph, expository language, propositional structure, and prose itself. While I must traffic in it here as one professionalized in the institution and in need of the rewards of such labor in which the corporate structure of academia mandates forms of knowledge production—the processes of review, tenure, and promotion; while I might even find pleasure in reading and engaging the expository propositional prose of my colleagues and elders, this book intends to push the boundaries of the form of discourse just a little bit by incorporating creative works as they are engaged here in the project as evidence of knowledge production, and as language that explores other evidences of knowledge production. Here poetry, narrative, image, video, and sound crop up in the text not as illustrations of a concept, but as a continuation of the discourse set forth in expository propositional prose. That is, engagement with artistic production here—my own and others'—is as integral to the prose more often given credence as rational and therefore communicable thought. More than understand, I want you to feel me.

The conditions by which artworks are produced very much function in the way that we will need to think about pleasure. Art *work* is also produced in the same world in which oppression and hierarchies of difference are produced—that is art *work* is dependent on labor and the structures by which capital, labor, and consumption depend. The value of art and its work is also valuated by the same regimes of knowledge that organize genres of the human and thus the work itself is in conversation with the effects of those forces. As *work*, art practice labors under the same forms of duress and coercion that any other work is produced. (As I stated above, so too, does this particular work that you are reading.) This means that art *work* is subject to and responsive to a market—its negotiations with knowledge are also within the parameters of that market and the market's logic. Nowhere else is this more evident than in the necessary and rich genre of the artist statement by which art may be translated and therefore valuated by logics of scarcity and novelty value inherent to capitalist art markets.

The Artist Statement—Methodologies and Methods

I research my mother's anger. What I really do is try to be a good daughter. While I do not purport to think exactly as all of them do, I do wish to attempt to "complete [her and their] thoughts."[67] My interest is in understanding who they are and the subtle tether between us that connects experience, knowledge, survival strategies, and strategies for thriving.

I could tell many stories about many mothers, first with my family and spreading outward to all of the Black women who have in some way nurtured me. I wish to make it clear that I do not wish to limit who these women are to the role of nurturers of anyone or anything but their own lives. For even as my own mother has in many ways nurtured me as a mother, what I have found most valuable and what I explore in my work are the ways in which she has nurtured her own life in art.

The first instrument that my mother gave me was my voice. It was an instrument that could not be taken from me unless I no longer used or cared for it (something that she warns me about even now). She demonstrated its purpose and power by using her own voice daily and for all occasions. When she was full of sorrow, worry, joy, or elation, she sang. She would put on a record or play her black standing piano and sing. She would sing in the car, me tightly buckled in next to her. Her rich, classically trained soprano would hit a note cleanly with no vibrato, yet something within me would shake. I would join her on such a note and something deeper within me would move. This sound and feeling would shift the air, alter the space; heavy feelings would lift, and there would be joy. She would perform and something would move within others—she shifted the energy of others, all while changing within herself. She thought of her voice as something that is to be used in service to the divine and others, yet the grace of it allowed for it to most dynamically change her life. She learned the power of creativity as something deeply personal and imperative for "feeling good" by example. When I was ten years old and showing interest in poetry, my mother set an unpublished manuscript of poetry written by her mother on the little white desk in my bedroom. These tools helped me to figure out my place in the world, and at the very least express my frustrations with it. It helped me to think about the sexism and violence in our home, it helped me to respond to the violence that was outside of our Los Angeles doors in the high tensions of the early '90s. That early desire for depth and understanding led me to poets, musicians, artists whose expressions touched on all of this—whom I could feel.

By focusing on the homegrown artistic practices through which Black feminist thought is created, I hope that my work highlights not only the contributions of Black women artists to feminist thought, but also the feminist practices within African American culture that place Black women squarely within a politic that is concerned with the status of women broadly and Black women specifically. Examining knowledge production beyond the academy or the gallery is important to a more holistic understanding of Black feminist thought. My research compels me to look at aspects of knowledge production that are so often avoided in the academy. Such knowledge production practices include spirituality, politics of emotion, and memory.

This kind of work requires me to work on levels of academic production that are both traditional and creative. This project oscillates between academic prose, creative writing, and other media in order to demonstrate the overarching artistic and scholarly approach I have to knowledge and creative production. As such, you may find that I refer to this book as a project—as it is imagined beyond its binding. I will primarily focus on expository propositional prose while incorporating as much as possible my own creative work that is set out to explore this topic.

In the process of writing this book, competing modes of meaning-making crowd my efforts. The research project, within the parameters of academia, requires a statement of project, a research question, clear and definitive declarations of meaning making. Scholars reveal not only our methods of research practice but also the methodology that informs those methods. We review and unpack theories upon which the basis of our inquiry is defined. Everything is seemingly revealed by this structure through expository propositional prose.

I am also impelled by practices, methods, and methodologies of art practice.

These practices have their own sets of methods and methodologies to consider because of the market in which they are produced. The rise of the importance of the artist statement in the art world, liner notes, prefaces, forewords, epigraphs by the poet, and astute interviews and lectures by all of the above, gives voice to artists who, otherwise, have said all that needs to be said in their work.[68] The artist statement and project description are outlines of the methods, methodologies, and theoretical frameworks of the creative trajectory of an artist's work—even over large swaths of time. What makes it compelling as a document is that it is intended to be both autobiographical and technical while also communicating some reason for the creative product's journey into being.

The artist statement is a document for which the primary use in the art world is business-related. Artists train to craft precise statements for grant opportunities, residencies, and gallery spots. The statement is as imperative to an artist's marketing as the art itself. The artist statement is also an artist's whisper into the ear of their audience. Its informal uses of personal pronouns and sometimes erudite use of academic language performs the artist as both deeply introspective and well read. From it, we expect to learn not only about the art but about the artist's intentions. By foregrounding the market based uses of the artist statement I do not mean to imply that artist statements are disingenuous. What I mean to point out is that these documents represent knowledge in markets similar to the academic market of project statements and proposals. That is—we are all compelled to produce knowledge in expository form, for exposition is the privileged language of positivist discourse wherein process, logic, and reason are seemingly simplified, universally shared, and thus consumed. In short, exposition makes the opacity of creative thought legible to the rational market of consumer-based capitalism and expository propositional prose is the mandate to be legible to the regime.

But we do what we must, right?

To describe my methods is to contribute to a circle of knowledge in which creative processes are as informative to truth and experience as the art that is produced. The creative practices of Black women artists *are* also their lived experiences, and as such, are included in my analyses of their work. *Feelin*'s central argument is founded on the idea that art is experience. That is, that Black women's creative process is also experience. Informed by Black feminist critical theories in the fields of literature, I include and highlight Black women's lived experiences in the context of discussing their work. As such, archival research, interviews, and reviews of interviews conducted by myself and other scholars and journalists inform the framings of discussing these artists' work. Also, cued by Black feminist criticism, I deploy close readings of these women's poetry, photography, and music, which enhance and drive the modes of discourse and knowledge production I observe.

Feelin's objective to take seriously how oppression is felt and thus how resistance is felt necessarily finds use in Amber Musser's "empathetic reading practice," which "illuminates how subjectivity and power act in concert with embodied experience" and functions as a "critical hermeneutic and methodology in that it highlights how we can discern the structure of sensation in various texts/performances and it works to give those sensations meaning, which in turn allows us to read difference in a sensational mode."[69] This kind of reading practice facilitates a sensitivity to tone and style in the artworks, which keys us in to the particular affective registers explored here.

23

ART PRACTICE AS RESEARCH

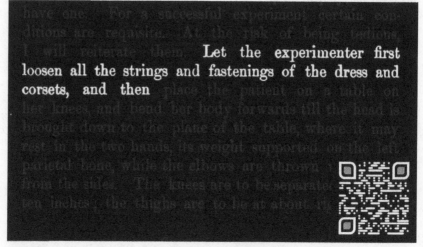

Figure 3. "Let the experimenter first loosen all the strings and fastenings of the dress and corsets, and then." Still detail of *Run on Sentence*. Bettina Judd, 2011, digital image. Hover your mobile device over this QR code to navigate to the full video at http://dr.bettinajudd.com /run-on-sentence.

My methods of art practice as research are informed by autobiographical experiences of knowing through creative production, affirmed by theories by women of color, as well as burgeoning scholarship that explores the inherent connections between ways of knowing and creative production.

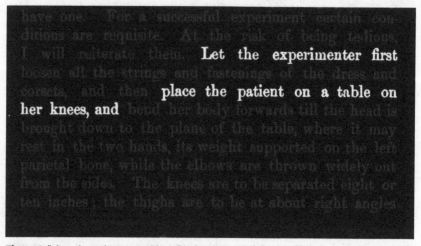

Figure 4. "place the patient on a table on her knees, and." Still detail of *Run on Sentence*. Bettina Judd, 2011, digital image.

These processes are representative in the series of images that recur in my project *Run on Sentence* in which I black out and highlight various passages from J. Marion Sims's book on uterine surgery. By highlighting parts of his text, I draw attention to the sexual, racial, and class tensions that are prominent in his work. These tensions are perceivable in this work through tone, space, and punctuation in his writing—particularly the frantic experience of reading this run on sentence in which Sims attempts to explain how to observe the female pelvis. His instructions read like a Harlequin novel while remaining cold and calculated. Eventually, Sims reduces the female body to a right triangle in order to sterilize the sexual anxieties barely hidden in the text.

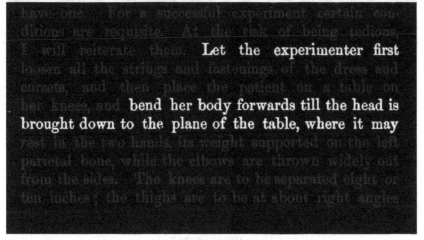

Figure 5. "bend her body forwards till the head is brought down to the plane of the table, where it may." Still detail of *Run on Sentence*. Bettina Judd, 2011, digital image.

This connection between the inner life and artistic production challenges notions of knowledge as exclusively located in empiricism. In order to postulate that art practice itself can be research, artist-researchers must also consider feelin and the inner life as valuable information. It is for this reason that artistic practice, the processes through which artists engage the inner life and create, is both method and data. This kind of information is unfixed, its contours developed by experience and context. In his essay, "On the Difference between Artistic Research and Artist Practice," composer Germán Toro-Pérez states that, "We can describe art experience as sensuous experience, and the result of artistic activity as form perceivable by the senses if we understand form not as solid shape, but as the possibility of relationship."[70] When we are considering the internal world of the senses to be valuable information, art practice is the research method.

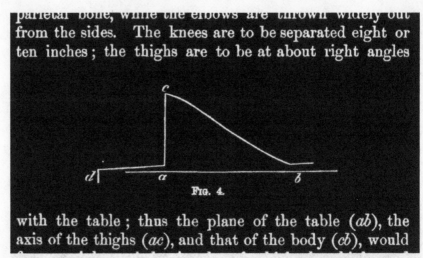

Figure 6. "diagram of the subject." Still detail of *Run on Sentence*. Bettina Judd, 2011, digital image.

Just as in scientific research, artistic research practices involve trial and error and ethics of rigor. Art practitioners are always experimenting with new materials, new concepts, and techniques as a part of the art practice in order to come to an end result. Rigor in the arts is tangled in opening up new opportunities for experiences of art.

> *There are no new thoughts, only new ways of making them felt.*
> —AUDRE LORDE[71]

Just like other inquiries in the humanities, art practice is grounded in the understanding of knowledge as relational. As artist-researcher and Black woman in the academy, I am prone to code switching, speaking in my multiple tongues, multiple modes of discourse. As I write in the mode of academic prose, I am also thinking in the poetic and attempting to fully capture the visual information that informs this project. This code switching is not only in language, but also in discipline, making this a necessarily interdisciplinary project. This project attempts to make connections between art practice and Black feminist knowledge production, newly felt. As Graeme Sullivan states, "The aim of research in the visual arts, as in other similar forms of exploratory inquiry, is to provoke, challenge and illuminate rather than confirm and consolidate."[72] Visual art practice is a form of knowledge production where transformation rather than fixed knowledge is the goal.

The art practice that takes place in this book is executed and represented in relation to archival research, theory, close readings of artists' work, and interviews. I include visual art and poetry that I executed before I began *Feelin*, and published or created while *Feelin* was still in progress. Including this work demonstrates the circular and ongoing nature of knowledge production and situates the project itself in the realm of experience. It reveals how my processes of developing questions explored here were seeded in creative practice. The artwork is in conversation with the Black feminist critical framework that operates throughout this project. It is also in conversation with the themes and concepts discussed in each chapter, including joy, the mystical, ecstasy, motherhood, and sexuality. Further, the art and poetry in this project converse with bodies of knowledge that exist outside of this book; as such that work has a secondary life. This fact highlights the scope and immense possibilities for what art practice as research is capable of accomplishing, and also reveals the relevance of the premise behind *Feelin* to further research/art projects. The goal is to make room for new thought—to be able bend toward new ways of thinking. As Anzaldúa states:

> Rigidity, means death. Only by remaining flexible is she able to stretch the psyche horizontally and vertically. La mestiza constantly has to shift out of habitual formations from convergent thinking, analytical reasoning that tends to use relationality to move toward a single goal (a Western mode), to divergent thinking, characterized by a movement away from set patterns and goals toward a more whole perspective.[73]

I would like to, for a moment, say a word about the structure of the texts and images in this project. As I stated above, this project deploys modes of code switching and cross-conversation in which image, academic prose, poetry, and lyric by me and other women artists are represented as "speaking to each other." I am influenced by the hybrid writing style of women of color cross-genre writers Gloria Anzaldúa and D. Soyini Madison in which border crossings occur at the site of language, critique, and poetry. I am also influenced by the performance writing mode deployed by playwright and director Sharon Bridgeforth, who, in an attempt to visually represent the improvisational jazz aesthetic that shapes the performance of her plays in her scripts, uses varied placement and font styles to represent different (and same) voices.[74] As I stated above, the creative work in text here is not intended to be illustrative nor addendum, but is the next sentence, the next paragraph, the next thought in what has been offered in expository propositional prose. Sometimes the forms of knowledge production live beyond the page as video or sound, and I hope that readers experience the next line of the book by using the QR code with your mobile device, or by navigating to the link to which the code directs. I invite readers to engage in this hybrid way of sharing knowledge as I, too, communicate through this broken tongue. I say it again: more than anything, I want you to *feel me.*

We begin this foray into feeling with a Black study of grief. This first chapter takes up my personal grief, yes, and places the experience of personal loss on the altar of Black studies, which—I argue—has been a study of Black grief. Influenced greatly by the interventions on the field of Black studies by Toni Morrison, Christina Sharpe, and Saidiya Hartman, this chapter reflects on how it feels to be left behind. As a means of refusing the expository which would, in my view, gloss over the intimacy and immediacy of feeling grief, the bulk of this chapter is a series of fourteen lined poems that find interspecies community with the grieving mother orca, Tahlequah, who in the summer of 2018, carried her dead baby calf through the Salish Sea for seventeen days. In writing these poems, I was able to access my own grief from having lost, not only my father that same summer, but at least thirteen other loved ones since my move to Coast Salish lands in 2016. The poems are a practice in affective sedulity, where I feel and think through the meaning of mourning through text. I acknowledge the presumed opacity of this form of writing and feeling in the series' introduction where expository propositional prose is relegated to footnote and video is offered as meditative guide to the text. By challenging form endemic to the book format requisite here, this chapter reveals the affective modalities of the expository, the poetic, and the visual in addressing grief.

Continuous with this exploration of grief as Black study, the second chapter, "Lucille Clifton's Atheology of *Joy!*," explores Clifton's poetic midrash on the Garden of Eden story as an intervention on discourses on the human in theological and humanist discourse. In a 2000 interview with Michael Glaser, Clifton frames joy as ethical and theological imperative made possible by acknowledging suffering.[75] This particular kind of affective sedulity—to deeply touch and acknowledge suffering—makes room for the possibility to experience the complexity of life. I use the term *atheology* after Ashon Crawley in order to mark the ambivalent relationship to any one religion or philosophy, especially western philosophies that would never acknowledge Clifton as a human subject. Beginning with one of her most famously known and deeply felt poems, "won't you celebrate with me," the chapter proposes that the central figure, one who is "born both non-white and woman," exists on a bridge between earthly flesh matter and Lucifer, the divine outcast, in order to make of herself something altogether new. The chapter then traces this atheology of joy through close readings of Clifton's poetry and creative process evidenced in her archive through reams of automatic writing and transcripts of conversations with the dead. I place Clifton's atheology of *joy!* in conversation with Womanist theologians and Black liberation theologies, as well as Black humanist theories, and find her in conversation with all of these approaches to the theodical question: Why do bad things happen? For Clifton, *joy!* explains how acknowledgment of the difficult, as well as pleasure, makes up a complex life.

Continuous on matters of the sacred and the sacral, chapter 3 goes on to unpack the ecstasy in the vocal work of Aretha Franklin and Avery*Sunshine's vocal performance. In order to listen to Sunshine and really hear her, really *feel* what she has to say, the chapter first exposits the aesthetic grounds by which Sunshine's craft might already be understood in the music of Aretha Franklin. There, we might observe the genre-crossing transaesthetics of the sacred sexual. Through such close readings, feelin is explored through the ecstatic sensation of singing, or as Bernice Johnson Reagon names, "running sound through the body."[76] Singing in both sacred and secular contexts emerges as a ritual that involves intense pleasures: the sensations of ecstasy—simultaneously one with carnal flesh and the divine on sacral and sacred planes that reveal the erotic's use in sacred sexuality. The chapter takes up L. H. Stallings's formation of funky erotixxx and sacred sex to argue that the craft of singing itself, the vocal tricks, the blues scale and harmonies are modes of practicing sacred and sexual ecstasy in the body. Where musicologists and those in cultural studies remark on the stylistic similarities of gospel and the blues, this chapter examines closely what makes those stylistic choices—growls, squalls, and layered harmonies—sacra-sexual.

Chapter 4, "Shame and the Visual Field of Black Motherhood," takes up the visual image of Black motherhood and its association with racial shame by analyzing the visual art of Renee Cox, Betye Saar, and Deana Lawson as visual practices of negotiating with the image of racial shame via the Black maternal figure. I analyze these images through the lens of Black feminist thought's critiques of the family and the myth of Black matriarchy propagated by the infamous Moynihan Report—including the critiques of Hortense Spillers, Angela Davis, and Tiffany King. I argue that feelin motherhood involves navigating these troubled and over-determining images of Black mothers—a navigation that is not necessarily blissfully joyous, but troubled with shame against the bodies, sexualities, and life choices of Black women.

Chapter 5, "Toward a Methodology of Anger," encounters feelin through method. It takes up the trope of the angry black woman as a signpost of subjugated knowledge and offers anger as a methodology to practice affective sedulity in scholarship and life—that is to follow where Black women's anger and the threat or accusation of Black women's anger leads. Urged by the foregrounding scholarship on Black women's anger and the insurgent image of Black womanhood by Audre Lorde and Hortense Spillers, I identify three texts of rage demonstrating how reading tone and homing in on the narrative and language of Black women accused of and experiencing anger produces otherwise subverted forms of knowledge. The first text is Nina Simone's "Mississippi Goddam," which serves as a document of Simone's rage at the murders of Medgar Evers in Mississippi and of Addie Mae Collins, Cynthia Wesley, Carole Robertson, and Denise McNair in Alabama and her own trajectory as an artist that was very much shaped by racism and segregation. I also take up the process of writing my first collection of poems, *patient.*, mining for the experience of anger that lay beneath the creative process, and finally, I revisit the transcript of the arrest of Sandra Bland, which led to her untimely and suspicious death, using Sharpe's method of redaction and annotation to focus on Bland's language, tone, and thus unwavering insight on the dangerous encounter with the officer which ultimately led to her death.

The book closes with considerations of the apocalypse. How might thinking through the pleasure-producing creative process inform the way we might thrive after yet another world-ending event? What does feelin matter when we are faced with the inevitable collapse of all that we know? Denise da Silva's Black feminist poethics anticipates the event and the import of Black feminist visionary creativity.[77] June Jordan spoke of always expecting the end of this world.[78] At this end of this book we return to the Black queer poetics that center Black women's pleasure as a locus of knowledge production—of interacting with the world. Taking Finney's metaphoric cue discussed earlier, Black feminist oceanographics urge for new and more depthful means of charting Black women's desires, where, like the ocean, there are unknowns, and largely our imaginations shape what we feel we know of its depths. This chapter takes up the work of Jacqueline Jones Lamon, Aracelis Girmay, Dionne Brand, Alexis Pauline Gumbs, Tourmaline, and Adjua Gargi Nzinga Greaves, all of whom, I propose, engage in this Black feminist oceanographic work. It is in the oceanic where *Feelin* sets out a claim for those of us interested in Black women's pleasure, interior lives, and Black feminist epistemologies: Black women's creative production demonstrates how Black women artists have their own means of charting pleasure, interior lives, and even our methods of knowledge production that are holistically grounded in mind, body, and spirit.

To return to the poem above by Nikky Finney, I ask, what are the things that we know that we know about the ocean?

This is the thing about engaging Black feminist thinking concerned with plea-sure: we are a part of this world that has developed our imaginations and the limits of our imagination. We take part in those limitations and occasionally are titillated by them, and we may wholly be invested in our pleasures toward them. The complexities of our lives find us squarely in spaces where how we have been read is what we have been reading. Which is to say that the language and ideology that we have to describe our lives snaps us right into a one-dimensional place. It's hard to see ourselves in this kind of maze. As Angela Davis notes, "What we often assume belongs most intimately to ourselves and to our emotional life has often been produced elsewhere and has been recruited to do the work of racism and repression."[79] What pleases us just might (and often does) please our oppressors. What do we do with that? Whatever it is that we must do, this book argues that we do it not by disregarding the internal life, but by engaging it in order to root out the structures by which we find our internal lives shaped.

There is already a legacy of Black lesbian poetry that has told us about this. Here, Nikky Finney gives us language for desire while critiquing Western modes of knowledge that would find clitoral pleasure small if insignificant. She chal-lenges cartography and also biology through the lens of pleasure. For what is the scale by which we measure the organ of pleasure for mammals? Which is another way to ask: Where does pleasure begin? End? This is what Black lesbian poetics has done, and a Black feminist pleasure poetics can do. Finney previously set forth another theory of Black queer women's pleasure in "The Making of Paper" while paying homage to her mentor Toni Cade Bambara. In the moment of situating herself within a tradition of Black feminist writing and declaring her dedication and love for Bambara, Finney recounts Toni Cade's final request of her: "some paper and what about one of those fat juicy pens?"[80] Bambara's sensuous descrip-tion of a pen marks the function of pleasure between the two women through the written word and the act of creating those words. It foregrounds the full-bodied response Finney writes. Finney's exuberant response to being the one to offer Toni Cade Bambara her last ream of paper and pen is that her pro-tree politics would not stop her from, in fact, chopping down the biggest tree and making the paper for Bambara herself and take deep hyperbolic pleasure in "slash[ing] its lovely body / into one million thin black cotton rag sheets."[81] Finney is offering here Black feminist theories of feeling that layer the daily possibilities of plea-sure with erotic pleasures. The creative process that is writing, the pleasure of being tasked by your mentor to assist in that pleasure and doing that work, the damage in doing that work, the intimacies that occur between two Black women in intergenerational creative practice takes up Lorde's "Uses of the Erotic," which proclaims the possibilities of pleasure in collective work and creative production among women and through the erotic. Lorde states, "That self-connection shared is a measure of the joy which I know myself to be capable of feeling, a reminder of my capacity for feeling."[82] It is the capacity for feeling that makes pleasure a possibility and rhetorical focus. The capacity for feeling at all, pleasure and pain, must also be addressed. The complexities of their coexistence and perhaps inter-dependence is the deep diving work that must be done as messy, slippery, wet though it might be.

It is at feelin where I would like to begin. A concept that not only encompasses pleasure, but centers it in a wide capacity of experience that would otherwise be denied to Black women. I want to talk about feelin the way that my people talk about feeling. The ways of knowing in a complex world that make up who we are. Ways that are not simple, or neat, but quite messy and irresponsible. Feelin that is nasty in every Black sense of the word nasty: sexual, raunchy, rude, messy, unfavorable, and on. Feelin as sensation, and possibility that is practiced through creative practice. It is both heady and theoretically complex, and yet, every day regular-degular. Here, I will talk about our way of knowing: my mama, my cousins, the way alla-us know that we know that we know.

CHAPTER 1

A Black Study in Grief :: Salish Sea

Something in my chest is always wailing. Its constancy marked by the sudden jolt of feeling one has when one finds themselves to be wailing. First the crack, then the moment of opening, then the sound. **It is the sound that opens wide everything else**. The sound, the crack, the opening, each punctuated by a more tender picture turned morbid: the way I held her hands that would never get warm, how we pulled rings from her fingers, a single tear on her cheek. I am abandoned, or have I abandoned her? My opened-mouth utterances do not know the difference.

Once, an elder asked me, "Bettina, what are the Black studies people saying about grief? There seems to be a lot of stuff on sorrow, but not grief," and I paused because surely much had been written on grief. **It seemed to be embedded in the language of Black life**. "The blues?" I questioned. "No," she said. **"Loss?"** "No, Black grief," and I thought some more. I think I feel the difference. This grief thing had a weight to it that hung differently within and outside of the body—weather *and* habitus, more particular and yet more consuming than sorrow. I was coming closer to a felt understanding of what she was asking for. Grief had to have been written about because it's clearly here, it's all around. Perhaps this was a fish in water thing. **I know that we discuss grief because we are often *in* grief here on the page**. In what appears to be digression—**grievance**, **grifting**—grief is really a very visceral state of both *being* in between and *being aware of being* in between states of life and death, of remembering who is lost and—**how we too, the left behind, might be lost**.

What might it mean that grief is the matter all around us? That grief is the very lexicon of Black study? What meaning can be made of the accumulated corpses—the work of counting them? Who or what are we, after we have counted? Who or what are our dead? I opened up a recently acclaimed tome, it begins with a litany of loss, another spoke of survivors' remorse, another about the inevitability of death for Black women writers, another, a list. **The epi-thing of inquiry always recounting, negotiating, attempting to undo the inevitable tripping over the dead that comes from this line of work**.

As for me, in the summer of 2018, **I sat down to work on this very book and could only wail in poems**.

To be a study of Black study. **To be living a footnote to a text about Black life, which is inevitably about death**. I had an accumulated number already. In the summer of 2018, I'd packed up my too-expensive apartment and that very day was told that my father, James Russell Judd, had joined that number. I finished packing, wrote a poem, went to his funeral, read it, and went on to research joy in some archives. Carry on. The number, you see, of my very recent dead, the dead who had the nerve—or the patience—to die between the summer of 2016 and the summer of 2018 had climbed to eleven; less than a year later, with the death of my stepfather—twelve; in that same month, my cat; months later another great-uncle—and the number isn't the point. I am sure that the number is nothing to some losses, and that's what terror and loss gets you—comparisons to other terrible losses. **The number doesn't matter, shouldn't matter**. Logics of capitalism and all that. I live under capitalism. **This book has to be written so that I can survive it and I carried on, I carried it**. The number wasn't what was making my back ache, my blood pressure spike. It is the never quite slowing, never putting it down but appearing to have put it down, carrying the continued living of this life between and during each death. **This Black grief is an accumulation of feeling** unprocessed, un-process-able, untimely, and unnamed. It is the regret, the severed ties held barely by the once living now gone, it is the march of time and status: elder, eldest, new youngest, dependent, dependable. It is the questions around deaths and the possibility that they could be alive if—if there was no war, if medical care was fair and free, if doctors believed that Black people experience pain, if self-medicating wasn't so useful, if he didn't avoid the doctor, if there was no gun violence in Baltimore, if Black folks weren't so damned prone to dying young, if their heart hadn't been broken so often and without relief, if they were never on that boat. It is the loss of patience gifted by the light of life now lost. It is the dream of the dead and waiting for the dead in my dreams. It is having to be reminded they are dead because, how in the world could I forget? But I forgot because it is too much—too much to feel—to know at one time. Remembering takes it (what is "it"? life, breath, will?) out of you the same way you learned the first time.

They gone, remember?
Remember, they gone.

At the coffee shop. Leaving the doctor's appointment. Holding her hand. Coming home from work. Watching TV. Cooking dinner. In the middle of a fit of tears for another. ***Remember? They gone***. And what, publishers, reviewers, colleagues, tenure committee, do you write of that? And what, dear Black feminists, can I say of pleasure in that?

We carry it, we carry. Each life and the moment of losing that life. Each question, and missed chance for that last. You hold the living tight. You hold the dead tighter and some days you let go.

If you remember.

Salish Sea | A Grieving Meditation

For Tahlequah and her baby.

With gratitude to the Indigenous people and stewards of the lands and waters of the Salish Sea: the Coast Salish, including the Duwamish, Samish, Snohomish, and Puyallup tribes.

For Uncle Leroy
For Capella
For Jalan
For Nia
For my dad, Clifton Leo Taylor
For my father, James Russell Judd
For Aunt Cheryl
For Aunt Katherine
For Angelique
For Cousin Cookie
For Uncle Keith
For Aunt DeeDee (Lula)
For Kwame
For Cheney
For Cousin Derrick,
For my grandmother, Laura P. Grissom
all of these who passed on in the three years after
I moved to the Salish Sea.

Sail well.

Figure 7. Hover your mobile device over this QR code to navigate to the video poem at http://dr.bettinajudd.com/salish-sea.

A Note on Pronouns

I, we, us, me, our is Bettina Judd, poet among the now living. Also, collectively, the *we* now living.

Sometimes Bettina (I, we, us, me, our) transmutes into an orca, and at least once, into an orca's prey.

Don't worry about me. I'm just in my feelins.

That orca is real, given the name Tahlequah by a group of donors to the whale museum at Friday Harbor, Washington, USA. She was also given the name J35 by scientists. In the summer of 2018, Tahlequah mourned her freshly born and dead baby calf by carrying its corpse for seventeen days. The seventeen (plus one) poems here reflect those days. They meditate and mourn, when I could not properly bring my primate self to it. Sometimes, I look at Tahlequah to honor her grief, and sometimes in grief, we merge.

You is mutable and contextual.

They, she, he is the ultimate other—the dead, the divine, and the not yet living.

ONE

water unto water,
this world into the next.
the unborn orca shifts in the womb
& turns toward oblivion instead—
she slides down to blue and bluer,
down to warmer darkness. gravity is so
neutral, amoral. see her descend
away from exanimate placenta, away
from umbilical chord, slack, then taut, and let go . . .

no.

i dive for mine, lift my prize to angels of thicker air
limp, but god, mine.

oh, this body unfit.
oh, this sea, sick with grief.

TWO

o, this sea, sick with grief
salish, chesapeake, whatever we may call
saltwater made brown with the blood of many
massacres, former extinctions, here in the in-
between of disembarked ships and shore
we have been the market and the exchanged
have nothing to see for it but ourselves
hands open and pleading we call your names
Yemaya, Ko-Kwal-Alwoot, mother and maiden,
what might be seen before our excision?
before we are made martyr and relic?
what can be seen when our possibility
has given itself to weightless depths?
we carry you anyway, child, we carry.

THREE

a group of female orcas gather around J35 (aka Tahlequah) for two hours at sunset

we carry you anyway, child. we carry
our babe found in the sea.
we open sister, we open
the grave of moonlight's reflection.
it too, shall be gone in the morning,
but here, you will be. and we always
with you. we, with you. and you
a gift to the disappearing moon.
a gift to the disappearing we.
carry anyway child, carry
although we may not see.
carry anyway child, carry
and we, always with you.
and we, always with you.

FOUR

and we always with you,
laura. your daughters and nieces, your granddaughter,
your girls are holding your hands and you are not here.
after the whirring of machines, after the pastor, the doctors,
after the men leave the room, we bend over in that same
void where spirit hovers, to tell you that we
listened, we love you, we shape our gait to yours,
and you could shed this flesh if you
need to.
thank you, thank you, *je t'aime*, adieu
be sure to hear this as you go
how we are emptied and made full with gratitude.
through gnashing teeth and salted lips
every well wish, true and spiteful.

FIVE

every well wish true and spiteful
platitudes: *the world watches, mourns with you,*
and your species, *endangered,*
girl, people lie all the time.
especially when the fault is our own.
these ain't nothing but unanswered calls
piteous claims to reform regret.
to make of humans, a failed savior—again.
tahlequah, your name rolls off my tongue familiar—
round vowels and eloquent consonants
hewn by a tongue not your own. Tahlequah
a mourning mother, a black whale not made
to leap in a cage for human delight, but diving to
hold yours up to the light.

SIX

hold yours up to the light,
the click and shutter of infamy
into magazines and commemorative photobooks,
our coffee tables dutifully aware and artful.
mother, your back's a black sight,
a glistening cradle, an unsteady slick, a cooling board.
oh, empty belly and womb,
oh, untended hunger make room
for every mouth aching to compose this song.
we make feast in our flesh, we make famine.
we move this sea, make waters cold and rich.
we move the sea with deep blue sound.
sing mother, you
the one. make us free in your wake.

SEVEN

the one, make us free. in your wake
is nothingness and the fullness thereof—
perilous waters, its depth and bounty.
please make of us some use, take this faltering
mortality. you who make streams
reverse and feed multitudes, whose body
is our bread, who protects us in every—
your—salten waters. bless us, or take us
swiftly home. for who can bear to lose another
with no babies to joyfully replenish?
what is an ocean to our cheeks
fatless and deformed?
what can we ask of you
without fear of ungrateful sin?

EIGHT

without fear of ungrateful sin
i keep the ways. that which must be done will be
by my hand, still here. the pyre, the coffin
the tribute, the washing and anointing
of feet, perfume in my hair wrung and brushed
in supplication for the body prepared,
dressed for the hereafter and now to say
this flesh returned is beloved and already
missed. this i can do: keep watch, be
seen the one left behind, and comforted
by the uncertainty of my staying,
punished too. sometimes i dream of them. they
send messages. sometimes they just want to
remind me that they are dead.

NINE

remind me that they are dead
and some of us, still dying. some of us
unable to shoulder what we be made to carry.
to be where there's no possibility of
being, yet here we be—a cruelty.
grammar confounds, paces and stops in our throats.
present, now past tense, obsolete plurals,
nouns and verbs fight rigor for movement—a
meal becomes *repast*, wake to *wake*, *vigil*
a space between worlds of the mourned and yet
to be mourned. *homegoing* for we live between.
but they on the other side are always sure:
we are here, they sing. *you are there & here*
we shall stay 'til all are ready to gather.

TEN

we shall stay 'til all are ready. to gather,
we practice our wails in the soft flesh of
our chests where air billows, unwatered and deep.
we bow our heads, seek bounty and wait, waves
come back empty, indifferent. we ponder
stepping into the sea, never looking back
like they egbo landing, like she samish land.
call it sacrifice, call it example,
call on them with sirens of loss, *circles
and circles of sorrow* flailing, quieting, starting
up once more. we are without hope but not yet
hopeless—foolish maybe. we begin again:
unfurl blankets on the sand, feed each other with our hands.
wait for death, birth, and death again. again.

ELEVEN

wait for birth, death, and death again. again
a disagreement over the order
of services, the suit, the dress, her shade
of lipstick, the wig, his signature beard.
when we finally agree (we never agree)
it is all players to the stage of our grief:
it was a beautiful service.
you did good.
pastor preached a word, didn't he?
we fought hard enough for their memory.
after rites we take to our beds, tongues bloody,
lids heavy with new loss. discord as love's
final offering. cousin and brother become stranger
the heartache we held, ruptured new.

TWELVE

Chinook salmon, the main staple food for southern resident orcas, are also endangered. They are spawned in freshwater, travel through rivers and streams to the sea to live, and then return to freshwater to spawn and die. Climate change has affected the livability of their habitats.

the heartache we held ruptured new
seedlings refusing to grow, unable to absorb
oxygen tainted by blood and lead. do we
call this drowning? ain't no air here.
the hand on our throat made invisible, natural.
our barren gasps, hard as a bullet and just as true.
what I mean is we keep dying and I
don't know what to do but bury our dead.
who remembers how we create anew?
we the evidence of what we ain't, how we
didn't & with nothing in the till . . .
in the till   hunh . . .
whether the river, the stream, the sea,
we be killed by our salmon dreams.

THIRTEEN

we be killed by our salmon dreams
the hunt in us, haunted—a thing deferred.
some may crumble under this weight of unliving,
the paradox of otherwise being,
a pinpointed misdirection. whatever,
wherever we may be, we are done here,
aren't we? and where are we to go?
knowing the nature of water and air
what place is not here? tides will rise, encroach
and call us back home. we mammals after all,
creatures made for that which makes us drown.
         would you think of that?
our end? have you already dreamed it?
a dream about our nightmare?

FOURTEEN

a dream about our nightmare:
you carry the child into the world
body stretched between two worlds, their heart
the taut skin of a drum singing, *be be be*
you carry the child to school, to daycare,
you carry them to their friend's house, your sister's.
you carry them with arms, with skin, with plans
you think of it always, this carrying,
and to take the next step, to wake, to smile
don't think. one day they will come home shaken,
they have found out that they are not children.
but you are my child, you say. and they wonder
with new sight: *how can you be a mother?* you
hear the question. you have asked it yourself.

FIFTEEN

hear the question, you have asked it yourself:
am i of any use to them? your hand
rounds a voided curve. what you are touching
are future ghosts. two little ones, maybe more
in joy for each other and possible
through you, though possible (*yes*) without. you
hope to be such an honored vessel
you check your basal temperature. you pee
on sticks daily. you make a special account
call it "hogs for the farm," what your father
said he'd need when you told him your plans.
it still seems wrong to want for them the chance
that you prayed for—to live. because all of
you will suffer, and it will be your fault.

SIXTEEN

you will suffer, and it will be your fault.
die to see your name blazed in digital
light. each syllable a sting on black tongues.
ladle the melody like winter provisions.
remember the spring, we say. say their names,
say we matter—a chant, a question, a
demand that means, in this country, a riot.
amidst this, assume a life of quiet.
tonight, we fold in our coats and make
for still air. watch as we walk away from
ourselves. hope we return to our homes unknown,
unscathed, & common. oh, to be nameless
to the world. that would be enough, wouldn't it?
to choose breath at night?

SEVENTEEN

to choose breath: at night
the air wets, cooled by earth's shrug from the sun
its dank meeting arid atmosphere—an
ancient ritual of opening, closing.
so lungs know the ways of air, its changes
when saltwater arrives. i am concerned
that i hear my provision at night. the
plangent wind of my skull is no comfort
i monitor its inconsistencies
feel the dew in capillaries—how it
makes flesh feel soggy and swollen. face blood
hot and burning, chest expanding then huffing out and
recoiling *in* . . .

                        n . . .

                            n . . .

                                n . . .

                                          a . . .

                                        a . . .

                            n . . .

                  d . . .

            i . . .

        i . . .

    a . . .

      n . . .

       d . . .

           i . . .

              i . . .

                i . . .

                        . . .

                                  i . . .

                            i . . .

                i . . .

                  i . . .

                  i . . .

              . . .

              . . .

AFTER

...   ...

there is nothing   to hold
even   my weight   is too much
  too much already   and you,   beloved   are light
   i would forget   that i carry   you   if i could
forget   the forces   that pull

death, that imponderable and familiar flight.
   we   who remain   slaves to gravity
fight   the drifting   your   having drifted
the falling—   this   having fallen. we—
  i   give way to   the deep
 & your   matter   in me.   too much

too much already & you, beloved are light as air. as
     water   unto   water.

Black Notes in Grief

It is the sound that opens wide everything else.

We touch on death in Black studies because we must. Because the condition of Black life is so often described by our proximities to death.[1] (As in, "The only thing I have to do is stay Black and die.") In the study of Black death, one must touch (mustn't they?) the feeling of being in death's wake. I wonder, in the notes to this chapter, how Black grief is in the structure of Black studies—if not *this* Black study. The pursuit of this question, *How is grief structured within Black studies?* requires a distance from the matter of grief that I would rather relegate to the notes. This book is about feelin after all—about leaning into the affective sedulity of Black creativity and to pursue this question without attending to the experience of grief seems like an ironically performative byproduct of the "race for theory."[2] It's much easier to talk about than do or be in grief. In the context of this project, it would be disingenuous of me to pursue this question without feelin because the real question about grief in Black studies, about Black people and grief, is . . . . ? Because the real question is uttered in a language difficult to transcribe on the page. It is ineffable, this thing called grief, and expository propositional prose sanitizes its contents.

The content of this chapter *is* grief—as well as I could communicate it as I wade through my own experience of grief in the process of writing this book. I wade through grief *with* Black studies to do this work and also to make sense of Black terror, loss, sadness, and all of the other unnamed affective experiences that grief attends to. Even that attempt to structure grief is too clinical. In my grief, Black studies, particularly Black feminist studies has been my companion—a wrenchingly honest friend. Sometimes too honest, but always there. Such brutal honesty is what I hope to learn from word work—from Black feminist writing that I reference, and from my community of friends that take Black feminism to praxis. These notes are a contemplative commons, an acknowledgment of the "wake work," to invoke Christina Sharpe, that precedes my own.[3] The notes stop where the meditation on grief, here titled, *Salish Sea* begins in text, but the citations within these notes inform the poems on a cellular level. I thank Alexis Pauline Gumbs and Saidiya Hartman for crafting examples of this kind of poetic citational practice.[4]

As these notes close, I imagine myself in a room full of these cited thinkers that I feel. (Imagine, if you will, yourself in the room as voyeur, or if you feelin me, participant.) We are talking and sharing our experiences, we present evidence, pour over archival artifacts, and wonder at what we find. We pontificate, reference, and speechify. We might even laugh. There is a point at which they all must go home, away from the din of our party and as I close the door behind them, their words, thoughts, and feelings have not left me. But, in the silence of the room in which I physically (work with me) remain, I meet myself and all of what could not be said before and after our meeting full of life-breath and sorrow comes up through my belly into my chest, my throat, and eyes. It fills me and overflows—becomes the room. This is what could be recorded.

It seemed to be embedded in the language of Black life.

The blues is a Black condition. The roots of the musical genre are explicitly drawn from the processes of cultural, spiritual, and bodily displacement and subjection. It would seem that a study of the aesthetics that shape the blues and its descendant musical styles would also be a study of grief, if not grievances (a point I discuss further below). Grief and grievances are cellular to the aesthetics of Black music. As Amiri Baraka notes of the antecedent of the blues, field hollers "were strident laments, more than anything."[5] So cellular were these wordless affective musical riffs to Black music that for Baraka, they could be considered lyrics—lyrics that communicate the ineffable and the identifiable (i.e., This is *my* grief.) Follow me here. I know that the ability to think through the aesthetics of a genre does not a study of grief make. There are way too many tributaries, and often, they are less difficult to sit with than grief. But the blues would certainly be core to an aesthetic interrogation of a study of Black grief. The riff marks the communicative possibilities of expressing the ineffable contours of grief's feeling.

There is a story about Funkadelic's "Maggot Brain" that comes to mind here: for the record, George Clinton told Eddie Hazel to make grief out of his guitar. In his words:

> I told him to play like his mother had died, to picture that day, what he would feel, how he would make sense of his life, how he would take a measure of everything that was inside of him and let it out through his guitar . . . when he started playing, I knew immediately that he understood what I meant. I could see the guitar notes stretching out like a silver web. When we played the solo back, I knew that it was good beyond good, not only a virtuoso display of musicianship *but also an unprecedented moment of emotion in pop music.*[6]

The aesthetics of the riff—the circular ascending and descending repetition, the distorted and imperfect tonality of Hazel's guitar, the vocal-like melismatic divergences express grief as it is felt, sonically. Hazel's song-length solo was so mesmerizing that Clinton had the rest of the band dropped from the final recording save for a simple melancholic melody on second guitar that points to where Hazel occasionally lands. As the quote suggests, Clinton understands this song to be a signal of the band's maturity as musicians—that their ability to express emotion matched their technical proficiency. Emotional dexterity within musical proficiency is fundamental to the aesthetics of funk and blues—to be proficient in spanning affective registers through musicianship and grief made that clear.

The lesson of the riff is instructive here. As studies of Black folks consider the social conditions of Black people, so they must consider the structures of feeling by which Blackness in Black studies must operate. The "social experience *in process*" to borrow from Raymond Williams, is ongoing as we feel, think, study, live, write, and teach Black studies.[7] The aesthetics of the riff tells us that there is no singular note that encompasses a singular feeling (i.e., grief *or* pleasure *or* anger) and no singular series of notes either. Not a solid line pointing us in one particular direction, but "notes stretching out like a silver web." A study of pleasure would so encounter, nay, become a study of grief—such is the web of Black studies's dexterous structure of feeling.

"Loss?"

Recovery uncovers what stays lost. Mamie Till Mobley remembers the painstaking and dreadful process of recovering the body of her son: "I looked deeply at that entire body for something, anything that would help me find my son. Finally, I found him. And lost him."[8] Her son, difficult to recognize because of the brutality of racist violence that ripped him away from life and her mothering arms, is only recoverable through memory. Emmett's body both a recovery (through memory of his life) and a final rupture (violent death).

What is lost stays lost but the open chasm of *something was here* remains as memory. Saidiya Hartman notes, "the slave was the only one expected to discount her past."[9] This loss was the ongoing *process* of forgetting homeland, mother. Hartman goes on to describe the folklore of coercive forgetting:

> Everyone told me a different story about how the slaves began to forget their past. Words like "zombie," "sorcerer," "witch," "succubus," and "vampire" were whispered to explain it. In these stories, which circulated throughout West Africa, the particulars varied, but all of them ended the same—the slave loses mother.[10]

Perhaps this is the fundamental difference between discussing grief and discussing loss—loss does not require memory whereas grief does remember what has gone. Memory can be lost, too. Hartman's return to the site of lost memory intones grief through her encounter with memory, mind, and mother, by returning to the place of forgetting. This site-specific experience of remembering what was meant to be forgotten is what Toni Morrison calls rememory.[11] Rememory is the glitch in space/time between what is meant to be forgotten in a past and what is reencountered as memory in the present. Here she presents the concept in the voice of Sethe:

> I was talking about time. It's so hard for me to believe in it. Some things go. Pass on. Some things just stay. I used to think it was my rememory. You know. Some things you forget. Other things you never do. But it's not. Places, places are still there. If a house burns down, it's gone, but the place—the picture of it stays, and not just in my rememory, but out there, in the world. What I remember is a picture floating out there outside my head. I mean, even if I don't think it, even if I die, the picture of what I did, or knew, or saw is still out there. Right in the place where it happened.[12]

Whom or what reminds you, refuses release of the tether and makes past time as lucid as the present and carries some message about the future. Or as M. Jacqui Alexander says, "Spirit brings knowledge from past, present, and future to a particular moment called a now."[13] In this bending of space/time, rememory enacts sacred touch—witness from the dead, the unborn, and not to be forgotten. Hartman finds recovery to be illusive as the rupture between Africans and descendants of African slaves expands beyond the width and depth of the Atlantic Ocean. Whatever is thought to have been forgotten has been etched in rememory as hauntings, familiars, and familiar sites of terror that live with those who remember. Rememory means nothing is forgotten though it may be lost, and that memory, along with that loss, makes way for grieving what has gone.

I know that we discuss grief because we are often *in grief* here on the page.

Karla FC Holloway's book *Passed On* is a study of Black mourning practices as well as a documentation of the writer's grief.[14] In it, she is studying the very thing she is in while she is in it. This is curious to me as it is not just a self-conscious matter of doing Black studies while being Black or Women's studies while being a woman. Grief is assumed to be a universal condition, yet her study reveals that the universal experience of mourning is altered by the conditions of racialization on the living and the dead. Namely, that Black mourning practices and Black death tell us something about the social conditions of Black life. These conditions do not stop when sitting down to write or research. They don't even stop when you've decided to ponder on that particular thing we might call *Black death*.

grievance

Consider how grievance and grief might be an aesthetic of Black resistance. The anti-lynching parades of the early twentieth century that were silent, save for the steady beat of drums, are prime early examples of such resistance.[15] Meta Fuller's *Silent Protest* both references and enacts this form of protest. These dirges of well-dressed Black folks mourned both one person in particular and every lynching as an ongoing crisis. Grief is the ethos of such attentiveness to Black freedom movements because the stakes are death and death's left-behind. When the 2016 Baltimore Uprisings took place in the aftermath of the deadly police murder of Freddie Gray, it was as much a moment of resistance as it was a visceral state of making grievance for every murder before and the inevitable after. Similarly, the aftermath of the 2014 murder of Mike Brown in Ferguson, Missouri, attended to the impromptu wake that the violent circumstances of his death initiated. Mike Brown's body lay in the street for hours before it was attended to, which draws questions of course about whether or not medical attention could have extended his life. Those waiting and watching—doing that wake work—for Mike Brown's dying and dead body could be counted among the protestors that night and the days and nights after. The protests in the aftermath of this death were of a particular death and its mourning, and also of the circumstances of life by which Mike Brown's death would be regarded as inevitable.

The 1992 Los Angeles Riot is often understood as a response to the acquittal of the four police officers who beat Rodney King mercilessly on camera in 1991, but it is also a response to the actual murder of a Black girl by the name of Latasha Harlins. Latasha Harlins was accused of stealing a bottle of orange juice at King Liquor Store in Los Angeles. This accusation, made by Soon Ja Du, the store's owner, resulted in a physical tussle. As Harlins left the store without the orange juice she was accused of stealing, she was shot in the back of the head. Du would receive five years' probation for the murder of the fifteen-year-old. The subsequent riots were notoriously fueled by tensions between Black and Korean-American communities in Los Angeles as Korean-owned businesses were particularly targeted for looting and burning. The circumstances of Harlins's life which marked her as a criminal whose life could be traded for a bottle of orange juice, the racist gatekeeping of business loans that would disallow Black people to build and maintain businesses within majority-Black neighborhoods, and the violent and racist LAPD precoursed the events of late April 1992. The loss of life of Black youth recurs in the scene of

Black resistance to violence against Black communities either committed by the police or condoned by an anti-Black carceral system.

Notably, Anne Anlin Cheng revisits this scene through Anna Deveare Smith's *Twilight: Los Angeles 1992* by analyzing the monologue of Mrs. Young-Soon Han, who is described as being between forms of grief and thus identification as a racialized subject. The Korean shop owner at once identifies with the grief of the Black community and also the grief of the Korean community that is targeted during the riots. Unpacking Han's dilemma, Cheng states, "In the splintering landscape of grief, identification and sympathy are at once imperative and fraught. For whom do you grieve, and how do you do so, in this world of layered victimizations, violence, and enmity?"[16] The expression of grief manifest in the riot is something to which Han is sympathetic and also aggrieved—a liminal state of racial identification produced by racialization's "history of abjection and coercions."[17] While the murder of Latasha Harlins is not expressly discussed in Cheng's analysis of this speaker's monologue, the spectral presence of Harlins weighs Cheng's question with Mrs. Young-Soon Han. For me, anyway. And perhaps this is the "expression of grief" by which my identity or at least the Blackness of this black study is shaped.[18]

However, grievance is not grief. Grievance as the protest, the litigious petition, or the riot has operated as an important affective tool for Black resistance to anti-Black violence but cannot be mistaken for grief, individual or communal. The site of violent rage in grief vis-à-vis the riot, unlike the protest or the mindfully placed photograph, does not ask for redress. Its logics are not bound to negotiate terms of justice—it is chaotic action incited by the violence enacted through the juridical process, militarized police, and the state more broadly. Anger and grief co-function in the riot—in the decisive action which operates knowing there is no one to hear petitions. As Rhaisa Kameelah Williams notes in her essay on Black maternal grief, "If grief is uncontainable and prediscursive, then grievance becomes the finite expression of such affect that can stand up to adjudication and receive material reparation."[19] In its finality, grievance renders Black feeling into productive labor that may be co-opted by the state in order to produce false narratives of racial progress. Williams continues,

> In particular, it establishes illusory scenarios where acts of racial and state violence are resolved with penalties against the perpetrator and restitution for the victim's family. It provides closure for the American public and state, helping to maintain the democratic myth that the nation applies just penalty to those who have committed wrongs beyond reasonable doubt. As such, the messiness and pervasiveness of trauma and grief, induced by systemic violence, can be contained within a case file.[20]

The riot is afforded no such understanding of feeling. The riot is a chaotic and unproductive display of grief through rage and so unconfined, must be controlled by brute force and national narratives on racial progress: racism as problem within Black communities by Black communities (vis-à-vis Black-on-Black violence), and the militarized police who respond to the acts are narrated as brave first responders to a confusing and difficult racial climate. What differentiates grievance from grief is grievance's attachment to outcome. This chapter does not write itself into an outcome. Its questions have no particular desire for closure. It is interested in the depth of grief's expression.

grifting

In the future if freedom is to happen, we would have to steal ourselves. We will have stolen ourselves.[21] Or as Alexis Pauline Gumbs writes into a future looking at the past/our present:

> so they stole themselves, which was a break with everything, which was the most illegal act since the law that made them property, and they had to re-rhythm everything, re-tune bass in their chest, and immediately and perpetually they gave themselves away, the selves they had to give, the reclaimed flesh and bones and skin.[22]

In a past for which we are the future, we stole ourselves. Which is to say that we are grifting a future in the past-present circumstances of living under capitalism and being moved as property—or in other words, being property. Such an imagination of past-present-future tense stealing and having been stolen points directly to rememory's tether to our had-to-have-been present. The current condition's possibility that is echoed in a past-impossible or in a past lost but remembered—the confluence of time/space could be understood as Black modes of *being out of time*. What I am saying is as simple as: someone spoke of stealing away after being stolen in certain future tense and here we are, again. Some would call this state of having to steal ourselves repeatedly, fugitivity. Fugitivity would come to define Blackness and the study thereof. Fugitivity itself would come to be a knowledge-producing standpoint.

Having stolen herself out of slavery Harriet Jacobs makes way for her children's freedom to be purchased by refusing to return to her enslaver. Though close in proximity to her children, Jacobs remains a fugitive—a stolen self—confined in a 9-by-7-by-3-foot crawlspace, enclosed and yet exposed to the elements. A one-inch hole allowed Jacobs to view the outside world, her children, and the goings on of her former enslaver. The loophole of retreat is the position from which she can view the outside world, it is also the site/sight through which she is both confined and free.

While not freedom outright, the loophole of retreat was a place of her own making. In order for her children to be free she would have to have stolen herself away and she would have to be both nearby and far away if just in the Flints' (her enslavers') minds to successfully orchestrate the scheme. Jacobs bent reality in the crawlspace, writing from a different time and place to these enslavers to avert their attention away from her actual location. She had to be more vivid in their imaginations than she was in the flesh. Yet she knew that her flesh was already ablaze in their minds. In her Blackness, Jacobs had been animated as a wanton jezebel, a draptomania-inflicted girl, and a careless mother. In the garret of her grandmother's home she was altogether in that confined place, Boston, New York, and no place at all. She was present for her children and absent from her children. Such capacities to be not in one place, but in many possible times and spaces, allowed for her to be in a nowhere all her own—her own. The garret was "not freedom, not yet."[23] It was strategic confinement. I'm repeating this because it is important to remember that the conditions of enslavement made a debilitating seven-year stay in a 9-by-7-by-3-foot crawlspace a had-to-have-been space toward her freedom.[24] In the end, Jacobs had no desire to play the game of slavery with her own life. She did not think herself property to be bought or sold. To steal herself was the only way to be free.

how we too, the left behind, might be lost

Many things die. Here, we are tending to human life—or lives of those who we may submit to be considered human. This study in grief examines the edge of these considerations, including the condition of life in late capitalism's degradation of the environment and the creation of environments in which Black life would be forever in peril. Witnessing varied mass extinctions, we might then be forced to confront our own precarious mortality. We might even—gazing out at the wake of it all—feel a bit of survivor's guilt. C. Riley Snorton reflects on survivor's guilt in the wake of so many Black trans deaths, particularly that of the late Blake Brockington, a Black trans masculine youth who died by suicide, in relation to his writing about Black trans lives. It is the consideration of that guilt that moves him to "consider the conditions in which he [Brockington] would be understood according to his self-definition."[25] In grief comes the work of recovery and the impulses, the need to bring into recognition, that which is lost as valued life through the witness of love. The impulse works twofold: to bring into relation the identification of the dead with the living, and to challenge and name clearly the compound effects of loss on those left behind who must grapple with the fact of their survival. As Pilate declares at her granddaughter Hagar's funeral in Toni Morrison's *Song of Solomon*: ". . . like an elephant who has just found his anger and lifts his trunk over the heads of the little men who want his teeth or his hide or his flesh or his amazing strength, Pilate trumpeted for the sky itself to hear, 'And she was *loved!*'"[26]

The epi-thing of inquiry always recounting, negotiating, attempting to undo the inevitable tripping over the dead that comes from this line of work.

See Christina Sharpe's *In the Wake*, Jericho Brown's *The Tradition*, and Claudia Rankine's *Citizen* for recent examples of Black texts that propel or close with the elegiac.[27] This list could go on using texts otherwise cited here: Holloway's *Passed On* carries the thread of grief for her son throughout the study; Holland's *Raising the Dead* ends with an elegy to her brother, Greg.[28] Layli Maparayan punctuates the end of her book *The Womanist Idea*, which invokes the spiritual lens of womanist thought, by wading through the events surrounding the death of her daughter.[29] Dagmawi Woubshet offers a "poetics of compounding loss" to think through the ways that poets, activists, and poet-activists alike chart loss through elegiac memory aestheticized within Black culture by the spirituals and the Black poetic traditions that followed.[30] The anthology *Revisiting the Elegy in the Black Lives Matter Era*, edited by Tiffany Austin, Sequoia Maner, Emily Ruth Rutter, and darlene anita scott, explores the elegy as a constant creative form in Black culture and particularly in this current era. In the process of pulling the anthology together, Tiffany Austin passed on and the book itself is dedicated to her memory.[31] Elegies are a consistent feature in Black studies and the Black studies texts cited here are exemplary, but this is hardly new for Black studies. In addition to beginning each chapter of *The Souls of Black Folk* with phrases from a "sorrow song," W. E. B. Du Bois reflects on his firstborn son, who died as an infant.[32] His grief as a parent is not without conflicting feelings of his son's death under "the Veil" of racial difference that begins his text. He is aggrieved by the death of his son, happy for his son's escape from a life under the veil, and angry at the negotiation of these terms: death or death-like life.

I sat down to work on this very book and could only wail in poems.

I call this a whale/wail of poems. Much like a crown of sonnets, but named for the grieving orca whale J35 aka Tahlequah, who carried her stillborn calf for seventeen days after its birth. Like a crown of sonnets, the final line of each preceding fourteen-line poem starts the first line of the next poem and the final poem ends with the first line of the very first poem in the sequence. There is no master poem in this sequence, but it does consider what comes after.

To be living a footnote to a text about Black life which is inevitably about death.

Yet, here we are the in the notes trying to make sense of this wail of poems—trying to build some context for why grief is important for this study. What I am saying is that Black studies is enshrouded by grief. I am feelin Black studies in my grief. Grief is Black studies' affective sedulity. It is Black studies' errant and unproductive feeling that challenges Western civilization's organizing systems of knowledge. Even as Black studies asserts productivity—toward freedom, against academy, challenging knowledge itself—grief bookends such claims with "circles and circles of sorrow"—the repeating riff, the everything and nothingness to which Western civilization finds no order, use, or value, particularly in the living ghosts of not quite humans.[33]

The number doesn't matter, shouldn't matter.

This chapter is not about the dead but about the conditions of life for those left behind to live and remember. I may count the ones I mourn. They were my 11, my 12, my 13, but to count them just increases the number and forces me to ask myself, *who do I choose to mourn?* I recount their names in this wail. Their accumulation, their numbering is an effort to communicate a feeling of loss that cannot be neatly processed. As Woubshet notes of compounding loss in the early era of AIDS, "the pain, the confounded psyche, the exhausted body and soul—of each loss are compounded by the memory and experience of the losses just before."[34] The steps of grief, the periods of mourning, the promise of linear time's healing properties fail when accumulation becomes stasis. To count may give credence to the "mathematics of unliving" that, as Katherine McKittrick notes, produces Blackness through a sum of violence and violations.[35] What is missing, unrecognized—unrecognizable—in the archive and its tabulations is the evidence of grief. Grieving responds with the enumeration of the dead with its same song wail. Chaotic and uncontained. This Black study in grief is interested in that which is and must be unaccounted for.

This book has to be written so that I can survive it and I carried on, I carried it.

Black scholars and scholars in Black studies are often compelled to make allegiances to our disciplines and thus make sacrificial the lives of Black people in our work. We are expected to, as Sharpe notes, "discard, discount, disregard, jettison, abandon, and measure those ways of knowing and to enact epistemic violence that we know to be violence against others and ourselves."[36] We risk and do commit violence on the page when recounting anti-Black violence in order to make a point about the pervasiveness of anti-Black violence. Disassociating from Black folks—reducing ourselves to a population to be studied, and disconnecting ourselves from the lived experiences of being in the room of history as we add to its pages, describing our very existence but *in absentia*. We choose ourselves as present absences in order to be legible in Western knowledge—but there is a cost, a loss of knowledge formations that have allowed us to persist: those remnants of memory and will underneath our writing and the conditions which would allow us to write ourselves into history at all. But as Jacqui Alexander notes, those remnants are not left indefinitely: "Not only humans made the Crossing, traveling only in one direction through Ocean given the name Atlantic. Grief traveled as well."[37]

This Black grief is an accumulation of feeling

How do you grieve that which is ongoing? Or as Hartman queries, "How might we understand mourning, when the event has yet to end? When the injuries not only perdure, but are inflicted anew? Can one mourn what has yet ceased happening?"[38] Injuries, inflicted anew. For instance, the fear of police violence in the course of grieving. In the summer of 2016 when doctors told my mother, uncle, and me that my grandmother was absolutely dying and there was no other course of action to take to stop the process, I went into hysterics, crying and begging my grandmother to stay with us at her bed. Nurses called security as my uncle shook me into a calmer state, telling me that security would drag me out of the hospital. Sexist and racist medicine has so sanitized the course and culture of death and dying to make such an outburst of grief from a Black woman intolerable if illegible. By making death the domain of the (white) and male-dominated medical field, the family is estranged from the process of dying. My outburst is dangerous chaos, not a rational course of the grieving process that accompanies the death of someone *who is loved*. As Sharon Holland notes, "The family is constructed as unstable, relative to the 'neutral' and universalizing gaze of attending physicians."[39] The hospital, unequipped for the unruly knowledge of death and dying by the family, is however equipped, through its carceral allegiances, for the emotional outbursts of Black people via security systems and police force, violence, and confinement. Like Black deaths caused by state violence, there can be no Black witness—or rather—Black witness is disregarded as untrustworthy. If as Holland writes, "death, as an unspeakable subject in a hospital ward, is divested of its own language and is consumed by the scientific knowledge in the physicians' possession," Black grief is the language by which Black death is acknowledged—even its tone and pitch is wildly outside the aspects of bedside care that can be served in the medical field or Western knowledge.[40] To think that my own life or the life of my family members might have been in danger because of my expressions of grief is personally overwhelming, but also signifies on griefs accumulated and confluent. My Black grief grieved by the confines of ungrievability. There is no common sense for Black grief that holds space for grieving even as Black death is so common-sense, to be expected, and to be in fact so "juridically sound" as Sharpe notes, that the nation's functioning depends on the reproduction of Black death.

Black expressions of grief may take iconic status in the process of attempts at juridical redress as the widely produced photos of Mamie Till Mobley weeping over her son's coffin and the photo of Tracy Martin, Trayvon Martin's father's open-mouthed wail demonstrate. These images produce the narratives of grief as grievance necessary for certain kinds of movement building and are so legible as productive strategy. Grief itself, however, becomes lost in grievance's show. As the aftermaths of the attempts at juridical redress for Emmett Till and Trayvon Martin (and on . . .) demonstrate, no such reparation could be found. What else could we expect our grief to *do* if Black death is, as Sharpe notes, "a predictable and constitutive aspect of this democracy?"[41] What is our grief—loud and disruptive—if not for us?

Remember? They gone.

Holloway ends *Passed On* with such an illustration of the ways of grief to arrest—to flow forcefully through cracks unexpected or unexamined. On her way to view the site of Richard Wright's remains with her daughter Ayana, she begins to recount her childhood practice of collecting chestnuts to make necklaces, and then:

> We were relaxed and at ease until we got to the site where those who had been cremated were interred. There I stopped silent, stilled but for the tears that clouded my sight. I thought of my child, our son, her brother, and I could go no further. And so, we left together, her hand in mine, turned toward home.[42]

Grief is the perfume of our stifled air. Even in the most joyous of our days we may be caught by its waft—blown in by the weather and our weathering.[43] My knees might buckle from its sudden strength and bring me to the earth beneath, senses shaken by gravity's pull. All that is left is this sound.

Further Notes

Yemaya and the Maiden of Deception Pass (Kʷʔkwálʔlʷʔt)

Yemaya appears here as mother of the children of water and of water itself. Known also as Yemoja, Yemanjá, Iemanjá, and Janaína (all matters of geographic and cultural location), this orisha is revered as an embodiment of motherhood, nurturance, as well as communications and trade cross the waters. As Solimar Otero and Toyin Falola note in the introduction of *Yemoja: Gender, Sexuality, and Creativity in the Latina/o and Afro-Atlantic Diasporas* this orisha is "also associated with other water deities, such as Olókùn in Nigeria and Mami Wata across West and Central Africa."[44] For her followers in the Americas, she often has special meaning as a nurturing mother who protects her scattered children across the waters—connecting them to Africa's Western shores. As poet Olive Senior writes: "From Caribbean shore / to far-off Angola, she'll / spread out her blue cloth / let us cross over—."[45] She appears in relation to the Samish spirit/deity Kʷʔkwálʔlʷʔt (pronounced Ko-kwal-alwoot) also known as the Maiden of Deception Pass who wades around in the waters of the Salish Sea and sometimes in the wake of canoes.[46] Once human, she sacrificed herself to dwell forever in the waters with the king of the sea so that her people could eat.[47] She acts as a sea-dwelling guardian who provides her people with sustenance from the waters of the Salish Sea and the surrounding fresh waters. She continues to be a guardian of her people.

Figure 8. Bettina Judd. *Following the Bright Back of the Woman*, 2021. Gouache, pastel, collage, 27 × 19 inches.

CHAPTER 2

Lucille Clifton's Atheology of Joy!

The few times I've met Lucille Clifton, I approached her with a book for her to sign. *I usually tried to solicit a longer message as a signature—something other than her standard "Joy!" that she wrote in everyone's books. I'd recount my first experience with her poetry, how she influenced my writing, and so on, but every time, in her small and curvy handwriting she would write "Joy!" On one occasion I told her how all of her poems about the body were so important to me because I'd had an ordeal with medicine. She interrupted my sob story: "But always joy—right?"*

I was dissatisfied with "Joy!" because I wanted her to convey some brilliance about writing poetry to this young aspiring poet. I was also dissatisfied because, at my core, I was afraid of what it meant to experience "Joy!" Joy comes with a load of responsibility to my community, to my family, to my God. But Ms. Lucille's steady and unwavering signature, "Joy!," was the brilliant message. My consistent dissatisfaction with this signature amplified the importance of her writing it. It continues to be the answer to any of the questions I would ask her even now after her death: Ms. Lucille, how do I become a better poet? Ms. Lucille, how do I survive the way you have? Ms. Lucille, how can I love myself the way you do in "homage to my hips"? Joy exclamation point, joy exclamation point, joy exclamation point to all of the above.[1]

The answer is *joy!* I cannot complete the poem, I cannot begin the poem without having experienced some sense of joy. It is an inner-being experience that emerges from the deepest sense of myself. Clifton's *joy!* is a concept rooted in Black selfhood; it is a total experience wherein the miracle of existence in the face of deadly oppression is acknowledged. Joy is discussed here as a conscious choice and practice. What Clifton conveyed with her insistence on *joy!* was as simple as the declaration *you are alive* and as complex as the question *why are you alive?* Joy was in the miracle of life made evident in the poem. Joy was also in the completion of the poem for the poem's sake and what the poem signified—the evidence of her existence. This is why Clifton's work, although packed with difficulty, sadness, and anger, all points to her notorious iteration of joy-exclamation-point. She is alive. You are alive. In the face of destruction, we exist.

Anyone familiar with Lucille Clifton's poetry might wonder how a reading of her work over five decades could render joy as a pervasive theme. Her poetry deals with some of the hardest sufferings imaginable: death, childhood sexual abuse, her own battle with cancer, the loss of a child, genocide, incest, and psychological abuse—I could go on. Never shying away from the "terrible stories" of human experience, Clifton's poetry manages to grapple with the painful and routs out ways of seeing that might otherwise be left unattended. What may be found there are felt thoughts that might have been buried by loud, salacious, or consensus-driven information and situations. For instance, her poem "in the mirror" anthropomorphizes the single breast left behind after a mastectomy. We are witness to the grief of fleshy tissue that has lost, in the poet's terms, "her sister," and is in tears from the *tear*ing of familial flesh. The final lines teach us the pronunciation of "tear." They state, "it is pronounced like trying to re / member the shape of an unsafe life."[2] The enjambment of "remember" magnifies the metaphorical and etymological meaning of the word "member," here as part of a whole, and also part of a body while "re" invokes repeated action or status. The poem again reminds the reader of the violence of being split apart from flesh kin when the word "to" is read next to the enjambed "re" to make the word "tore." Even with this reminder of the stakes of grief, violence, and pain in the aftermath of surgery meant to treat breast cancer, the last lines of the poem speak of the pervasiveness of fatal danger in Black existence. "The shape," she calls us to re/member, "of an unsafe life."[3] The space left behind by the missing breast is also the shape of being left behind and living—the present absence of loss that accompanies us all in life. That living is not without danger—not without cost—but is a *kind of life*.

For Clifton, joy exists *with* mourning—with the terrible and with suffering. Within and underneath acute difficulty are the possibilities of life itself rich with sensation. Joy emerges through this tension. Reminiscent of the biblical scripture which commands, "count it all joy when ye fall into divers temptations," Clifton chooses joy within while suffering.[4] This perspective on joy is conversant with larger questions about the nature of good and evil, the divine and human. In her second collection, *Good News About the Earth*, the poem functions as a prayer: "why is Your hand / so heavy / on just poor / me?" Here, Clifton situates her line of inquiry through theodicy—the theological paradox that asks: If God is all powerful, all good, and all knowing, why does suffering exist?[5] The short answer is that there is joy in the mourning.

Joy! is a practice and a philosophy of complex personhood that I call Lucille Clifton's atheology or way of joy. While I have the impulse to place Clifton's insights on joy, her reading of the fall of man and on, as philosophy—as theology, I am liberated by Ashon Crawley's critique of theology-philosophy which tells us how "theology and philosophy would come to work together to target the object of blackness."[6] Crawley offers "atheology-aphilosophy" as the performance practice against theology-philosophy that would instantiate the racialization and gendering that would rob Black folks of the joy of which Clifton speaks. Though explored in this chapter through her poetry and creative process, her perspective on joy may also be found in a 1999 interview with Michael Glaser:

> **Lucille:** It is not a completely intellectual choice. To choose life, that's reason enough to know that the whole of life is more than an intellectual life. I don't believe that one should always try to take the easy road. And when you do, you should know you're doing it. But suppose once in a while we choose joy. That could almost be enough, you know?

Michael: And you can't choose joy unless you acknowledge the darkness?

Lucille: Absolutely.

Michael: But to acknowledge the darkness and not choose joy is—

Lucille: Is sin.

Michael: Wow! 'To acknowledge the darkness and not choose joy is sin.'

Lucille: It's sin against the spirit. Against the self. It's sin against what made us.[7]

The dimensions of joy outlined here are: (1) the complexity of human experience (i.e., "the whole of life"), (2) acknowledgment of the difficult, and (3) conscious, habitual, and deliberate choice. This tripart and cooperant atheology embraces joy in its complexity because life is complex. It acknowledges the feeling as hard-edged, multifaceted, exuberant, and inclusive of the difficult. It posits joy as a choice made by hard-won and defiant will. Clifton's atheology of joy is fundamentally concerned with what Patricia Williams and Avery Gordon call complex personhood, because it embraces aspects of being and living that are contradictory: gracious *and* selfish, powerful *and* powerless.[8] Though humanist in its foundations, Clifton's atheology proposes a different kind of being *in-process*, forged from the silhouette of that which is "both non-white and woman."[9] Clifton's stance on joy is predicated on deep engagement with felt experience—feelin—that makes up a complex life. That is, as an *a*theology of joy, Clifton's poetry is deeply connected to a set of aesthetic practices and experiences that, as Crawley notes of Blackpentacostalism, "illustrate how enjoyment, desire, and joy are important for the tradition that antiphonally speaks back against aversion, embarrassment, and abandonment, against the debasement and denigration of blackness."[10] In such an atheological framework, God is not infallible and Lucifer ain't all that bad as God and Lucifer, the avatars of good and evil, are entwined in co-created meaning. A self-made insurgent subject is the outcome of this atheology because the very ideology upon which the human is formed in negative space is yet another one of those bad things to have happened. *Joy!* is the practice by which one makes, affirms, and yes, celebrates the complex self.

In this chapter, I will follow the outline provided by Clifton's atheology of joy as discussed with Michael Glaser. I begin with her assertion of complex human experience by first attending to the spiritual inquiries into the origins of the universe manifest in her personal spirit writing and poetic midrash—or biblical reinterpretation—of the book of Genesis's telling of the origins of man. Her use of the story of Adam and Eve in the Garden of Eden attempts to make sense of the world in which certain acts are codified as good or bad (or biblically speaking, obedient or disobedient to God). She centers Eve and the serpent rather than Adam (who would come to represent the human vis-à-vis "man"), as intentionally contradictory, self-made, and fully actualized subjects. To draw on the biblical origin of man, and thus the mythological framework for suffering by which she and much of the Western world has been acculturated, Clifton's atheology of joy also manages to intervene on both theological and secular humanist ideologies.

The insurgent subject embodied in Eve and ultimately the poet herself posits another kind of being self-formed between that which is made of the same stuff as Adam and that which is divine.

The next dimension of *joy!* discussed in this chapter will be the acknowledgment of the difficult. It is by acknowledging the difficult that Clifton embarks on the theodical question. Through the perspective of Lucifer, we can see how *joy!* exists within the difficult—as the sweet funk of life. In a series of poems set up as a conversation between Lucifer and God, the poet asks why humans had to be expelled from the Garden of Eden and made to suffer when God could have intervened.

The third dimension—conscious, habitual, and deliberate choice—is the art of being, what I call the art of *i be* demonstrated by the collaboration of Eve and Lucifer, and declared in Clifton's signature poem "won't you celebrate with me" which reads:

> won't you celebrate with me
> what i have shaped into
> a kind of life? i had no model.
> born in babylon
> both nonwhite and woman
> what did i see to be except myself?
> i made it up
> here on this bridge between
> starshine and clay,
> my one hand holding tight
> my other hand; come celebrate
> with me that everyday
> something has tried to kill me
> and has failed.[11]

In this poem, the reader is witness and entreated to celebrate the creation and practice of an otherwise self: a self that has faced adversity, the possibility of not existing, and built a life anyway. It is fitting that Clifton considered it a signature poem, because it concisely speaks to the urgency of joy in her life as a practice of self-making.[12] It functions as a clarion call for a way of being that challenges the idea of the human in favor of a more complex personhood. This way of being, this practice, is *joy!*

While I focus on two specific series that explore the fall of man, I place them in conversation with collections dating from Clifton's second book, *Good News About the Earth*, to her last collection, *Voices*. These selections serve as a glossary of sorts—offering context for the meanings of terms such as *light, darkness, star*, and *brother*. Clifton is a poet known for her concision, and it is precisely because she loads so much meaning into the context of a single word that understanding the tapestry of one word's meaning through other works is necessary to perform a proper exegesis. This chapter considers Clifton's interviews, archival material, and autobiographical insights rendered in her poetry.[13] I take cues from her conversations with spirits that she calls The Ones. Clifton does not distance herself or her spiritual practice from her work, and neither will I in this reading. Her poetry is in conversation with the many interviews and discussions she has given in the context of her poems.

I also place Clifton's atheology of joy in conversation with womanist and Black liberationist theologians who also consider the nature of God, suffering, and evil. The poet who insists on joy grapples with suffering because she must; *Why do Black folks suffer?* is a high-stakes question for the poet, the Black theologian, and the scholar of Black studies. Theodicy poses a particular problem for Black folks globally, as anti-Blackness manifests in violent forms across continents. It is founded in a set of philosophies already designed to desecrate the body, mind, and spirit of a Black woman poet. In agreement with Ashon Crawley's assertion, "to think theologically, to think philosophically, is to think racially,"[14] I understand Clifton's atheology of joy to be a way of reading theological and philosophical constructions of the human with the literary and spiritual tools she has as a poet and as a "natural channel"—thinking through and ecstatically against what Crawley would name "the epistemology of western constructions."[15] Further, I consider Clifton's writing on Black suffering in the context of larger dis-cussions of Black suffering and death in Black studies and Black feminist thought that counter the violent mode of being that is "the human and its . . . repetition."[16] Clifton must consider Black life under surveillance, threat, and in the wake of enslavement, yet faithfully insists, "always joy—right?"

"The Whole of Life": The Complexity of Human Experience and the Insurgent Subject

> *I never learned to cut feelings off. I never learned that you were supposed to contain your feelings if you were an educated person, a sophisticated person. I did learn that I had to see things wholly and I learned to feel wholly as well, especially the complexities of what it means to be human and the complexities of what it means to be me.*
> **—LUCILLE CLIFTON IN AN INTERVIEW WITH BILL MOYERS[17]**

Clifton insisted on a holistic approach to telling the story and used the language of "wholeness" when in conversation about her work and the human condition. Her approach to knowledge considers the complexity of existence and centers those whose existence is deemed a problem to the concept of the human. As a way or practice that centers complex life, Lucille Clifton's atheology of joy does the work that Kelly Brown Douglas asks of theologies of "survival and liberation/ wholeness," which is to "be accountable to the 'least of these' . . ."[18] Clifton's devel-opment of an atheology of joy considers "the least of these," and is based on her understanding of a wholistic life that encompasses material as well as spiritual experience and knowledge evidenced in her own mystical spiritual and creative practice as well as her experience with biblical text. In an interview with Charles H. Rowell, Clifton speaks of the wholeness of knowledge as inclusive of feeling. She states: "The whole truth is that we're not all just our head and what we think. Logic is very useful; so is feeling."[19] The wholeness of human experience extends to the complexity of human thought and the production of knowledge.

While the sparse yet complex language of poetry attempts to, as poet Rita Dove has said, communicate a greater "inner truth," the trouble with critical interpretation is that it seeks to foreclose. [20] In its hubris, literary criticism can flatten the complexity of an idea, a population, and even a poem. This is how we like our ways of knowing. In expository propositional prose we can control the chaos of the world, ordering it with diagrams, outlines, and a concluding chapter so that we are at once comforted in the feeling of having known a thing and having struggled to learn that thing. Yet, there are limits. What amount of exposition can define the experience of joy?

In order for joy to be at all contained and unequivocally one's own, knowing must be placed in the body. Feelin is in itself a tool for interpretation, and it may also be interpreted. In the African American tradition of signifying, joy means joy when one means it. Joy also means life when one means it. Joy means the complexity of life when intended because joy is a thing that is felt so that it can be understood.

Feelin is not foreclosed knowledge. It does not matter whether or not you agree with the conclusion of the story or one perceived meaning of the song. The point is that you feel how it moves along, the motivation, the tools, and the experience that leads to the conclusion. I do not intend to foreclose the meanings of Clifton's poetry. I do not "interpret" her poetry for readers—other writers do this just fine—when they do it. What I address is the evidence of her atheology in action. Because feelin is not foreclosed knowledge, it has room for those who feel it and those who don't. As a theory in the flesh, it is both rooted in physical reality *and* mutable. [21] Open for revisions, it thrives in *both/and*. For Clifton, poetry operates in the *both/and* of intellectual engagement and intuition. In an interview with Rowell Clifton, she says, "Poetry, it seems to me—what I tell my students—comes from both intellect and intuition. One doesn't separate oneself out. It's not either/or; it's both/and again."[22] The power of feelin as a form of knowledge is in its ability to operate in the *both/and*. Joy operates in such a place.

ONENESS AND WRITING [WITH] THE SPIRIT

As someone who sees the antecedent to her writing as "good preaching," Clifton's poetry is notably in conversation with Black church and folk ways of speaking and seeing the world. [23] Her poems, in concert with these other ways of knowing, explore why she suffers, why in turn, Black folks suffer, and why suffering exists at all. Although not a very religious person, spirituality and biblical text informed Clifton's poetry and worldview.[24] She considered writing an integral part of her spiritual practice, and poetry was a way of distilling her experiences as a spiritual person into form. In her last interview, Clifton calls herself a carpenter, the same trade for which Jesus of Nazareth is known. She states, "I do carpentry that is needed for what's going on, in the carpenter's rule, not the poet's rule."[25] The theme of making good use of herself runs constant in her public writing, interviews, and even her personal reflections, and they are always imbued with spirituality.

Clifton's personal history with the Black Southern Baptist church places her use of midrash in context, but as a person who described herself as "more spiritual," Clifton's religious background was also influenced by a metaphysical relationship with spirits she calls the Ones. The Ones act as muses, guides, and ghostly figures who speak to the mysteries of the universe. They appear in individual poems in the section "Messages from the Ones" found in the book *Mercy*. There, she writes of being chosen by the Ones in order to share their messages. Clifton communicated with these spirits by multiple means: Ouija board play, life regression, sitting/listening, and automatic writing. Automatic writing is the practice of tarrying with spirits (sitting and listening) and allowing that sensation to move pen across the page.[26] It is in these writings that an engagement with questions about the origin of the universe and notions of good and evil emerge. In an automatic writing dated March 20, 1977, Lucille/the Ones appear to write:

> We wish to begin by discussing the origins of / the universe. We will discuss it / in a manner that you can understand / The universe was born in a mind of / the universe was formed from the mind of / the creator it was / his plan to make perfect [. . .][27] (figure 9)

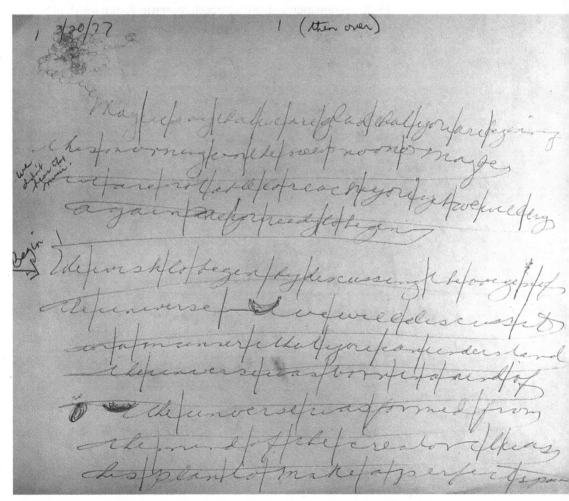

Figure 9. "Spirit Writing, 1977" copyright © 1977 by Lucille Clifton. Stuart A. Rose Manuscript, Archives, and Rare Book Library, Emory University; Lucille Clifton papers, box 30, folder 1. Used by permission of Curtis Brown, Ltd.

The writing at this point gets less decipherable, then becomes clearer as Lucille/ the Ones suggest that the earthly channel write on a new page (figures 10 and 11). It continues:

> May we begin again. Just as your world is a place / of singular materi- ally so is this world in / which we are a world of singular energy / we are a part of that energy [more] of the / spirits were curious about the effect of this / on selves and the creator devised a place / where it could be [used on earth?] of the spirits was [. . .] the choice [often] the / world on not and many refused but / many decided to try and were trapped inside this is the reason for the doublethink organ of the [. . .] circle of return / though materially so she spend energy that we will discuss this with / you so that you can understand / and then perhaps write a book about / it so that others can understand [. . .] you can be a help in these times / you have been shown to be a [. . .] good channel for this information and / we have been chosen to share it with [. . .]"[28]

Figure 10. "Spirit Writing, 1977" copyright © 1977 by Lucille Clifton. Stuart A. Rose Manuscript, Archives, and Rare Book Library, Emory University; Lucille Clifton papers, box 30, folder 1. Used by permission of Curtis Brown, Ltd.

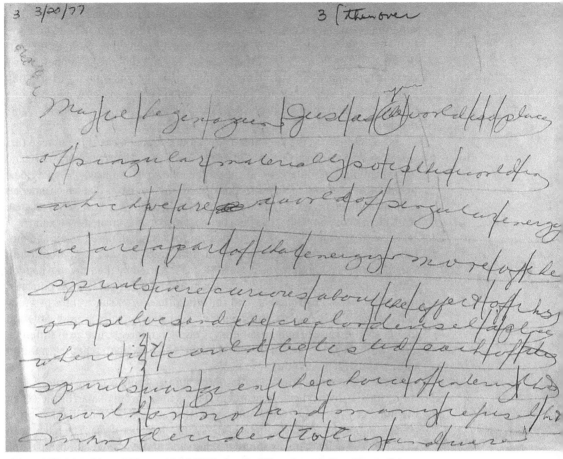

Figure 11. "Spirit Writing, 1977" copyright © 1977 by Lucille Clifton. Stuart A. Rose Manuscript, Archives, and Rare Book Library, Emory University; Lucille Clifton papers, box 30, folder 1. Used by permission of Curtis Brown, Ltd.

Clifton's spirit writing and midrash demonstrate an adherence to and development of a spiritual creative practice that is informed by both a religious background and a metaphysical belief and practice. This pantheist spirituality and her creative practice allows Clifton to grapple with the theodical question with a more robust set of tools than biblical text alone. Writing is a technology by which Clifton is able to explore the mysterious and perplexing problems of good and evil. In her midrash, Lucifer's divine origins are not taken for granted—in fact Lucifer's divinity means something quite important about the value of good and evil on human life. There can be no sense of goodness without this figure who sheds light on what differentiates the good from the bad. There can be no joy without a sense of the complexities of feeling.

Informed by her religious background and spiritual practice, Clifton revisits the biblical events in the Garden of Eden, also known as the fall of man, to explore the roots of suffering and the nature of evil in its relationship to pleasure.[29] If we revisit the story Clifton may be referencing when she states that to refuse joy is to sin against "what made us," we can garner some insight into the contours of joy, suffering, and this concept of sin. Clifton seeks out "what made us" and finds joy. In her capacity to seek and know joy, she refutes the logics that would assume she does not exist at all, much less experience joy. Joy and suffering are nonexclusive, non-dualistic experiences that structure human life. Joy and suffering exist within and because of each other, and this interlocution is what makes it possible for a being that is both "non-white and woman," a being outside of the notion of Man, to exist.

As an origin story, the fall of man offers foundational ideas of the human that would become medieval Christian ideology. By casting Adam (who comes to stand in for man) in God's image, we are given the following: an image of God as ideal man, man as *in process* to the perfection of God, and woman as that which emerges from man un-whole. From God, something related to but less than God is created: man. From man, something less than but related to man is created—woman.

The woman's alliance with the serpent and evil through the baseness of temptation and desire precipitates man's fall from grace, forever away from God's Paradise. Man's potential to be close to God is thwarted by the woman who foolishly brings humanity closer to the evil whims of the serpent. Man is punished with labor, harsh environment, and thus the difficulty of survival for listening to his lesser.[30] Thus divine ruling names woman and her voice as unreliable and ultimately the cause of human suffering. This hierarchical structure of suffering, along with Eve's birth out of the rib of Adam, sets into sharp relief the status of women as divinely subordinate to men.

While Enlightenment-era notions of the human would claim to write against the script of a divine theological order vis-à-vis the concept of Man birthed from the mind of God, the lasting imprint remained sacrosanct. Christianity would come to support scientific notions of the human and vice versa. The fallen man would now be defined not by sins of the flesh and his inverted relationship to the divine, but to a higher order of his own mind beyond the natural world.[31] This new construction, however, continued to rely on splitting the flesh apart from the mind and spirit, and mind would supersede spirit. This system would also construct formations of the human that presume fundamental moral difference, such as the mark of Cain, and forge into sharp relief binary gender logics vis-à-vis Eve and Adam's opposing female- and male-ness.[32]

As this story draws a template for notions of the human, it also produces questions about the nature of God and the function of evil. If God is all-powerful, all-knowing, and all-benevolent, how and why do bad things happen—beginning with the fall of man? Why didn't God stop Eve from being seduced by the serpent who bid her to eat the forbidden fruit? Why did the serpent exist at all for her to be tempted? It would bring this writer to wonder: Why, if God exists, do any such logics that would retain my oppression exist at all?

Clifton's way of joy, which revels in the mind, spirit, *and* the particular fleshiness of the body, identifies an insurgent subject, self-made like the human, but also otherwise and whole. This entity emerges as a testimony to joy amid the terrible things that may happen. Embodied in Eve and made possible by the luxocratic work of Lucifer, this subject emerges from the biblical fall of man as an otherwise being—complex and full of light. The next section of this chapter ruminates with Clifton's midrash on the fall of man in order to fully render this subject and thus make sense of the residue left behind by the break from the flesh upon which the construction of man of reason/human stands.

Here on This Bridge / The Bright Back of the Woman Is the Formation of an Insurgent Subject

I've said that I know there's Lucifer in Lucille, because I know me—I can be so petty, it's amazing! And there is therefore a possibility of Lucille in Lucifer. Lucifer was doing what he was supposed to do, too, you know? It's too easy to see Lucifer as all bad. Suppose he were merely being human.

—CLIFTON IN CONVERSATION WITH HILARY HOLLADAY

Let my childhood pastor, Sunday school teacher, and James Weldon Johnson tell it, the world started like this: In the beginning, the earth was void, dark, and uninhabitable. God, who exists above and beyond this void, decides to make a world.[33] According to Johnson specifically, it is because of God's loneliness, which is only salved by the creation of humans, that the world is made. After creating the sky and earth, orbs of light that would rule the day and night, waters, mountains, land, and plants—even after creating every kind of animal that lives in the sea or on the land or flies above—God is still lonely and wishes to create something in God's image. So, God, "Like a mammy bending over her baby, / Kneeled down in the dust," to create man.[34] It should be noted that Genesis provides two versions of this story. One describes the making of "humankind" in plural; the other describes making Adam, understood as the first man, and his helpmate Eve. The second version of the story explains more than creation. This is the story that tells us not only how the world was formed, but what disobedience is, how disobedience is punished, how gender is structured by subjection, the cunning of evildoers, and why human suffering is a part of God's will. The fall of man story teaches religious followers that suffering is divine punishment for the original sin committed by Eve and Adam in the garden. More specifically, gender and sex *difference* are explained and *fixed* through the discursive punishments endured by Adam and Eve.

When Eve and Adam confessed to eating the forbidden fruit at the behest of the serpent, they were swiftly ordered to leave the garden. The serpent is damned to slither on the ground for the rest of its life, Eve is punished with subordination to her husband and pain in childbirth, and Adam is punished with a lifetime of toiling on the earth to feed himself and his family. Why did God allow this fall to happen? Why was there a tree that would make possible the knowledge of good and evil available in the garden, and why would an all-powerful, all-knowing, all-good God put it there? Clifton's midrash attempts to answer these questions, and in doing so she positions woman (through Eve) and Lucifer (through the serpent) as agents who know of a greater good. At the center of that good is pleasure.

Lucille Clifton takes up Adam and Eve and the story of their expulsion from the Garden of Eden in two series of poems across two books: the "tree of life" series in *Quilting* and the "brothers" series in *The Book of Light*. Central to both series is the perspective of Lucifer, imagined as the serpent. Lucifer—born the prince of light, the morning star—is also a fallen angel, God's first son who was once close to God in heaven and then laid low for their attempts to usurp power from God.[35] The "tree of life" series begins with the origin of Lucifer noted in the biblical passage Isaiah 14:12. Isaiah 14 is largely a praise song for the downfall of the King of

Babylon: "How art thou fallen from Heaven, O Lucifer, son of the morning?"[36] Lucifer's beginning as an angel in heaven, as the "morning star," is invoked here as a familiar, and Lucifer's name, which shares the same root as Lucille Clifton's, further invokes the other shared root by which Lucifer's task is set out—light. [37] While the biblical victory song celebrates Lucifer's being expelled, Clifton asks of his whereabouts. Because the morning star has been banished from heaven, light itself has gone and heaven is dark without him. The poem laments, "bringer of light / it is all shadow / in heaven without you."[38] Though angels in heaven sing prayers of thanksgiving, the voice of the poem is witnessing a powerful shift in the dynamics of heaven.

God, identified here as the "solitary brother,"[39] points toward the garden where God's new creations have committed the first sin, taking the fruit from the tree of knowledge of good and evil and now, "light breaks / where no light was before / where no eye was prepared / to see."[40] The first sin has inaugurated a new quality of light due to the hijinks of the lost brother of heaven, who has lit up the world for unready eyes; "oh lucifer," the voice laments, "what have you done."[41] This poem acts as a preamble to this story in the voice of another who has the vision between heaven and earth and the unique perspective of heaven. The poems that follow take up the perspectives of the players in the story of the fall of man: Eve, Lucifer, and Adam. There is also an omniscient narrator later in the series, but that voice is distinctly different from this voice that opens the series, speaking directly to Lucifer, asking, "what have you done?" and "where have you fallen to?"[42]

It is this voice that can remember Lucifer as a sympathetic being. The second poem in the series, "remembering the birth of lucifer," recounts Lucifer's birth as one of grandeur and curiosity. The quality of light that Lucifer was born to maintain was "too much for / one small heaven."[43] The seraphim, the highest of angels, were wary of this new angel, "and began / to wait and to watch."[44] The kind of light that would be overwhelming for heaven appears to be the reason for Lucifer's fall. This is key because Lucifer's purpose for being—to bring in morning light—results in Lucifer's fall, and it is Lucifer's fall that in Clifton's interpretation of the serpent, precipitates the biblical fall of man.

In "whispered to lucifer" the familiar voice from the first poem in the series asks Lucifer why they left. "was it the woman / enticed you to leave us[?]"[45] To choose the word *entice* invokes the sense that seduction is at play. From this vantage point, the sympathetic speaker asks if it was the woman who lured Lucifer, yet the voice highlights the possibility of mutual sexual excitement for both the serpent and Eve, "was it to touch her / featherless arm / was it to curl your belly // around her[?]"[46] While close to God and "going about [their] / father's business," the angels in heaven are also "less radiant / less sure."[47] This ending couplet pairs the quality of light with safety and trust. Heaven is not the same without Lucifer—a startling revelation that the presupposed enemy's absence in heaven is such a loss of certainty.

Clifton's reading of Lucifer's character as doing his work as the bringer of light wherever it is needed highlights her complex view of the nature of evil. The biblical enemy is not evil itself but the seduction of the will to discern good from evil. Thus, the concept of evil appears to exist within the will of humans but largely as a neutral force. Lucifer comes to understand his position and his actions in the poem "lucifer understanding at last." He begins on these terms with God: "thy servant lord // bearer of lightning / and of lust," and describes his duties on earth as, "thrust between the / legs of the earth / into this garden // phallus and father

/ doing holy work."[48] Thus the project of entering Eden and enticing Eve to eat of the forbidden fruit is pictured here as another kind of conception—a sexualized and phallocentric injection of light imagined as lightning: dangerous, lifegiving, and quick. Lucifer's work is to bear light as awareness—new knowledge—and this new knowledge is pleasure itself, "oh sweet delight" he says, "if the angels / hear of this /// there will be no peace / in heaven."[49] As such, pleasures available on earth would be envious in heaven. Thus, the work of Lucifer can be described as holistic—what results in suffering, the punishment for eating the fruit of the tree of knowledge of good and evil, is also vast sensory experience that is pleasurable as well.

For the poet, the garden is a metaphor whose meaning is in flux and reflects on the reader more than the garden or the very nature of God. The garden of delight is pleasure and pleasure's meaning: "for them" she writes, "it is a test."[50] As for Eve, she has taken up her lushness, her relationship to sensuousness and pleasure, and ushered it into human existence. As Adam struggles to name the two, Eve thinks, "tonight as he sleeps / I will whisper into his mouth / our names."[51] This Eve is not passive. In this midrash, the poet restores Eve's voice, rejects the subordination of the woman ordained in Genesis and, in centering her voice, also centers sensuousness and sexual pleasure. Eve describes Lucifer as a "smooth talker" who "slides into [her] dreams,"[52] and fills them with forbidden fruit. Eve testifies to seduction here, the seduction of her own lush life and body. In the second and final stanza she says, "it is your own lush self / you hunger for."[53] This perspective of the seduction that leads to eating the forbidden fruit indeed posits Lucifer as the seducer, able to penetrate Eve's dreams and leave her wanting what is forbidden. What is forbidden is the fruit, sure, but we also see the fruit as metaphor for Eve's own desires—a want of her fleshy self that alludes to her own sexuality.

So, humanity goes forth, in light, knowing carnal desire. The omniscient voice narrates the exit of God's clay creation, Lucifer, and Eve from the garden: "so they went out / clay and morning star / following the bright back / of the woman."[54] Eve now bears the shimmering light and births a new world devoid of the chaos in which the divine being begat the world according to Genesis 1:1, "as she walked past / . . . / into the unborn world / chaos fell away / before her like a cloud / and everywhere seemed light // seemed glorious / seemed very eden."[55] Eve's descent into the world beyond the garden was the birth of a new world filled with delight—as the poem goes on "the road led from delight / into delight." It is the quality of light, borne first by Lucifer, that makes such discernment possible, and thus the experience of pleasure possible. This delight is characterized by the "sharp / edge of seasons" and "the warm vale of sheet and sweat after love."[56] Clifton is noting a special kind of unsanitized delight that can be described as the "funk" of life. Toni Morrison describes funk in *The Bluest Eye*, "The dreadful funkiness of passion, the funkiness of nature, the funkiness of the wide range of human emotions."[57] The funk of life disrupts the sanitized and sinless world created by a perfectly patriarchal God.

The series ends with Lucifer reflecting on his role in this particular bearing of light and his role as first son of God, ". . . it was / to be / i who was called son / if only of the morning."[58] Yet his position as first son also meant that he had some omniscience, that some would suffer if he did not take their place. He saw "that some must / walk or all will crawl," and thus Lucifer's illumination brought the possibility of free will and seduction.[59] For it was not new to Adam and Eve that they had a choice to eat of the forbidden fruit. What was new was that the choice had previously undisclosed consequences—knowledge of good and evil. This was, apparently, worth the risk. Lucifer would know, as they had already been expelled from another Paradise. Lucifer's job, however, is not read here as outside of the will of the God who created them. As they say, "i the only lucifer / created out of fire / illuminate i could / and so illuminate i did."[60]

An Acknowledgment of the Difficult

James Cone, the architect of Black liberation theology, considered the God of Jesus of Nazareth as one whot suffers with the oppressed and calls the followers of Christ to common struggle against oppressors.[61] Womanist theologian Delores Williams questions the biblical notion of redemption through suffering as demonstrated by Jesus Christ's suffering on the cross because of its implications for sanctifying Black women's suffering and justifying our pain as historical and rhetorical surrogates.[62] In agreement with Williams, Kelly Brown Douglas asserts that resistance to a surrogate reading of Christ's sacrifice is not in service to what she calls "ordinary" Black women.[63] She calls for womanist theology to affirm the "wholeness" of Black women who suffer, and reject the logics of redemptive suffering.[64] William Jones and Anthony Pinn suggest human-centric theism and strong humanism, or atheism, respectively, as an answer to the conundrum theodicy presents.[65] These theological and counter-theological readings of the nature of God through theodicy share a common concern with Lucille Clifton, and that is the condition of folks whose suffering is systemic and ongoing. Along with womanist theologians, Clifton does not go on to glorify suffering but instead chooses to consider it while embracing the wholeness of human existence. As such, Clifton centers the human as theological and secular humanists suggest, but because there is a mysterious *something else* there, something spiritual and unaccounted for in the mysteries of the Ones who speak of the great unity of all things, Clifton's approach to the theodical question invokes unity as a persistent force. The "brothers" series sets up this unified reading of biblical text by making the divine agents of eternal good and evil co-conspirators rather than rivals.

Set in a time "long after" the fall of man, the series depicts a conversation only heard from the perspective of "an aged" Lucifer.[66] The series is in eight parts, arranged with one poem on each page in the voice of Lucifer and conversational in tone.[67] The first poem, "invitation," is just as much an invocation as it invites God into conversation with Lucifer in "creation's bed," the Garden of Eden where Lucifer has long been banished. The familiarity with which Lucifer can speak to God is perhaps highlighted by the poet's decision to age Lucifer, to have him come into a kind of maturity to speak with God on frank terms: "let us rest here a time," he says, "like two old brothers / who watched it happen and wondered / what it meant."[68] Something is afoot with Lucifer's proposition to reflect on the events of the garden *with* God—as if Lucifer is gearing up for a confrontation, a difficult conversation that challenges God. Wouldn't the all-knowing God, having orchestrated the events of the Fall and everything after, simply know what it meant? Lucifer's proposition suggests that there is some mystery after all of this time, that either God or he would benefit from reflection.

The poem goes on in the ceremonial structure of worship. Having begun in invocation—the poem moves on to exhortation. Part 2, "how great Thou art," is so titled for an old hymn of the same name. It continues Lucifer's musings in the established conversational tone and talks about the nature of God's understanding of Godself; "listen," the poem begins, "You are beyond / even Your own understanding."[69] Lucifer goes on to describe God on the same terms as God's human creations: "that rib and rain and clay . . . / is not what You believed / You were, / but it is what you are."[70] When Lucifer says, "in Your own image as some / lexicographer supposed," he is referencing biblical text that purports that God made humans in God's image and scoffing at the possibility that God's image is in any way describable. The thesis of this section of the poem is that the creations God made *are*, in fact, God. That in creating matter from God's own mind, God merely re-created Godself in humans. Lucifer commands, "the face, both he and she, / the odd ambition, the desire / to reach beyond the stars / is You. . . ."[71] Even the qualities that interpreters have understood as God's motive for creating the world and its imperfections, Lucifer says, are ". . . all You. / the loneliness, the perfect / imperfection."[72] God's qualities are those of the people that God creates: lonely, curious, full of wonder beyond the self; and thus, God's flaws are perfect.

What makes Clifton's exploration of theodicy so peculiar is that she considers the nature of Lucifer as well as God. As such, she takes up the concept of evil personified and explores its projections incisively. This is not to say that theologians do not consider the nature of evil itself; they do.[73] What is compelling about her poems as theodicy is that she considers the nature of evil personified in Lucifer with the kind of rigor and interest that is lent to the nature of good and God in traditional theodicy. The theoretical paradox could possibly read as: *If Lucifer is all evil, an enemy of humans and God, why has God not destroyed them?* By answering the theodical question with the notion of faulty human free will, Augustine of Hippo is credited with moving the theodical conversation away from the serpent or the embodiment of evil in one persona.[74] Clifton's intervention pursues an unanswered question in Augustine's contribution: *Why would a perfect God create beings capable of such evil?*

In "as for myself," Lucifer moves from reflecting on the imperfect perfection of God to his own nature in relation to the personifications he is often given. He calls himself, "less snake than angel / less angel than man," and asks about his consciousness as a serpent: "how come i to this / serpent's understanding?"[75] This is the perspective of one who was made both before the world *and in* the world. The serpent's position is a vantage point from below, belly to the ground, "watching creation from / a hood of leaves."[76] Lucifer's underdog status allows him a particular and otherwise unexplored view—a subversive knowledge if you will. Lucifer's eye is on the creation of Eve as she represents a watershed in the creation of the world. He says, "i have foreseen the evening / of the world."[77] Here the poet, cleverly playing with Eve's name, makes the first woman an action happened upon the world: the eve-ening. The serpent has indeed watched God create day and night—the onslaught of darkness that promises light in the morning. The serpent has also witnessed the birth of this new post-clay creature. Lucifer would have some interest in the bringer of night to do his work as the morning star. She is also peculiar to Lucifer for her ability to feed from her body and self-create— something only he and God have yet been able to do. Calling her "the breast of Yourself," Lucifer cites Eve as a "separated out" and exposed part of God's being.[78] Eve is sent to do work on God's behalf as well, and is thus expected to come back into the fold. Lucifer goes on to describe the shared continuity between God, Lucifer, and Eve: "as sure as her returning, / i too am blessed with / the one gift you cherish; / to feel the living move in me / and to be unafraid."[79] Here, the poet emerges within Lucifer, as one who can create and know of what they have created. Adam is credited with the birth of Eve, but he never knew of her existence within him as he was made to go into a deep sleep to allow for her birth. The Genesis 3:16 curse that Eve receives in punishment for her sin, pain in childbirth, is reset to highlight the ability to give birth. This Eve is not set apart for her particular way of suffering but has the agency to create as God does. This midrash pushes against the concept of inherent subordination and suffering to which women are biblically and biocentrically conscribed; it eschews what Snorton calls the logics that sustained racial slavery that are also within the "expression and arrangements" of sex and gender.[80] In Clifton's midrash, it is Eve who comes up with her and Adam's names, and it is Eve who imagines a world beyond the garden heralded by her "bright back."[81] Eve's particular is not her suffering; it is her ability to make another thing and to name herself in the process.

Clifton's affinity for Lucifer goes beyond the shared Latin root of their name. Clifton was also intrigued by Lucifer's capacity for pleasure and self-making—the shared trait between Eve, Lucifer, and God. To be "between starshine and clay" is to be between the self-making Lucifer, who chose to fall from the ultimate manifestation of Paradise in order to have a world their own, and the fallibility of human existence embodied in Adam. Lucifer identifies with this ability to self-name and create, though he was cast out of heaven for it. Taking imagery from the "tree of life" series, Lucifer goes on to compare the shared fates of Eve, Adam, and himself. They begin, "in my own defense / what could I choose / but to slide along beside them, / they whose only sin / was being their father's children."[82] Lucifer's self-defense disturbs the notion that Adam and Eve had free will and accuses God of negligence, having the power but perhaps not the will to intervene: "only You could have called / their ineffable names" he says.[83] But Adam and Eve became new, having been excommunicated from the garden with "a new and terrible luster / burning their eyes."[84] Could that luster have been placed by the light bearer himself? Is this not the work he was sent to do as discussed in "the tree of life?" This luster, truth, the ability to see evil and good, sensuousness—is all ahead of them in the world *outside of* Eden. The world that Eve ushered in, flanked by morning star and clay.

A SILENT GOD :: A DEAD GOD

In the wake of the end of the perfect world designed by God, God goes silent. One of the problems of theodicy rests on the conundrum of God's unwillingness if not inability to end suffering. A God unwilling to prevent evil is just as unnerving, if not more disturbing, than a God unable to prevent evil. In this understanding of the nature of God, God lacks the omnibenevolence believed to be the nature of God. An idle God is no comfort to humans prone to suffering. An idle God is perhaps as useful to humans as a dead one.

This silence is at the heart of the theodical question, and Lucifer asks it directly in the poem that follows, "tell me," he says, "tell us why . . . / You neither raised Your hand / nor turned away, tell us why / You watched the excommunication of

/ that world and You said nothing."[85] Lucifer's question exposes the silence as a dynamic actor in the scene of the fall: God has the capacity to bring worlds into being by speech, as demonstrated in Genesis, and said nothing—belying God's omnipotence;[86] God watched Eve and Adam commit acts that would excommunicate them from the world of God's making, through punishment of God's design, and said nothing until it was time for them to be punished. Insight into this may be found in the section's title, which takes the line "the silence of God is God" from Carolyn Forché's *The Angel of History*.[87] The context of Forché's line is the Holocaust in Nazi-occupied Europe, and this musing on the nature of God is as complex as it is simple. Silence to the question of *why?* in the wake of human catastrophe and suffering takes over the consciousness—it is an existential crisis resolved only by its echo. It is a mystery beyond human understanding and thus takes up the mysterious nature of Godself—if one is to maintain that God is inherently good. In the garden where God's presence is primary and overwhelming, God's silence after the fall of man *becomes* the nature of God as fallen humans know it. Humans after the fall do not know the God that walks in the garden with them—humans know absence, silence, and mystery.

Lucifer admonishes God for this silence during the apocalyptic consequences of the fall. The excommunication they mention is specifically of *that* world, the tense and object here indicating both another time and place. Eden is a world in the eternal past, an origin where humans may never return, its geographies stipulated in Genesis, though unseen since.[88] The ending of that world has ushered in a new one, but the question still remains why God would allow for apocalypse, this ending, and the many catastrophic endings since. Black studies and Black feminist thought would tell us that apocalyptic conditions are the structures of Black everyday life. The wake of enslavement is life after the end of the world. Considering the mining of finite resources of the land, disposal of toxic waste that returns to the water supply, war and climate change, apocalypse is expected—anticipated for us today.[89]

In an earlier poem titled "the beginning of the end of the world," Clifton imagines that the end of the world would begin with the declining population of roaches.[90] Clifton has often written about roaches—particularly her murderous tendencies toward them—but alongside an understanding and respect for their persistence towards life.[91] If the roaches are dying, humans, she concludes, must also be dying. The end of the world is an ongoing event, a world with its own beginning. What happens after the end of the world, and what afterlife of ending are we enjoying in this life? This is a theme mentioned by Lucifer, who speaks of foreseeing the end of the world (the eve-ening) at the moment of creation.[92] Lucifer's vision of the end of the world is simultaneous with creation. This makes sense as Lucifer witnessed many apocalypses: their removal from heaven, the creation of the world which was also the ending of what was before, the expulsion from the garden was another ending, and the new world heralded by the Fall was yet another beginning that is also an end. Lucifer, the morning star, exists in this constancy of existence and reminds us that Eden is just one end of a different beginning—one beginning of an end to something else. What beings are created from these new endings and beginnings? How do we go on living when the world has ended, will end again and again?[93]

The idea of a dead God (note, not just an absent God, but a God who was once alive and now dead) was a captivating conclusion for Western post-Enlightenment philosophy. As scientific reason ruptured and replaced Christian *theologos* as the governing order of knowledge, the corpse of God could be replaced by Man with all of the powers and capacities to create therein. However, the creativity of the Enlightenment also produced conquest and the ratiomorphic apparatus that naturalized the biocentric idea of the human and the human's exclusions. So, when Friedrich Nietzsche famously pronounces that God is dead and "we" (man) killed him, he is citing specifically the logical outcomes of scientific reason that would end religion and belief in the mysterious.[94] The silence produced by scientific reason in the wake of a dead God is the silencing of the Other. As Charles Long states in his classic text *Significations*, "those peoples and cultures who became during this period the 'pawns' of Western cultural creativity . . . were present not as voices speaking but as the silence which is necessary to all speech."[95] The loss of the mystery of God co-witnessed the enforced silence of the colonized, the inhabitants of the non-Western world—people of a darker hue. God and the chaotic Other were irreconcilable in this construction of Man. Of the chaotic Other, Sylvia Wynter notes, "the 'negro' . . . was not imagined even to have languages worth studying, nor to partake in culture, so total was his mode of Nigger Chaos."[96] As such, the silence of the speech of chaotic others and God allows for uninterrupted Western prattling.

That very silencing makes heard and read speech possible for the chaotic Other. According to Long, "silence is a fundamentally ontological position, a position which though involved in language and speech, exposes us to a new kind of reality and existence."[97] Such silence would be an anxiety-producing, inevitable end of discourse for the progeny of the Enlightenment. As Long notes, "In the very pursuit of authentic selfhood, the Western world has come face to face with silence, with the exhaustion of the forms of the world. What more is to be said after Buchenwald or after a flight to the moon or after one has said that God is dead?"[98] Speech becomes a series of declarative statements—of concepts that overdetermine meaning upon the silenced Other that can only expand within finite human experience.

If God's silence after the Fall and once again after Enlightenment produces the possibility for human utterance and manages to terrorize post-Enlightenment thought into existential quiet, then perhaps it is silence to which we should attend. That silence persists in the everlasting question about the meaning of existence, in questions unanswered and unknown to ask, in questions beyond finite mortal existence that Western structures of knowledge refuse in its hubris. It is in the awareness of silence that Oneness is made apparent—the concept of Oneness being that which connects the universe, all beings across species, all objects, all celestial bodies, all thought. And it is awareness of this Oneness or what the Ones call "a world of singular energy," that makes creativity possible.[99] Stay with me: In the beginning, the world was void. In the beginning, God was lonely. God was quiet with Godself and it is this moment in which the universe is created. That is, the poet in her quiet, stolen or structured, alone on that bridge between starshine and clay made a kind of life. As Kevin Quashie notes, "The quiet subject finds agency in the capacity to surrender to his or her inner life. If there is a fearlessness in this surrender it is because of the freedom of falling into what cannot be known entirely, as well as falling into all that one is."[100] That poet would also, in her quiet, tap into unknowns, give her body over as a spiritual channel and poet and make her a world from that place.

The penultimate poem in the "brothers" series, "still there is mercy, there is grace," reflects in the silence bemoaned in the previous poem. Having questioned the silence of God, Lucifer finds themself questioning their own existence and own possibility of survival: "how otherwise / could i [. . .] "curl one day safe and still / beside You / at Your feet, perhaps, but, amen, Yours?"[101] If God is omnibenevolent and omnipotent and the serpent is the embodiment of evil, why has the serpent not been obliterated? For Lucifer to ask the theodical question is to ask why they exist at all. But Lucifer *is* alive, and what a mercy for the serpent's sake.

In the final poem in the "brothers" series ". . . . . is God," silence and Lucifer's revelation fold back on themselves to reveal Oneness. The title of the poem revisits Forché's line and performs the silence of God on the page. The page, Lucifer's recounting, and Clifton's poems cannot contain the mysterious nature of the question, so ellipses attempt to communicate that quiet. Within the ellipses, Lucifer considers their emergence with and from God. After wild accusations, blasphemy, and the end of the world, there is still silence. Lucifer meekly begins with "so"—and as with the sound of a guest clearing their throat after a short, awkward hush at a dinner party, we are made more aware of the noise of Lucifer's speech.[102] After the noise of that revelation—the fact of his own existence—after the silence which follows, Lucifer recovers, "having no need to speak / You sent Your tongue / splintered into angels."[103] Having been the nearest—though fallen—angel, Lucifer is implicated in this: "even I, / with my little piece of it / have said too much."[104] In reflecting on God, Lucifer has reflected on themself. They have had a job in this fall of man, thus the creation of a world, and are therefore not separate from God. He goes on "to ask You to explain / is to deny You / before the word / You were. / You kiss my brother mouth. / the rest is silence."[105] Lucifer ends here on the sentiments of the psalmist, David, who said, "be still and know God."[106]

As Long states, "It is a silence which may no longer terrify us, and it is a silence which in its showing might give us an understanding of the human mode of being which moves us beyond conquest, enslavement, and exploitation."[107] Clifton embraces the mystery of God and the possibility for becoming *with* God. She imagines God and Lucifer as forever connected being(s). She embraces the silence of God, as life is chaos *and* being. *Being* is the everlasting answer to the question of theodicy. It might not be sufficient, as no answers would suffice for the atrocities in which lives, species, languages, and worlds are wiped out, and for that we might, as she has said, "cry forever," but within Oneness, that which is difficult is also made of the same matter as that which is pleasurable and present within us all.[108]

Where Black humanists might argue for a rejection of the existence of God in favor of charging humans with the job of ending human-made suffering, and Black feminist thought and Black studies critique the post-Enlightenment concept of the human, Lucille Clifton, on "this bridge," favors a self-made subject that is divine, human, and capable of doing "great good as well as great evil."[109] Her affinity with the shine of the "morning star" reveals a reading of Lucifer that rejects the binary of human and nonhuman, good and evil, and insists on the production of an otherwise being because there is simply no other option *but* to create. Clifton's insistence on "making up" her "kind of life" at the location of the bridge between starshine and clay as described in "won't you celebrate with me" might also be understood by what Kai Green and Treva Ellison call tranifesting. That is, making up her kind of life functions as an "epistemic operation" that "challenge[s] the categories of man and woman as ontological givens."[110] If, as Calvin Warren suggests, that tranifesting is merely seductive, that its possibilities are limited by the perpetual mutedness of Blackness, what Clifton offers in *joy!* is the *is*ness of her be-ing at the foot of a muted God.[111] This is the art of "i be"—a celebration, a call for others to join in with this newly imagined hybrid subject molded between heaven and human.

The Art of "I Be": Conscious, Habitual, and Deliberate Choice

> . . . *come celebrate*
> *with me that everyday*
> *something has tried to kill me*
> *and has failed.*
> —LUCILLE CLIFTON[112]

> *To live is to escape the soft familiar call of the tether, threatening the*
> *ankle, the neck, the voice, threatening to infect the voice with its voice.*
> —DAWN LUNDY MARTIN[113]

> *Resistance is the secret of joy!*
> —ADAM, OLIVIA, BENNY, PIERRE, RAYE, AND MBATI
> VIA ALICE WALKER IN *POSSESSING THE SECRET OF JOY*[114]

Life is a matter neither wholly intellectual nor easy. One could choose to succumb to the voice, to accept the states of disaster in which Black women find ourselves.[115] But life is not a given—a matter of not being dead; it is working against "somethings" that threaten death, worthlessness, erasure. Clifton's "won't you celebrate with me" foregrounds the joy of self-making, of her life both divine and earthly born. The motifs, woven heretofore in her exploration of the nature of God and the fall of man, come together in this *art of i be* that asks that we begin in celebration for what she has "shaped into / a kind of life."[116] Her phrasing here, of "a *kind* of life" draws our attention to the precarity of life itself, what constitutes life made from her Black and female flesh. She was "born in babylon / both nonwhite and woman," left to make up a "kind of life" with "no model."[117] Here, Clifton is speaking of the practice of being in action. She does not name being *human*, but names it *life*—an action ongoing and visceral—a joining of the "*being* of *being human*," to quote Sylvia Wynter.[118] Life ongoing and otherwise imagined from the vantage point of subjects excluded from the domain of the human.[119]

An ars poetica (translated as the "art of poetry") is a poem that describes guiding principles for writing poetry. The Roman poet Horace is cited with composing the first of this kind of treatise, and his influence has prompted many poets since to attempt their own ars poetica. In its modern construction, the ars poetica can be a space for the poet to name their philosophy for coming to the page. Clifton's take on the fall of man provides thinking room for the questions that theodicy asks, the answers that humanism claims to offer, and the concerns that Black studies and Black feminist thought present about the concept of the human. It is in light of Clifton's theodical exploration that this reading of the poem, I argue, serves as an art of "i be"—an art of the practice of *being*.

Clifton speaks of making up a *kind of* life. Shaping it into being. *Shaped*, as in formed from another matter altogether incomplete—flesh unnamed, without its verb. She *shaped* this kind of life "here on this bridge between / starshine and clay," and it is here that the motifs from her midrash on the fall of man find their place in this ceremony of self-making. She who makes herself between the one made of clay (Adam) and starshine (Lucifer) is a kind of being named Lucille. Her reclaimed Eve/self is another kind of subject—a more daring, as Hortense Spillers would say, "insurgent female social subject," fully embodied and monstrous, leading Adam and Lucifer out of the garden and into a divine *and* human experience.[120]

Ever aware of her singularity in this making and having to make oneself without example, she does this work alone, "one hand holding tight / [her] other hand." But this is no thought to mourn; she invites others to enjoy self-making within such precarity, "come celebrate / with me . . ." she says, "that everyday / something has tried to kill me / and has failed."[121] Celebration is centered here as communal acknowledgment and understanding of the miracle of being. A miracle because, as Audre Lorde notes, "we were never meant to survive."[122] Celebration is the joy in Clifton's atheology of *joy*, it is the communion of the practice of self-making that revels in joining flesh with the divine to forge an otherwise life—a life precarious and lush, a funky life that can stand in the wake of its having been assaulted *and still be.*

In order for *joy* to become a practice, a "once in a while" choice, the exercise of it must be self-generated.[123] *Joy* must be self-sustaining. Perhaps this is why Clifton chose the singular word whenever she was asked for her signature; it may have functioned as a self-sustained practice of choosing joy in a body that is under constant threat. Celebration is the cause and practice through which resistance is manifested. Resistance is compulsory—every day—as in: "Every time I walk out of my house, it is a political decision."[124]

Death is inevitable. In some beliefs it allows for humans to join with the silent God. Lucille Clifton, the mystic and spiritual poet, had a less final, less quiet idea of the outcomes of death. If the reams of spirit writing, conversations with the dead through Ouija boards, and poems in the voice of her mother speaking to her in spiritual form tell us anything, it is that, at the very least, Clifton believed in a kind of consciousness or way of being that extends beyond the limits of the physical body. She also believed in the ability to speak with these beings, to write poems with them, and for spirits to write poems through her.

The ultimate silence of death was not a guarantee of Clifton's voice being lost—not if we follow the direct instructions in "won't you celebrate with me." I wondered during that community celebration the summer after her death if it were truly appropriate to read the poem. Had it now lost its meaning because she had died? I wondered if the everyday somethings finally found their way to her and won this time. By engaging with Clifton's poetry with a focus on her way of joy, this question has an answer. Joy does not promise physical immortality. In acknowledging death, joy accepts its existence in favor of choosing life. Choosing joy is the failure of those heinous somethings that seek to kill. Death is a part of the complexity of human life, but its inevitability does not foreclose the possibility of *joy!*

Conclusion: Joy in the Mourning

I have to ask, and perhaps you can feel the despair with which I write this: *How, how, how can I choose* joy in times like these—when the world is ending? How can joy be a practice when I just ruminated on the ways that Blackness is inured by grief? The planet is shifting to make up for the effects of human destruction driven by capitalism, authoritarianism seems to be taking stronger holds globally, greed and selfishness exacerbate the death toll of a global pandemic, and what of the very personal losses that overwhelm? What of the loss that serves as the weather of our lives? How do we feel through that? I turn to Clifton's *Blessing the Boats* for such answers, and find that even in mourning and grief, there is much to know, much to feel, and *always joy, right?*

In "grief," Clifton returns to the garden of Eden and begins with contemplating the grass beneath Adam that bears his weight and witnesses the birth of Eve. The voice of the poem positions grief through empathy by asking that we consider feeling the grass that bears the weight of Adam—chlorophyll darkening at the broken edge of its blades, what she calls, "the original bleeding."[125] The voice imagines the grass itself as something to grieve for, unrecognized and disregarded, belonging to the "horizontal world," differently orriented from the upright, or vertical human.[126] With just that idea of the horizonal world, the reader is invited to reorient themselves toward feeling beyond our own habitual understanding. She goes on to ask that we pause for the raced differentiations of the "human/animal in its coat / of many colors."[127] Clifton gives us imagery from the ground, from beneath that grass, to the animal upright, and finally to a thing called human. We might see where Clifton is going here—she is asking that we grieve the loss of worlds before, including the land and nature that bore, in both the natal and suffering sense, the human animal. The poem ends with a cross species expanse of feeling: "grief for what is born human, / grief for what is not."[128] To begin with the grass is to begin with another vision of the world beyond the human species as she, too, has not been so considered human. The capacity to feel, even in grief, might remind us of the unity of our collective being.

Lucille Clifton's atheology of joy demonstrates how felt knowledge is multidimensional and resists binary modes of categorizing lived experience. Her assertion does not affirm evil nor adopt a theology in support of redemptive suffering. Her approach attends to the practicality of theology's humanism and an earnest concern about genres of the human. Joy serves as a way of navigating toward an otherwise way of being. Joy is not a fleeting experience that feels good, it is an orientation toward knowing and doing something else, even if one has to invent it for themselves. Joy is not without mourning or sorrow. It is inclusive of sorrow as a complex experience of being that is the exuberance of life.

Joy is political because it operates in the everyday survival of a Black woman. When she discusses writing about "the whole of life" with Michael Glaser, Clifton is talking about the complexity of human existence. When she talks about writing "the whole of what I am" with Charles Rowell, she is speaking about the complexity of her existence in her work.[129] And when she refers to herself as a "grown woman" and her poems as "grown woman poems," she is referring to her sexuality and experience as a Black woman.[130] In joy, Clifton claims life for herself in the face of the "somethings" that "try to kill" her, daily.[131] These somethings would aim to kill all manner of lived experience that could be named in joy—"the warm vale of sheet and sweat after love"—pleasures for which Eve risked it all.

The next chapter takes up the erotic—namely ecstasy—as an intentional creative practice that generates from a place both sacred and sacral. It is here, where the *both/and* of Lucifer's light (and previous act as the minister of music in heaven) comes into form directly in the body through the functions of breath and vibration that make singing feel and sound so good. If we have learned anything from the emergent subject self-formed between starshine and clay, it is that what is divine is not without a little dirt on it and that may be the best thing we have going: pleasure's greatest possibility in the sweet funk of life.

CHAPTER 3

Ecstatic Vocal Practice

Singing is running this sound through your body.
You cannot sing a song and not change your condition.
—BERNICE JOHNSON REAGON, IN *THE SONGS ARE FREE*

I have a hard time writing this because, to be quite honest, I get over-whelmed. In listening with, thinking with, singing with Black women vocalists about and within our aesthetics of excess that make way for ecstasy, I just—whoooo . . . lose myself—have to get up from this computer, have to stretch my body, to sing, gyrate, contort my face a little. My neck rolls—some muscles tense while others relax, my pelvis warms, I'm limp and then I'm up again, I have been taken somewhere. I am trying to explain this feelin on the page so you can understand what I'm writing about when I say that this singer has done me in this evening. *Has done me innnnnnnnn*, and how do I write about this feelin? Writing don't contain it; her singing it don't even contain it, my listening has been unable to contain it. It is too much, which is right about enough, which is exactly what I needed—whooo—whoooo. Amen? Amen.

Breathe.

How does one sit down and structure a chapter about feelin this excess of feelin—this ecstasy—without leaving something out, without performing some kind of dissemblance to ensure I am being understood in a scholarly way, when in my hearing and listening the feelin takes over? Bear with me as I do not wish to contain this thing, but I do want to talk about it, share it, make it make sense in this particular format. If I could write this chapter right, it would sing for you. And it would sound like Rachelle Ferrell at any venue but especially when she is in her bag, as it were, at that piano—head reared back and mouth wide, feelin herself and doing so in front of all of us to witness with our whole senses. It would squall like Chaka Khan at the vamp. It would lead us to that which is just shy of the tonic note like Billie Holiday. It would growl and run like the Clark Sisters, take us into other worlds on Minnie Riperton or Lisa Fischer's whistle notes, and rock us in the exacting tones of a Roberta Flack or the texture of Dionne War-wick—whoo—at some point we'd have to rest.

There will be rests, there will be starts that dive into the feelin with no partic-ular promise of conclusion. I promise I'll get you there if only you allow yourself to feel as I have decided to do—to be on this page in the closest way I know how.

Listen with me. I recommend it. And if you need to fall out, get a drink of water, take time for yourself, do that. I'll be here. I've been here. It's the only place I've ever wanted to be:

*It resonates through the head, lower tones vibrate in the chest. The highest note lifts the scalp from the skull. Belly distended with air, mouth gaping, feet firmly planted and apart. **Sing it through your face, as if you are pushing it off of your head**.[1] Adjustments are made; the whole body is an instrument: The torso a reservoir of wind, limbs alternative control devices. The head is the horn, the speaker, the amplifier, and output. There are cracks, then at the trill, a note breaks, and something else: a tear. **It is the job of the vocalist to emote, not to get emotional**.*

I gather myself but the song has gone beyond me. It is not sadness but an overwhelming vibration of feeling and I cannot identify those feelings just yet. The song is about immaculate conception, or working, or something else I don't know because it is in a language I haven't learned. But a sound has broken through my body and it carried me, or I have carried it to a place where it spun and resounded.

I first encountered anointed sound in my mother's car. Her voice was legendary in every church we'd attended—the prize of all qualities one could have is the ability to move people deeply through song. Her voice was described in the supernatural, as if one had to be born with it or endowed with it by the Holy Spirit. Exclusively used for the uplift of His kingdom. There was no amount of practice that she could do to have this quality bestowed upon her. Anointing was a holy thing, but ecstasy ignited by that sound happened not in a church, but in a car, the studio, my bedroom floor while listening to Jill Scott or Sarah Vaughan, the living room where I mimicked each warm note Toni Braxton sang. The quality that I experienced didn't feel relegated to Sunday morning (or Friday night rehearsal), but the language for it was there.

Sangin, blowin, tearin it up, peeing on it, anointing, are concepts that I've understood to mean a quality of singing that encompasses musicality and the metaphysical.[2] These are terms meant to describe an aesthetic practice that values spiritual and bodily transformation through song or, as Farah Jasmine Griffin would say, "a voice capable of casting spells."[3] Black women's vocal practice demonstrates feelin as embodied knowledge at its most magical core and is never coy about this fact. Sisters will ask you: *You feelin the spirit? You feelin me?*

In the engagement of the first instrument, voice and body stretch and open into expansiveness, and that expansiveness allows the production of sound and textures of the internal instrument: the throat, the skull, the soft palate, the tongue—the body in its vibrational capacities. There is the enmeshing of the very physiological fact of vibration within the body, what historian and singer Bernice Johnson Reagon calls "running sound through the body," and the feelin it produces by this "tampering." Bernice Johnson Reagon states of this practice as an aesthetic:

> I am talking about a culture that thinks it is important to exercise this part of your being. The part of your being that is tampered with when you run this sound through your body is a part of you that our culture thinks should be developed and cultivated that you should be familiar with, that you should be able to get to as often as possible. And that if it's not developed you are underdeveloped as a human being.[4]

Reagon was teaching songs to a group of community members in Virginia Beach when she said this. Describing the sensations in her own body at the time she said, "I'm a little flustered up here. My temperature—I'm a little flushed, and I open my mouth and I do one of these songs and my whole something is different and I can just *feel* it."[5] It would be no surprise to some that the sensuous experience she describes refers to Black religious music—spirituals—and her physiological response to them remains erotic. She's feelin her own self singing this song, *and in public*.

This chapter is interested in the excesses of Black women's vocality that are intended to produce transformation. Ecstatic vocal practice, I call it—that does what it transmits—tampers, casts spells, flusters, brings to climax for the singer and for the audience and participants that the singer has enthralled. I argue that ecstatic vocal practice is a creative practice that performs and induces feelin as transformation through embodied vibrations within the body and audile transmission which shares that breath. This is no trifling matter. Vocal practice operates on levels that are sacred and sacral, what Audre Lorde would call a "use of the erotic," what L. H. Stallings would call sacredly profane sexuality that "ritualizes and makes sacred what is libidinous and blasphemous in Western humanism so as to unseat and criticize the inherent imperialistic aims within its social mores and sexual morality."[6] In line with the operations of transaesthetics, described by Stallings in *Funk the Erotic*, ecstatic vocal practice goes beyond genre, which would serve Western notions of that which is sacred or secular music styles, commercial differentiations of style and audience structured by the racialized and profit-driven interests of the music industry. Ecstatic vocal practice does more than bend genres. It is antecedent to bending the sacred and the sexual. Ecstatic vocal practice—simply—is sacred sex. It operates within community to mandate shared ecstatic feeling which challenges delusions of subjectivity in the individualist sense and performs the power of interconnected vibration of feeling. This shared feeling is sacred and sacral, performs and invites vulnerability. The importance of ecstatic vocal practice is to change one's condition, to be tampered with and into shared communion, to remind us of this Oneness.

Instructive to my discussion here are the words of Black women singers themselves. The rigorous intellectual labor of Black women singers should be studied as seriously as any other artist or scholar on Black life. In addition, I pay attention to scholars of Black culture, many influential in Black feminist thought, who have pointed to the production of excess ecstasy and otherwise in their music as an imperative to their craft and way of living. Avery*Sunshine, an Atlanta-based singer whom I initially interviewed for this project in 2012, said to me about the importance of feeling that thang:

> The older you get, the more you're going to want to get it. The person you love may not have that same [urge]. But it's like, 'I have this thing in me, what's that?' . . . There is a spiritual realm where this thing happens as well and, ideally, to me, it would behoove us to . . . explore that early on. But nobody talks about that. Your mom ain't going to sit down and talk to you about spiritual ecstasy—let alone, shoot, physical ecstasy; ain't nobody talking about that.[7]

And perhaps my momma didn't, but I did get the message of the importance of a feelin that was desired in the sacred place of worship and demonized there too.

95

(I was raised Baptist, we're funny like that.) To describe this "resource . . . firmly rooted in the power of our unexpressed or unrecognized feeling" is to encounter the struggle of making effable and expository this feeling and its (seeming) contradictions.[8] I do know this: Avery*Sunshine wasn't lying. Ecstasy is something that I do wish to explore, again, and again, and again. Which is to say—I practice.

It seems counterintuitive to give you a map to where this is going, but convention says I have to give you something to look forward to. I'd rather give you something you can feel. I begin with a framework embedded in vocal practice. In this first movement of the chapter, we have demonstrated the presence of *this thing* that is felt in practice, and next we will explore the aesthetic principles behind its practice, that is the transaesthetics within Black women's vocal practice that privilege the sacro-sexual through the theory in practice of the Queen of Soul, Aretha Franklin.

In line with this book's larger project of feelin as a mode of knowledge production practiced, honed, and made tangible theory in the studio and onstage, I must engage the work of one of the most prominent Black women thinkers in the field of ecstatic feelin and vocal practice. Aretha Franklin's body of work reveals the depth of what I discuss here at the cusp of sacred and secular, or rather in the space of sacred sexual sound. Wholly holy, Aretha's particular musical aesthetic, through the power of her musicianship as a pianist, vocalist, and songwriter, takes quite seriously the importance of feelin in Black women's singing. She is so deeply embedded in my way of thinking through Black women's vocal work that I couldn't even get far into this chapter without passively invoking Franklin's performance of Curtis Mayfield's "Giving Him Something He Can Feel." By looking at her live album performances of "Wholy Holy," "Dr. Feelgood," and "Spirit in the Dark," I discuss three core dimensions of her ecstatic vocal practice that will prove valuable to later discussions with other artists, writers, and scholars on the subject of sacred sexual ecstasy in Black women's vocal performance: (1) the transaesthetics of sacred sexuality, (2) vocal techniques that draw on aesthetics of sacred sexual breath, and (3) transmission of feeling and oneness within ecstatic vocal practice.

With the groundwork laid, I will further elaborate ecstasy and the transaesthetics of sacred sexuality with L. H. Stallings, Daphne Brooks, Farah Jasmine Griffin, Ashon Crawley, and other scholars whose interests in the erotic and Black women's performance inform my further reading of Avery*Sunshine's music and performance. Further, I will place my own conversation on Black women's vocality in dialogue with longer discussions on Black music, the upending of genre, and the dichotomy of sacred and secular forms. Many of these concepts are rooted in myth, and so too are counter to ideas of spiritual and sexual deviance and derivation. The next subsection takes up this theological position within the frame of analyzing the vocal practice of singer and preacher Kim Burrell. In this reading, I discuss her technical use of vocality within the framework of a practice of ecstasy while also reading the cultural codes by which her performance of sexual purity and carnal ignorance are undercut by the very aesthetics practices she deploys to shame her congregants and differentiate her erotic work from that of queer folks'. The end of this section focuses on the vocal technique of the growl and melisma as examples of the sacred and sexual performance of ecstatic experience. Never far from the music that will always shape this inquiry, the music plays on with the reading (and my writing) of this chapter. Jill Scott, Karen Clark Sheard, her daughter Kierra "Kiki" Sheard, and others will make key appearances in inquiries of "pitch, tone, and mood" that characterize Black women's vocal styling.

Following that, I will discuss my particular encounter as audience/participant with R&B singer—and at the time of our interview, choir director—Avery*Sunshine at a backyard barbecue during Black Gay Pride in Washington, DC, and then with the song titled "I Need You Now" from her debut album. While there is something to witnessing and experiencing ecstatic vocal practice in person, what Alexander Weheliye calls "sonic Afro-modernist possibilities in technologies of sound" are engaged to meditate on Sunshine's music.[9] I think with the sonic differences between the intimacies of the record and the intimacies of public performance to consider the ways in which vibration and breath can be shared beyond the singular moment of performance. In my listening practices here I am influenced by Phyl Garland and Daphne Brooks—although my writing style can, at times, veer into the technical, I have largely refused to write about technical aspects of the music with classical training in mind. Garland makes the astute decision to write in clear, nontechnical language about music, since technical language is both alienating to general readers and lacks a means of describing the experience of listening. "The music is its own best witness," she says.[10] In that spirit, I have included a playlist to listen to along with this chapter. It can be found at http://dr.bettinajudd.com/feelinecstasymix, or loaded at the QR code in figure 12.

Figure 12. Use your mobile device over this QR code to navigate to the playlist. You may also navigate directly to: http://dr.bettinajudd.com/feelinecstasymix.

I have found the use of technical language for thinking through the vocal styles to be less helpful than one would think. For instance, in my discussion of Aretha Franklin's "Spirit in the Dark," I describe the end of the song as a "praise break" rather than the "coda" or "vamp" that sheet music and traditional notation and music writers might suggest. The function of that section of the song is to break in praise, and it has all the technical sonic points of what we would call a "praise break" in Black Pentecostal and Black Baptist church settings. As Brooks and Garland demonstrate, writing about Black music is an inherently inclusive, interdisciplinary endeavor. Garland goes so far as to acknowledge Amiri Baraka (no doubt for his own music writing work) and Gwendolyn Brooks as writers to whom her work is indebted.[11] I agree with Emily Lordi that a deep engagement with song should foreground modes of listening that reach toward the experience of the sound itself.[12] Like Lordi, I draw on my own musical background and experience to feel with the audience that particular way of "running sound through the body."[13] I engage with deep listening to lyrics, sure, but most importantly the embodied practice of singing, the sonic experience of listening to that practice, and the environment produced by the sound. I will try to contain myself as best I can.

Finally, I return to this notion of changing one's condition. What is the ultimate meaning and power in the transcending, sacred ecstatic voice? What are its stakes? A few thoughts here: the necessary undoing of genre that ecstatic vocal practice transcends; the embodiment of flight, pleasure, and otherwise possibilities of feelin that have the capacity to heal, salve, and—like the latter's shared etymology suggests—save; and finally, the mandate and compulsion to transmit this good feelin as it undoes concepts of self-containment and "takes back the air" from oppressive forces that would make it so that we cannot breathe. For if we cannot breathe, we cannot sing. Think about this section as a bridge by which we can find ourselves on the other side, transformed by new rhythms and harmonies. Ecstatic vocal practice is developed by aesthetics that privilege transformation situated in the sacred-sexual—to climax in consecrated communal place. Thus, to climax in a sacred place would be not sacrilege, but make our gathering here that much more holy—much more whole.

Aretha Franklin's "Wholy Holy"

(You can press play now, if you haven't already.)

THE TRANSAESTHETICS OF SACRED SEXUALITY

While the documentary footage makes "Wholy Holy" the first track performed at the two-night concert that would become Aretha Franklin's *Amazing Grace*, the album lists the track as number 12 and opts instead to begin with "Mary Don't You Weep."[14] But to begin her concert with a tune by her R&B/Soul colleague Marvin Gaye, a crooning sex symbol, might be a commentary on what this album is intended to do: though it is a gospel album first and foremost, recorded in front of a live congregation with the backing of James Cleveland's Southern California Choir, Aretha Franklin is neither conceding nor apologizing to the church folks for her life as a secular artist. She is both, and she manages to be both in this church and on this album where she also makes gospel Carole King's "You've Got a Friend," Simon and Garfunkel's "Bridge Over Troubled Water," and Rodgers and Hammerstein's "You'll Never Walk Alone." Franklin's creative decisions to maintain her perfectly picked and patted afro at the concert (as we are now able to see in the recently released video footage) also reflect the underlying political message of Gaye's genre-nonbinary tune. The song calls for community unity and peace in the midst of the ongoing Vietnam War and the liveliness of global Black Power movements as much as it passes along a Christian message of Jesus's love. The re-release CD cover art also reflects these layers of meaning between the sacred and secular body and the political backdrop of the album's original release. It pictures a cut-out cross and within it the visage of Aretha as the body within the cross. Upon opening the first layer of the cut-out cross, one can see Aretha in her full dashiki sitting on the steps of a church house. The church is as much her domain as the dominion of soul and its Afrocentric aesthetics by which she has been named queen.

Franklin starts the song with a series of dreamy quarter notes on her piano that set the slightly slower pace of her version of Gaye's tune. That dreaminess, though not present through the same sound in Gaye's original, manages to capture the mood of Gaye's original composition. In the original "Wholy Holy" Gaye comes in on the first bar as the introduction to the song also serves as the vamp to "Right On," the previous track on the album. Franklin's vocals, which rise into the first note from a few steps down, still manage to come in about a measure later than the original song calls for, giving the audial impression of her answering or continuing a song that started before her. Notice her over pronunciation of the "w" in "wholly" to sound more like *Whoa-ly*. "Whoa" is an artful enactment of breath referred to rather consistently in gospel, rock, R&B, and soul music. Some may understand it as a vehicle by which to carry notes that are outside of the lyrical structure of a song, but "whoa" specifically is its own word that carries the affective meaning of reacting in wonder. Its definition also invokes a command to stop; it commands attention and aestheticized breath that sets and affirms the mood of a song. Her attention to the "w" in wholly allows her to play up the double meaning intended in the song's use of the homonyms "wholly" and "holy" while also invoking the mood that she injects into "whoa" as the first word uttered in the song. She is feeding to her audience the *both/and*-ness of this music, ensuring that the holy rollers hear the whole in holy and not attribute the lyric to another Baptist tune named "Holy, Holy." Gaye's song enacts and calls attention to the transing of sacred and secular—soul/R&B and gospel—through the homonymic relationship between "wholly" and "holy." What is holy must also be whole. This call ushers the secular artist into sacred space, or rather invites the sinner and the sanctified (and sanctimonious) into the temple where the sacred and the secular/sexual are one. She invites the congregation into what Margo Perkins might call "the church of Aretha," where spirit dwells in song. "When i [*sic*] listen to Aretha," Perkins says, "i know that there is a holy spirit because nothing else could make me feel so alive. As far as secular music goes, vintage Aretha is about the closest i come to 'getting happy.'"[15] The "Arethasized" version of "Wholy Holy" amplifies the sacred secular two-ness—both audially and in improvised lyricism which speaks of followers "moving and grooving in love" (a lyrical borrow from her "Spirit in the Dark") as well as Jesus's love. Her own voice as soloist is backed by James Cleveland's choir who, along with the ringing of chimes, continue the dreamy soundscape of the song with the altos' and tenors' "ahhs." These deeper notes are the choral wall that respond to the angelic soprano trio who act as backup singers to Aretha, whose select work is to offer the "wholy holys" that seem to keep time to the dreamscape of the song.

Aretha Franklin often called out the politics of genre in her albums and maintained her sound regardless of what the genre dictates. So when she exquisitely performed Puccini's "Nessun Dorma" in place of Luciano Pavarotti at the 1998 Grammys, *in his key, mind you*, she maintained that she was doing as she has always done: transcending genre through *her* sound. Franklin didn't take up classical style to do so—instead of a rounded ending at "vincero!" she maintained her brighter, face-resonant vowels and ran her way out of the song. Transcendent indeed.

VOCAL TECHNIQUES IN AESTHETICS OF SACRED SEXUAL BREATH

What isn't talked about nearly enough is how "Spirit in the Dark" on *Live at the Fillmore West* is preceded by "Dr. Feelgood," which absolutely sets us up for a sacred ecstatic experience.[16] There is something beautifully intentional about these two songs butting up together in this way on the record as if to deliberately construct an orgiastic congregational feeling for listeners at home. While Jeffrey Wexler and Arif Mardin are credited as producers, Franklin also had creative input on the final record, as is the case with many of her albums at this point. Both songs offer praise breaks in the style of Black Southern Baptist and Pentecostal worship. Before "Dr. Feelgood" starts, Franklin asks the crowd if they feel like hearing the blues; her question is met with enthusiastic yeses. Then, Cornell Dupree's electric guitar and Billy Preston's organ start those familiar bluesy chords and bring the crowd to a frenzy.

As soon as she starts into the verse, "I don't want nobody, always . . ." a voice in the crowd responds, "SANG IT!" Already we're in church. Aretha's voice continues in the melodic blues tradition of singing between talk and melody. The lyrics exceed the twelve-bar structure of the song, which she fills with repetitions and extended phrasing. For instance, in the next line, "sittin' 'round me and my man," Aretha extends the *s*— into a long hiss. The sound doesn't bring up the kinds of sweetness that vocal emphasis on the *s* might otherwise invoke, as I discuss later in this chapter. This *s* is nasty, a sound to ward off any snooping or meddling folk that just might sssssssit around her and her man all the time.

She continues to intentionally drag her vocals behind the already slow-dragging blues. This forces slight changes to the lyrics that at times privilege the lyrics and at other times feature them through melisma and squall. She also injects other vocal forms of lyrical and melodic interpretation when she insists that she doesn't mind company "every once in a while." On the repetition of this line, she is stressing each syllable of the phrase and adding the word "great" for exceptional emphasis, so that we know "eh-vuh-ree once in a while," is quite rare (so don't come 'round here assuming now is one of those times). After that phrase we get the audial gist of what she is doing—or would rather be doing—instead of having company; there is no need to sing the lyrics, "But oh, oh, when me and my man get to lovin'"—we hear exactly what happens. Franklin howls and shouts with "oohs" and "whoos," performing orgasmic release through the end of the phrase. These aestheticized moans get louder and louder until the final lines of the verse are nearly overtaken by the Memphis Horns, who seem to reflect the building intensity of the song. It is here that Franklin finishes the lyric interrupted by orgasm, "I just don't have time / To sit, and chit, and sit and chit chat and smile." The audience sings the chorus along with her: "Don't send me no doctor / fillin' me up with all of those pills." But this isn't the end; Franklin shouts through the ending notes of the song, punctuated by bass and edged on by the organ. The organ talks back to her melodic "yeahs!" filled with more power and breath as they ascend to outright shouts. Moans shift into hums that slide up and down. The occasional trilling soprano from her background singers, the Sweethearts of Soul, enhances the air of ecstatic release that would appear to be improvisational.[17] Here, Franklin is ushering in sacred sexual ecstatic feeling through transmission. As Lordi observes, "Franklin's ad-libs brought everyone higher," through what she calls the "gospel idiom."[18] This ad-lib—which extends for more than three minutes—sounds like the rousing precursor to intense worship; after the formal song has ended, squalls and shouts of "yeah" carry over from the enactment of orgasm in the verse and extend the song into instantaneous revival.

The bass rumbles, and the organ talks back to Aretha as she hums and sings, "It's gone be alright." The energy mounts again as she ascends into more shouts of, "It felt so good, I just gotta say yeah!" and begins to testify, her backup singers helping her out here in brackets: "I get a little fearful about things that I don't understand sometimes. Sometimes it's good—aw hear me now—it's good [*trilling soprano*] to sit there, [*yeah!*] cross your arms, [*yeah!*] cross your legs, [*yeah!*] look on up to heaven and say [*trilling soprano again*] yeah!" Now the song outrightly invokes religious worship within this sacral/sexual performance. This testimony conjures imagery of a particular kind of praise where the worshipper is in a pew and on the verge of shouting. The key to such worship being the affirmative power of yes. In his discussion of the praise song "Yes, Lord," Ashon Crawley muses on the function of the melodic *yes* in ecstatic worship: "'Yes' is for otherwise possibilities. 'Yes' is holy."[19] Aretha instructs the crowd in holy call and response, asking them to say "yeah" if they "understand what [she] mean[s]." She does this four more times before the song mellows into a quieter praise. Aretha's shouts might have gotten her happy as she continues with more exuberant testimony. In the full concert version, now available to both see and hear, we know that the testimony became more of a full-on sermon on the night of March 6, 1971. Aretha directly tells her congregation—err, audience—"Don't put worry on you before worry gets to you," and "You gotta keep your arms around us. You gotta do that for us, Lord." The album version uses the take from the second night which, in light of the performance the night before, makes much more sense in context when she sings, "Come on home and watch over me." I hear this both as the melodic ending to this kind of musical interlude and as a phrase that emerges from the free performance of ecstatic worship in which the sacred sexual spirit takes hold in the room. The "feel good" that the good doctor provides is made possible by the divine will of God.

"Dr. Feelgood" transcends its function as a sexual blues into a sexual bluesy worship song. It overcomes the limitations of genre to do important sacred sexual work through vocal stylings that perform ecstatic experience: chants of "yeah," melodic preaching, strategic use of background singers as demonstrating call and response, and vocal punctuations like the trilled soprano. As Dennis Wiley notes:

Stylistically, it began as blues, but it is ending up as gospel. Emotionally, it began at the Fillmore West, but it is ending up in church. Artistically, it began as a song, but it is ending up as a sermon. And, erotically, it began concerning a *sexual* union between a woman and her man, but it is ending up involving a *spiritual* communion between a woman and her God.[20]

Franklin's sacred sexual performance exemplifies stylistic vocal techniques that cross genre *and* in doing so ignites erotic spiritual response. Her voice at the edge of its limits, signaled by the occasional cracking, her growl and squall, her incantation and affirming divine presence—the performances of ecstatic pleasure and worship happen on every end of the song. It is not hard to forget the substance of Dr. Feelgood's meaning even as she continues in religious worship. These are not competing concepts. One could hear her navigating the communities of secular and sacred music—the saints might forgive Aretha's raunchiness for the fact that she is saving souls, but she's inviting those saints into sacred sexual communion as well.

TRANSMISSION OF FEELIN AND ONENESS IN ECSTATIC VOCAL PRACTICE

As I said above, though the version of "Spirit in the Dark" on the album was recorded on a different day, its skillful placement on the record and in the original concert produces its own kind of listening community. What I am saying is that Aretha Franklin an'em knew what she was doing. Her listeners would be taken into the sonic whirlwind of collective feelin by the end of "Dr. Feelgood," and then, when she asks, "Are you gettin' the spirit in the dark?" she has already transformed the audience into a shouting congregation. The answer to her question is yes and, apparently, we are going deeper. To place this song here is to further shape the orgiastic church vibe that Aretha's music invokes.

The song begins familiarly enough. Aretha plays the opening chord and starts to sway and sing those beginning lines of the chorus. The Sweethearts of Soul hum in response. The song picks up tempo at the verse, "Tell me, sister, how do you feel?" The rhythm section really gets grooving here with the bass taking more prominence. At the bridge the rhythm picks up even more and she sings, "It's like Sally Walker sitting in her saucer," which is both a reference to a child's hand game, a folk song, and to Rufus Thomas's "Little Sally Walker" that oozes sexual undertones as Thomas sings for Sally to "ride Sally, ride."[21] Aretha sings as a midwife to Sally Walker's sexual abandon. Instead of "letting [her] backbone slip" as the original lyrics demand, Aretha sings for her to "Put your hands on your hips / and cover your eyes a groove with the spirit."[22] This song isn't about dancing as a spectacle for others; it is an invitation to lose oneself by being "in the spirit." As E. Patrick Johnson notes, "Franklin's song uses the sacred notion of 'spirit' as a metaphor for sexual ecstasy [. . .] she endows Sally Walker, the innocent and chaste little girl of the famous children's nursery rhyme, with sexual agency as Franklin encourages Sally to 'ride' the spirit in the dark."[23] Sally Walker functions as a stand-in for the listeners whom Franklin instructs to "groove with the spirit." The bridge leads us into a bona fide praise break.[24] The bass walks double time, signaling that we now act on moving with the spirit. We have already been given instructions after all. Aretha herself takes this moment to emerge from behind her piano and cut a step around the stage and into the crowd. During the praise break, the background singers keep the pace with "Move in the spirit."

In the reprise to "Spirit in the Dark," Franklin emerges from backstage with Ray Charles asking, "Did I move with the spirit?" She introduces Charles to the audience and accompanies him while he gets comfortable in the groove of the song. He improvises more sexually direct lyrics than Franklin's original—at one point singing, "I gotta find me a woman tonight, cuz I feel the spirit!" Between some stellar piano solos by Aretha and Ray (as well as a sax solo by Andrew Love that doesn't make the official recording), the groove does change. The bass is no longer walking double time to usher in shouting; the Memphis Horns take a more prominent role; the sound is much more "funk" than the straight-up gospel style in which the song was initially penned. Aretha announces, "It's funky up in here," speaking to the new groove that Ray Charles inspires in the song. At one point, Ray brings the sound low for the audience to hush and listen to the groove with him, "Come on listen to this. [A few beats] Can you feel the spirit?" he asks and follows up with, "When you hear Aretha sing, y'all, can you feel the spirit?" The song goes out on this groove, and Franklin acknowledges Ray Charles once again, calling him the "right reverend"—a reverend of the one and same church over which Aretha presides: The Church of the Spirit in the Dark, where sexuality is sacred and the ecstatic is sexual, holy, and to be shared and improvised with, where ecstasy is structured in the song. Not a happenstance but structured and performed *every time* to make way for spirit to come.

What I have outlined here, through close listening to three of Aretha Franklin's performances, are three aspects of ecstatic vocal work that I find to be important to this discussion: the first is Black transaesthetic principles that resist genre; the second, vocal technique, vulnerability, and sacred breath; and the last, transmission of feelin—or oneness that allows for embodied expression to be shared in communion. Neither this list nor the analyses of these songs are exhaustive, but they do the groundwork that taps into why feelin ecstasy matters and how it manifests through Black women's vocal practice.

Phyl Garland describes the particular genius and power of Aretha Franklin's sound through her capacity to *feel* and transmit that quality of feeling to an audience:

> She sings of life, of love, and of the terrible thrill-driven torment of lust with an uncompromising honesty of feeling that leads one to believe that every twisted note, every conjugated cadence and imploring lyric, has been ripped from the bowels of her very own soul. She *feels*, and so she is, and thus she sings. To hear her is not to be entertained; it is to undergo a baptism of emotion that leaves one weak and yet fulfilled, as in the aftermath of good sex.[25]

What she describes here is an ecstatic conduit. In conversation with Garland, Franklin describes her tutelage as skill infused with and transmissible by feelin. She quotes Franklin describing learning from James Cleveland in this way: "He showed me some real nice chords and I liked his deep, deep sound. There's a whole lot of earthiness in the way he sings and what he was feelin', I was feelin', but I just didn't know how to put it across. The more I watched him, the more I got out of it."[26] Franklin was taught through feelin, and as a pianist who played by ear, she relied on the senses that went beyond musical notation. Aretha embodied her music—that is, her body is what makes the sound, the whole experience of her music, possible. Aretha, a round-bodied and brown-skinned woman, was the emblem of a gospel sound and quite sexual.[27] She transmitted it all: a sacred sexual healing that is wholly holy, and wholly embodied in flesh considered profane even in secular spaces.

Ecstasy and Aesthetics of Sacred Sexuality

Tone, pitch, and mood also have a function in erotic attunement for women who might be classified as sluts elsewhere. Tone and mood enable a manner, mode, or way of living. Alternating among the various tones and modalities of emotion and experience at their disposal, individual women cull a new purpose for funk and women—namely sovereignty . . .
—L. H. STALLINGS, *FUNK THE EROTIC*

What does it mean to be feelin a song? Not just listening to music or engaging in lyrical interpretation, but the experience of vibration that a song puts the listener/practitioner through? There is, to borrow from Hortense Spillers, an interstice here between singing and being the emblem of song that the Black woman vocalist (note the singularity of this figure) represents.[28] Not simply to be the one singing a song or listening to a song, but to be the embodiment of song as well. This might very well be co-opted into a kind of iconography—that is, the particular kind of politics of representation that makes of Black women singers a tool for nationalist structures of feeling, as Farah Jasmine Griffin describes in "When Malindy Sings." There, Griffin talks about the extractive labor of Black women's vocality in representing an "American voice"—a "version of the United States as it wishes itself to be."[29] As with much co-optation comes the reduction of Black women's vocal ability to natural talent, as opposed to practiced technical proficiency that is honed in the studio, or what Fredara Hadley calls "Black music's greatest conservatory"—the music ministries of Black churches.[30] What exists before an audience can come to clamor for Black women's voices, is a practiced embodiment of song that is (as the kids would say) for the culture and for the self. An experience of "running sound through the body" in which the haptic and Black musical aesthetics merge to produce qualities of feelin that characterize whole genres: the blues of \blues, the jazz of \jazz, the soul of soul, the gospel of gospel (and on and on), and all the erotics therein implied.

Farah Jasmine Griffin talks about Black women's singing voices that evoke and transmit a kind of longing: "the black woman's voice as the source of black artistic creativity, the voice expresses a quality of longing: longing for home, for love, for connection with God, for heaven, for freedom."[31] What longing might sound like and what the vibrations of those sounds might feel like are within a set of creative considerations made by a singer in her ecstatic vocal practice. These considerations involve technique—Black feminine genius, to use Hadley's term—passed down through generations that includes methods and sounds which evoke and emote and also necessitate being within the technique—enthralled by the body in haptic and aesthetic response as well as capable of ensuring its execution.[32]

To climax in a sacred place, to open myself to breath and to release that breath, leaves me open. There is a sacred vulnerability to singing that is made possible by the communion of breath. "Once you start to put sound out on that level you're out," says Reagon. "There's no hiding place, you're exposed, everybody in the room has heard what you sound like, you know what you sound like and you can't go back in."[33] To be touched by sound and to fundamentally attempt to reach out and touch others with this breath—its vibration and sound—is a kind of reaching out that one hopes can be received, but that could fundamentally be rejected, laughed at, scrutinized, ignored. The sound and vibration could come out uneasy, wrong. But that tender breath which vibrates the inner sanctum spiritually, if not the inner organs physically, has come out of me and into the world to be shared. Within the aesthetics of gospel, that vulnerability is shared, is gold, and reveals how such vulnerability makes possible otherwise ways of being, seeing, and sharing in community. Singing, then, using this framework, is a practice of sharing sacred breath and vibration, of revealing that which resides within to an outside world and thus resists finite constrains of singular beingness in favor of interconnected wholeness.[34] Examining what it would mean to be feelin a song would take into account this communion of breath and vibration, or as Weheliye notes, "a more accurate theory of listening might consider the dissolution of subjective boundaries."[35] Far from natural or inherent to Black women, this embodied practice is learned and taught through gestures of communion.

Take the following for example: In 2006 at a gathering of Black women artists and activists, Bernice Johnson Reagon spoke and led us in song. She told me to start singing—"any song," she said, and the rest would join. Now, of course I was afraid, but I was given a mandate by an elder whom I particularly revered, so I began to sing the soprano for the choral version of "Jordan River" that she'd taught the Spelman College Glee Club during the two weeks that I was a member. The rest of the group did indeed join, in their own voices, in harmony. The gift of that experience was the handing-off of song, and the greater lesson was to trust my own voice as a leader *and* follower in community. The act of singing in that group was not that I would show off my vocals, but that I would select a song useful for the occasion of singing together—getting us right and on one accord. Lordi notes, "The singer has to trust her own sensual-musical intelligence, as well as her right to express it. Her self-trust does not develop in a vacuum; it is born of communal engagement."[36] I offer this anecdotal tidbit to provide a sample of singing within the teachable moment. This isn't inherent skill. It is learned, practiced, shaped, and reshaped over time. I learned so much in that moment: trusting my own voice, leading the song in a sharable key and in a recognizable melody, and as the community rises in song blending *and* leading, falling back and again trusting that exhalation of breath will bring us all there.

The erotics of this practice might be well understood within the frame of L. H. Stallings's invocation of funk studies as a study of the erotic within Black transaesthetics. Funk studies, the aesthetics of Black sexuality, sexual cultures, and politics eschew logics of the human that frame sexuality within medicalized discourse. Funk flags the ways in which Black sexual cultures can exist within regimes of capitalism, beneath and among asexual and medicalized logics of sexuality and sexual discourse while remaining protective of the capacities for Black sexual ecstasy. If there is a difficulty in articulating Black women's sexual pleasures while also engaging the problem of capitalism, violence, chattel slavery, and colonialism, we need look no further than funk to guide us toward understanding the depth, the interiority, of sacro-sexual subjectivity as a multifaceted, multivocal, tonally complex set of cultural practices by which affective experience is practice. Funk presumes complex Black interiority that expresses through transaesthetic practices rooted in Black sexual cultures. The Black ecstatic is an aesthetic and ritualized practice that prioritizes interior and exterior human/nonhuman/spiritual experience. As Stallings states:

> Black sexual cultures offer an alternative sexual geography in which two seemingly opposite elements, the intimate or intimacy and the ecstatic and ecstasy are placed alongside each other. Intimacy is conceptualized as deep-seated interiority, while ecstasy is expressed as a state of being "beside oneself." Intimacy prioritizes humanness and human relationalities, while ecstasy accepts that there are human and nonhuman relationalities occurring in spiritual, sexual, creative, and pharmaceutical activities and expression. These sexual cultures can be about the metaphysical plane between the living and the dead, or human beings and inhuman forces. Funk studies demonstrate that we need only acknowledge these new metaphysics of struggle.[37]

The cultural work of genre would prove antithetical to Black transaesthetics. That is, the capitalist, imperialist, and racist organization of modes of creativity that permeate Western culture's understanding of itself—from the discourses of the high and low arts to the differentiation of the sacred and secular—are not useful ways of thinking about Black cultural production. As Maureen Mahon notes, "Genre categories do cultural work. They place artists and listeners into and outside of meaningful categories of identity and belonging."[38] The very concept of funk as a genre, for example, was created to draw a market line between rock and roll by Black folks and rock and roll by white folks.[39] The gag is that all of that music, rock and roll, funk, the blues, and soul, is nurtured, cradled, developed, and performed not only by Black folks in a wider sense but often by *the same* Black folks. One song, one *artist* can travel through each of these genres seamlessly. Stallings's intervention then, brings to the fore Black *trans*aesthetics which challenge the taxonomized notions of sexuality, gender, erotics, pornography, art, and sex that funk itself represents. As Ashon Crawley notes, the dueling genres of normativity and morality, the sacred and the profane, are constructions baked in with notions of race, gender, sex, and class. These endless taxonomies are, in Crawley's estimation, "a problem of modern thought" as they are complicit with racialization and maintain racialization as a necessary means of thinking about humans.[40] With such an understanding of cultural value without genre, one might see where it is not only possible but inevitable *and intentional* for one to climax in a sacred place.

It is my contention that Black women's vocal performances are sites where metaphysics of struggle are embodied, performed, and ritualized through ecstatic vocal work. Because we are talking about a culture, or a set of cultures, that values ecstatic engagements like "running sound through the body," we are also inherently engaging those practices that ritually and publicly incite Black women's ways of being that are intimately interior while expressive and thus on the edge of human and nonhuman praxis. By engaging deeply with the aesthetics of Black women's vocal performance, we tarry with the spiritual, the emotional, and the political experiences of engaging with asexual and medicalized logics of sexuality and the human. Namely, vocal practice is intent on changing one's embodied condition.

The aesthetic practices engaged here take up functions of "pitch, tone, and mood" employed in technical proficiencies of anointed sound. That is, the subtle and not-so-subtle aural aesthetic choices that affectively engage erotic, sacred being that Stallings might name—sovereignty. Vocal performance's potential for such ways of being is in its *already* being, as opposed to asking or demanding such sovereignty. As Stallings notes, "When women clarify the terms for sexual desires through tone, pitch, and mood, as well as words, they highlight why stating, asking, or demanding the conditions for sexual autonomy and freedom is not enough."[41] Black vocal ecstatic expression asks for nothing—it is what it does.

Daphne Brooks explains to us precisely how Black women's musical practices are modes of knowledge production and goes so far as to call them revolutionary because such practices "both forecast and execute the viability and potentiality of Black life."[42] This attention to the work that Black women's music *practice* does is of particular interest to my exploration of ecstatic vocal work as the "potentiality of Black life," made flesh by way of Bernice Johnson Reagon's definition of singing as "running sound through the body." Which is to say that ecstatic vocal work is knowledge production that documents and enacts revolutionary—that is *transformative*—praxis by being within and transmitting song made to change one's condition. In her recounting the intellectual and musical work of Abbey Lincoln and Pauline Hopkins, Brooks highlights how the Black aesthetic of mood is "the conduit through which historical forces shape our lives and the instrument that enables us to recognize and reckon with historical forces."[43] The function of mood is to transform and shape not only our knowing, but our way of knowing—in particular, a Black woman's singing voice becomes a "method for mining the archive."[44] To be feelin something is to also know something in *that* way—a particular and otherwise form of knowledge that colors knowing itself.

Blues Notes and Blues Bodies

Most preachers tune up in the key of A.

The term "tune up," in this context, refers to the practice in African American Christian churches of singing or chanting part of a sermon for climactic effect. I don't know if this bit of trivia is true, but, for me, it was part of a search for the note or series of notes that were most sacred, most exalting—most likely to make one catch the spirit. I wanted to figure out how I got these complex and overwhelming experiences from notes, melisma, and intervals I heard and sang despite the lyrics.

Initially, I was taken by the concept of notes and their spiritual qualities when in my freshman year of college I learned about *diabolus in musica* or the flatted fifth. It is the most dissonant interval in European music and named for the devil because of its darker qualities. That it has been so heavily used to connote the gothic, the demonic, or dark in many genres of music seemed to solidify this concept for me. Further, the idea of the flatted fifth resonated with me because it is a familiar interval in Black music. The flatted fifth is essential to the blues scale.[45] This would seem to be musicological proof that perhaps it is the devil's music, as church folks and legends have always said. But if blues music is the work of the devil often described as interchangeable with Lucifer, many Christians are implicated in blending the sacred with the profane as they utilized the intoxicating qualities of this music in worship.[46] In an interview, when asked about her assertion that music brings listeners back to the spirit, Avery*Sunshine references a biblical verse:

> Music was so important music was such a force that it almost was in competition it was revered . . . I wish I could pull up the scripture now and talk about Lucifer himself being the instrument. His body being the drum his lips being a horn for God to have an angel that is music is the personification of music like it was something versed out of spirituality.[47]

Lucifer, once again, emerges as a complicated force—a minister of *both/and*. As the previous chapter discussed, Clifton's meditation on Lucifer presents him as the darkness within God's will. Lucifer is the prince of light as well as the prince of darkness. This duality of the devil is presented in his Yoruba relative, Esu or Elegba.[48] It is Esu, a gender-ambiguous trickster and guardian of passage to the afterlife, who, when crossed with the Christian devil, becomes the minister of music on earth. *Both/and*—sacred/secular—angel/devil. If music is in fact the devil's work, it is within the divine will of God.

The devil's interval persists in the blues because the blues and the musical traditions from which it comes do not exist on the Western scale. They are most accessible through the voice because Western instruments often have to be ingeniously altered to achieve them.[49] These notes, played "between" the Western standard division of notes, are often invoked on instruments by playing adjacent notes—one note and the next note—this *and* that. This duality of notes and the way they must be achieved on Western instruments symbolically and sonically achieve *both/and*.

My search for the quality of a note, a series of notes, turned into this study of ecstasy. I went looking for the note, and I found myself in the places where I first practiced singing—Baptist and Pentecostal churches. In the church, the term used to describe the ability of a singer to evoke emotion and spiritual ecstasy through music was "the anointing." The anointing is also a biblical notion, and the gift of song through the anointing is a concept that describes one's connection to the divine as much as one's ability to carry a tune. It is defined as a skill that could not be taught on an earthly plane.[50] Unable to be learned or taught, the anointing is a gift from the divine that uses the flesh as a vessel.[51] In a worldview that perceives the flesh as permanently disabled through sin, anointing is divine ability.[52] It is empowerment from the divine to rule or even to pass on a message.[53] Despite the definition of *anointing* as adept singing skill appearing nowhere in the Bible, the use of the word as a barometer of divinely inspired singing persists.

The anointing describes authority, and for the singer it is an authority to invoke the Holy Spirit. In the church setting, the anointing is a subjective quality that speaks not only to a person's ability to sing but to the person's ability to move the congregation into an enlivened state of spiritual ecstasy. Because of its subjective aspects, the anointing is a tricky quality to negotiate in the church. In the church, anointing is the quality in which one's connection to the divine is perceived. A barometer of a person's salvation, the anointing is also a confirmation of "good singing." As Sunshine notes, "I absolutely believe in anointing, and I think everybody is anointed to do whatever that thing is. I do believe that, but it may not touch everybody the same way."[54] I bring the anointing up as a relational barometer of musical and spiritual quality. It is this very quality of relativity that most closely acts as a measure of ecstatic experience in vocal performance.

I found it difficult to find a term for this measure, and I am not the only one. In her dissertation on pedagogical strategies for gospel vocal training, Trineice Murlene Robinson-Martin defines the qualitative difference between singing and sangin' across the lines of technical and emotive skills:

> When a singer is regarded as being able to 'sing,' he or she typically has a nice timbral quality to their voice, can sing in tune, and demonstrates technical and harmonic skills with the use of 'runs,' 'vocal ornamentations' or the soulful elements. However, the singer . . . typically lacks the ability to display a personal connection to the music in a way he or she would by 'sangin'.' . . . 'Sangin'' is not about technique; it is having the ability to relate to the audience in such a way that the audience feels as if the singer is telling their story.[55]

Yet, even this passage does not adequately describe the experience of this particular quality in a voice. Although sangin' describes the emotional quality of being able "to relate to the audience," the "anointed" voice is described in biblical terms that invite divine presence. Whether or not most churches would agree on the theological implications of this is not the point here. In fact, because it limits the way in which we listen to vocal artists, some would say the term is overused. Avery*Sunshine does. In our interview I asked about the concept of "anointing" in voices, and she replied that the term is, "Overused and abused."[56] The concept itself is subjective. Yet, something *is* experienced, even if only on the individual level of the audience or the performer.

Adding another term to describe this quality seems superfluous, but this lexicon of terms—anointing, sangin, blowin, witnessing, testifying, or putting it down—is rooted in a culture that understands singing to have powerful, enigmatic qualities that move people. These powerful qualities are so valued because they can "change one's condition."[57] The power to change one's condition might also be reflected in what Robert Farris Thompson calls *àshe* or "the power-to-make-things-happen."[58] Thompson goes on to say: "A thing or a work of art that has àshe transcends ordinary questions about its makeup and confinements: *it is divine force incarnate*" (italics mine). Àshe is the experience of the divine on earth, and it is also a force that exists within an aesthetic. Àshe is a force that is experienced through its representation. He goes on to say: "As we become noble, fully realizing the spark of *creative goodness God endowed us with* . . . we find the confidence to cope with all kinds of situations. This is àshe. This is character. This is mystic coolness."[59] The concept of anointing in US Black religious expression echoes the qualities of àshe in which "creative goodness" is "endowed" by God. Through àshe, style meets and *represents* the divine and the divine's power to change.

Ecstatic experience is the catalyst for changing one's condition, and it is the practice that makes change possible. Ecstatic expression through song exists on an arc where secular life and sacred afterlife are part of a single continuum of human experience. It is for this reason that Black women's vocal expression exists between the spaces of secular and sacred musical genres, between sexual and spiritual ecstatic experiences.

BLACK WOMANIST THOUGHT AND THE BLUES BODY

Ecstasy, the divine erotic experience, happens in the body. Black women musicians of religious or secular music must, regardless of genre, negotiate issues of embodiment and sexuality that are projected onto their bodies. Blues women are most often associated with their brazen sexuality, and this characteristic of their musical content and performance has been considered the most liberating aspect of their legacy. Scholars such as Hazel Carby, Angela Davis, and L. H. Stallings have already told us about the blues woman performer as an arbiter of Black female sexuality without regard for respectability politics.[60] Kelly Brown Douglas, inspired by blues women's unabashed embrace of their own sexuality, describes something called a "blues body" that connects body and soul through sensuous experience. The blues is a form of music in touch with the sexual. "To be sure, sexual themes are prevalent within blues, especially those sung by women. Blues women sing, seemingly without shame or restraint, about their sexual needs, desires, and preferences."[61] Black women whose bodies have often been subject to scrutiny and Western projections are embodied symbols of sexual desire in blues, yet they shape the dimensions of their own sexual desire. Douglas goes on, "Blues is in touch with the feelings of blues bodies. Blues does not begin with ideas in the head, but with the experiences of the body. Blues listens to the call of the body and responds by conveying what the body is communicating, making visible that which is invisible."[62] Blues women become high priestesses, experts of sensuous experience in their own bodies.

The blues body is a body on the edge of society—a body in touch with sensuality and ecstatic expression. It yearns for sensuous experience, and sensuous experience can occur in the church or in the juke joint. As described in blues woman Bessie Smith's "Preachin' the Blues," Sister Green, a character in her song, is as uplifted by the power of the blues as she would be by the Holy Spirit. Douglas notes, "Resonating to the message of the blues, she cannot help but jump up and shout/shimmy. . . . Through the blues, she is put back in touch with her body."[63] Put back in touch with her body, Smith's Sister Green breaks barriers expressed in the church, where piety and silence around sexuality are preferred.

The shout and the shimmy become indiscernible expressions of ecstasy in the flesh. Blues singer Ida Goodson reiterates this experience in the documentary *Wild Women Don't Have the Blues*. She says, "When I play the blues I feel something going on and next thing I know I'm feeling good . . . then you go and play church songs and then that feeling come back . . . The devil got his work and God got his work."[64] Goodson's statement both highlights and rejects the Christian division between sexual and divine sensuous experience. Her acknowledgment, certainly, gives room to the saints in the church who continue to view the blues as the devil's music because of its sexually explicit content. Yet, she also rejects the notion that because of this association with the devil she, too, must reject the experience. Both the devil's work and God's work are deemed valuable. This could be read as ambivalence toward good and evil or a recognition of the co-reliance of the natures of the devil and God. I'd like to take this idea that God and the devil each got their work as a standpoint for sacred sex work as vocal practice. It is a position that suggests there is room in the aesthetics of sexual sacred work for both, one that often turns the very concept of morality on its head and leaves as much room to critique the so-called nature of God as that of the devil. This is a valuable cultural position that would come of use for a people who have histori-cally sat in the same churches where pastors preached a gospel that marked them as inherently devalued, intrinsically deviant, and born to be enslaved.

THE PREACHER'S SADOMASOCHISTIC SEX ACT

When rumors swirled about Kim Burrell releasing a secular album, the president of the International Music Department of the Church of God in Christ (COGIC) Judith McAllister issued a statement in an attempt to assure the church that, in fact, Burrell's upcoming album was not secular and that Burrell was still con-ducting her life according to COGIC "holiness" standards.[65] Although Burrell distances herself from the term "secular" to describe her album, songs on the album deal with secular themes of romantic love and relationships. For example, she has a timid remake of Earth, Wind & Fire's "Love's Holiday" which begins, "Would you mind if I touch, if I reach out to hold you tight," consciously changing the lyrics that mention kissing.

Every precaution Burrell took to make a seemingly "clean" album that featured secular songs did not fool certain segments of the religious crowd. Numerous blogs criticized her efforts, but none of this criticism foiled Burrell. In an interview at one of these blog sites, she defends her decision to sing songs that may be considered secular. She said, "I have a range of lyrics because we need to learn to speak about love without having to preface it with a scripture. . . . If you have this God in your heart, you can have a conversation without men-tioning Jesus and God and the Trinity and all that, and people will know that there's love in you."[66] Burrell's belief in the divine presence outside the struc-ture of religion is reflected in her vocal performance, which many reviewers describe as jazz-inspired. While Burrell denies the claims that she deliberately attempts to sing in secular forms, she proves that her musical inspiration comes from her authority to interpret song—any song, as scripture. At the very publicized funeral of Whitney Houston, where she was scheduled to sing Houston's semi-gospel song "I Believe in You and Me,"[67] Pastor Burrell went off program to sing "A Change Is Gonna Come" by Sam Cooke. Burrell consistently tries to define herself outside of genre yet remains connected to the religious community. She is a musical mentor to countless secular musicians, including Houston, and remains an influence for others such as Avery*Sunshine.[68] This influence is evident in musical style as well as philosophies on the connection between the sacred and the secular worlds.

When I speak of vocality here, I am largely describing singing voices, how-ever, the practice of vocal ecstasy has no disciplinary limits. The vocal practices I describe here are also evidenced in oratory traditions manifest in gospel preach-ing (like "tuning up" and whooping). The sermon is also a space in which sacred sexual work takes center stage to the ritual of church and offers a good study of pleasure, sexuality, and the ecstatic. It is through the vocal that we can see how pleasure as an affective register is not necessarily ethical and is enshrouded by the circumstances under which pleasure is made possible—namely through negotiations of power and control.

Burrell's infamous homophobic sermon released to the public through cell phone camera footage is an example of vocal practice that ushers in ecstatic pleasure and erotic titillation through sexual shaming and damnation. Burrell's sermon, or at least the section of it we are able to see, is focused on the concept of perversion: "That perverted homosexual spirit is a spirit of delusion and confu-sion and has deceived many men and women and has caused a strain on the body of Christ," she says and then, with ample urging from her congregation, goes on to say, "You as a man who could open your mouth and put another man's penis in your face, you are perverted and you cannot tell me what thus saith the Lord! You are perverted! You are a woman and will shake your face in another woman's breasts—you are perverted!"[69] Burrell seems to be on the verge of whooping, and paces from one edge of the stage to the other. It is at this moment that the preacher could be swept up by the spirit and the sermon and divinely invited to dig deeply into or prophesy about the unsavory and specific parts of the congregation's indi-vidual lives. The preacher may give a nod to her own sexual indiscretions as a way of being able to speak frankly about sexuality in general.[70] This preacherly performance signifies on the supposed decorum of the holy desk that is willfully ravished by the Spirit of God and shakes up the presumed dignity of the church.

What Burrell performs in this sermon, however, is a wielding of sacred sexual vocality while professing no such knowledge of her own capacity for (homo) sexual knowledge. Ignorance, in the case of Burrell's sermon, is also deployed as a form of dissemblance which shrouds Burrell herself as too holy to imag-ine or understand lesbian sex acts that involve genitalia while simultaneously asking her congregation to imagine male on male oral sex. As Snorton notes, the multimodal function of ignorance in Black performance is irreverent of social decorum, a manipulation of spectacle, and a practice of disavowal of the param-eters of moral order.[71] Ignorance in this instance is a kind of aesthetic practice by which notions of inherent value and authenticity rest.

What I offer here is an example of how pleasure's possibilities may also be caught up in that which may harm. Amaryah Shaye Armstrong reminds us that Burrell's performance tells us a lot about the function of power and control in conversations about sex in the Black church. They note that Burrell's sermon was in fact preached to bring a particular kind of masochistic pleasure to her congre-gants, who could share in the explicit demonizing of queer and trans people in the church.

> Burrell's performance works to get the congregation excited, to make people happy to participate in denigrating the sexual lives of those sexual minorities who are likely among them. . . . We must understand that pleasure, as an affective register or a practice of enfleshment, doesn't engender an ethic that sustains life or transfor-mation without communal discernment and accountability[72]

In short, pleasure is not neutral. Congregants and the pastor herself are able to find moral authority through the pleasures of this performance. To agree loudly, as one congregant exclaims "That is real!" in the video, is to stake a claim in the work of distancing oneself from the queer figure imagined as sacrifice on the altar—the embodiment of carnal sin. As Terrion Williamson notes, "the black female body both marks and is the boundary of normative sexual behavior and desire as it is evinced within the black church."[73] And so we might see the purpose of Burrell's rant—to move the figure of sexual immorality away from her and onto the ever present scapegoat of perverse sexualities: the homosexual.[74]

Burrell was engaging not only in a form of theological terrorism but in a religious sadomasochism by which deep pleasure is taken through the denigration of silenced, though presumed to be present, others. Her sermon enacts the very homoerotic functions it claims to preach against. Burrell not only pleasured her congregation through the aesthetic practices foundational to Blackpentecostal churches, but in her "off the rails" (ign'ant) sermon, she explicitly titillates by describing gay sex acts in odd detail in the moment of collective ecstatic passion. Her sermon denounced and demonized queer people through a seemingly innocent heteronormative imagination of queer sex acts, but it did so by enticing the congregation into the fully embodied and imaginative space of queer sex. Congregational bodies open and ready for spiritual penetration would hear this message, take it within, and leave having received "spiritual nourishment" directly from the Holy Spirit. The impact and influence Burrell has within the gospel industry and in Black music cannot be denied. Yet, Burrell has both influenced and been influenced by Black musical styles and cultural practices built by Black queer folks who endure this oft repeated and damaging act by many pastors, gospel singers, and evangelists.

Another experience is possible, concurrent, and counter to Burrell's damaging message. When I think of "Mother" Shirley Miller leading "Oh Happy Day," with her breathy and deep contralto, or her wife Bishop Yvette Flunder singing "Thank You," I cannot succumb to the toxic version of God's ecstatic presence promised by Burrell. On "Oh Happy Day," Miller leads the choir in a flatfooted coolness much like Dionne Warwick, the upbeat tempo of the song grooving beneath her voice. She sings "Oh, happy day" and the choir returns the line: "Oh, happy day / when Jesus washed / when Jesus washed / He washed my sins away."[75] Usually, when any reference to sin and the washing of it occurs in the songs I grew up with in the church, I think of the moralizing codes that debase and demonize queer folks and women: the sexual lasciviousness projected onto Eve and her role in the fall of man, Jezebel, Mary Magdalene, and of course the use of verses in Leviticus and Corinthians to demean queer folks. But when Mother Miller is singing this song, she is not apologetic, she is not lamenting, but offering a pronouncement of being—*happy*. Miller declares with a growl at the vamp, "*When* I get to heaven," and the choir ascends with her—she is certain of this future destiny not in spite of who she is and loves, but inclusive of who she is and loves.

Bishop Yvette Flunder's lead on Walter Hawkins's "Thank You," is yet another performance of Black lesbian contralto that has managed to move spirits and bodies in pews. Walter Hawkins's opening lyrics to the song—"Tragedies are commonplace / all kinds of diseases / people are slipping away"—no doubt refer to the HIV/AIDS pandemic that was ravaging queer and Black communities and, notably, the gospel music community at the time.[76] Her voice slightly brighter than Mother's (a term affectionally used to reference Miller in the community of believers in the fellowship of faith to which Flunder's church, City of Refuge, belongs) she thanks the Lord for "love," "power," and "protection" from all of the obstacles, the "commonplace tragedies" or what Lucille Clifton would call the everyday "somethings" that have tried to kill her. The vamp of "Thank You" invites the congregation into praise through call and response. Bishop Flunder continues to sing this song as a kind of calling card to her place in the center of gospel music tradition. She now leads the Fellowship of Affirming Ministries and her "risky experiment," the City of Refuge UCC, founded in 1991, that has roots in Black Pentecostal tradition but maintains an open and affirming stance on LGBT folks.[77]

To return to the value of vocality here, Mother Shirley Miller and Bishop Yvette Flunder's long term musical collaboration with Edwin and Walter Hawkins was, too, a space that influenced their gospel careers *and* their partnership. On Walter Hawkins's *Love Alive IV*, the same album on which Flunder's performance of "Thank You" appears, there is a duet between Mother and Bishop (Miller and Flunder) titled "Full and Complete." Mother opens the song in her deeper and wispy contralto with, "The devil told me that I could not stand / all the sin and the darkness / that spread throughout the land . . ." and Flunder follows, "then the lord said to me / get your eyes off of what you think you might see / and put all your trust in me."[78] Together, in the chorus they sing: "He will give you salvation, joy, and peace / he'll give it full and complete . . ." Bishop begins to preach in the bridge, which Mother vocalizes and hums, building up until the choir vamps the song out. The very idea that these two sing this song, "Full and Complete," as they are also joined in romantic pairing and Flunder would soon after this record's release found her church means that certainly otherwise is possible through the vocal practice intended to usher in spirit even squarely within the confines of the church. Listening to Mother Shirley Miller and Bishop Yvette Flunder sing these songs and still *be* publicly in love, partnered, within *and* alternative to the spaces that demean queer folks I can feel how, as Crawley notes, "Alternatives exist— *already*—against the normative modes under which we endure."[79] The space of music making from which these two emerged as singers was also the space that united them as romantic partners. The context of their coming together was also one in which deep rejection and pain would endure for queer folks. Yet, these two opened a space for healing through their use of sacred sexual vocality. Further, their work in Oakland, California, that founded affirming church and fellowship invited queer folks into ecstatic expression within the Blackpentecostal tradition that had otherwise made it difficult for them to thrive.

THE TONE AND TEXTURE OF SACRED SEXUALITY

When I asked her if there was a difference between Denise White, her given name, and Avery*Sunshine she said, "Avery*Sunshine is Denise and Denise is Avery-*Sunshine. The only difference is Denise is going to say a few curse words."[80] Avery*Sunshine has public relations management whereas Denise "keeps it real." Sunshine takes up sexuality and spirituality in her music and her musical mission, and she sees the divine as present in religious and sexual contexts. In an online interview she said:

I think that we put God in a box, that is such an overused term but it's fitting. We put God in a box when we say, "I'm only going to do this, and I'm only going to be . . ." No, I'm a person. I am a sexy Black woman. I want to talk about being sensuous, I want to talk about not feelin good, and I want to talk about God being present while all of that is going on in my life. God is never outside of that, ever. Ever. Even when we so-called sin, God is there. God is there, and I feel like I'm supposed to say that.[81]

Musically, these connections are clear. Interviewers notice this enough to ask why she didn't pursue gospel. In one interview Sunshine responded that it would be "like pulling teeth" for her to be a gospel artist. "Because I'm not just gospel music, I'm soul. . . . God is present [in] every song I sing."[82] For Sunshine, gospel was a genre that would limit her ability to express herself as a whole person. She goes on, "There are times I just want to talk about [how] 'I don't feel good today.' . . . I need to be able to do that. I can't really do that if I say I'm just a gospel singer . . . they don't want to hear that. They want you to say [starts singing] 'In Jesus . . .' I don't want to talk about Jesus right now! I want to talk about what happened today. I ain't feelin good and I want to talk about that."[83] However, White, at the time of our interview, continued to sing in church, lead the choir, and, as I mentioned above, record and perform gospel music as Avery*Sunshine.

By straddling the fence, she does risk rejection. The line between sacred and secular is thin and treacherous; artists such as Aretha Franklin, Sister Rosetta Tharpe, and others who crossed over into secular music received pushback from the religious community. This pushback dates to the emergence of the blues from the legacy of the "seculars" of enslaved people in the US South. James Cone observes, "The 'secular' songs of slavery were 'non-religious,' occasionally anti-religious, and were often called 'devil songs' by religious folk."[84] By calling the blues secular spirituals, Cone asserts that they share a common thread of existential crisis with sacred music but with fleshy urgency: "They are secular in the sense that they confine their attention solely to the immediate and affirm the bodily expression of black soul, including the sexual manifestations. They are spirituals because they are impelled by the same search for the truth of black experience."[85] Philosophical and theological connection aside, blues music itself is implicated by religious music and vice versa.

Though the cycle of influence is rather transparent, some gospel artists who crossed over did have popular audiences, such as Sister Rosetta Tharpe and Willa Mae Ford Smith.[86] If church folks heard Bessie Smith in Willa Mae Ford Smith, it is because she was there. Mahalia Jackson, one of the most recognized gospel singers, was mostly influenced by Bessie Smith and other blues singers. According to Horace C. Boyer, "she listened for hours to the recordings of popular blues singers Mamie Smith, Bessie Smith, and Ma Rainey and attempted to capture their nuances and volume."[87] Jackson blended the vocal styles of blues singers to create the signature sound that epitomizes vocal worship in the gospel genre. Specifically, Boyer notes that the "deep and dark" resonances of the blues singers coalesced with that of "sanctified singers" in the church to shape Jackson's singing. Right down to *vocal styling*, the evocation of praise and worship is implicated by a genre which, according to Angela Davis, "challenged the most powerful African-American institution, the Christian church."[88]

Many artists across genres attest to ecstatic experience during singing performance. On the video for her first solo release, Karen Clark Sheard described a holy spirit descending on her and her sisters at the beginning of their careers.[89] Gospel singer Rita Wilson described being "in the spirit" as an out-of-body experience: "Sometimes it is embarrassing. But I can't control it. When the Spirit begins to come into my body and dwell in me, I can't stop, I can't control it."[90] In an interview with *Rolling Stone*, Whitney Houston described her desire to sing was because she, too, wanted to move people as her mother did: "When I used to watch my mother sing, which was usually in church, that feeling, that soul, that thing—it's like electricity rolling through you. If you have ever been in a Baptist church or a Pentecostal church, when the Holy Spirit starts to roll and people start to really feel what they're doing, it's . . . it's incredible. That's what I wanted."[91]

As much as these artists are asked about the methods behind production, the concepts surrounding their art, and how they consider the connections between sacred and secular genres, it is often assumed that their experiences of singing the genres would differ because of the lyrical content. As former blues woman Annie Pavageau relates, "It does seem to me, though, that you're bound to feel different when you sing for Jesus than when you sing the blues, because *then* . . . you are inspired by the Holy Spirit."[92] While gospel singers are expected to experience divine presence in their sacred music performances, they are not expected to have similar experiences while singing secular music. Yet, secular artists describe the experience of singing in similar terms; themes of losing control, being out of the body, and being vulnerable are repeated in their descriptions of musical vocal expression. In an interview with *Kick Magazine*, Avery*Sunshine said, "there's something about the vibration of music that brings you back to the spirit."[93] With me she described the experience as "euphoric" and expanded on that concept: the spirit is ". . . that indescribable nudge, that thing that is very present that you might not be able to touch but you know it's there." This nudge is the change agent within that ". . . either keeps you from doing something or encourages you to do something and it definitely is more felt than seen—and I mean internally felt."[94] Feelin the activating nudge of the spirit in music, Sunshine not only enacts her own philosophy of the secular and sacred as one but also her philosophy of music as an essential and dynamic force in human expression.

Singing God in the Body

My greatest teacher in singing gospel music was the minister of music in the church we attended in the deserts of the Los Angeles suburbs. First Lady H was a slight woman from Chicago who played the piano with such finesse that the congregation would get worked up by a mere four bars of her elaborate intros. As both the minister of music and first lady (pastor's wife), she was also an example of respectable Black womanhood. I could go on about her delicate mannerisms matched with her strong will and dynamic personality. I could write a book on her hats and their matching outfits, clutches, and heels. But this is about the best lesson she ever taught me: how to growl.

The song was Vickie Winans's version of "Long as I Got King Jesus." I felt out of place. Her daughters were selected to sing backup for this high-energy song, and they were the prize singers in the choir. The lyrics, anchored by the stock phrase "I've been 'buked / scorned / talked about sure as you're born," made the song sound older than it actually was. As we practiced, my timbre wasn't right. Sister Hackett told me to dig deep, presuming I had somewhere to dig at sixteen. "Haven't you been lied on?!" she exclaimed. On the spot, I dug up a story from the recesses of my childhood, a third-grade incident when the popular girl blamed me for a nasty note she wrote about our classmates. First Lady H, wanting me to get in touch with those feelins of betrayal, made me repeat the girl's name. Thinking about it as an adult, the whole incident seems funny, and even at sixteen I could appreciate the humor of recounting the troubles of an even smaller child. But just that little bit of emotion put some strength in my voice at the very first phrase, "I've been lied on / cheated . . ." a strength that didn't seem right coming out of my body and vibrating through my throat. Such a sound seemed relegated to older women who'd actually been through something.

Not only did I seem to lose my childlike soprano, but the chest note had gristle. When I got to the phrase "talked about sure as you're born," I had a grown-woman growl that excited me. Our rehearsal of this song went on longer than we needed to learn it. The feelin needed practice. It would be my first time on the praise team. My newfound growl would be a part of the practice of ushering in the Presence.

I include a discussion of the growl here not to presume that its use is always indicative of transcendence, but to discuss the way it and other vocal tools may be used to express and invoke divine presence. The power in its use are the element of surprise and placement on particular lyrics within a song. Like all vocal tricks used in blues, gospel, soul, and R&B, such as melisma and runs, the growl can be overused and rendered hollow of meaning. When I asked Avery*Sunshine about the quality of an "anointed" voice and the use of these skills, she rejected the notion that vocal tricks alone have the power to move. "For a minute," she said, "I thought that the only anointed voices were the ones that could do runs, do all kinds of stuff, the vocal melisma with their voices . . . I thought that was anointing until you listen." She goes on, "There are people who . . . you know the whole song is nothing but a run. It's been executed wonderfully but I didn't feel anything."[95] Despite this, Sunshine and other notable singers use the growl, blasts of vibrato, melisma, and runs to express emotional connection and emphasize the meaning of a lyric or draw the audience's attention to a note.

Many voice instructors might find the trick of "growling" a rather elusive skill to teach safely. It happens in the throat and resonates through chest notes. It creates an explosive vibration less subtle than the typical vibrato. Its use signals that divine presence has taken over the singer's voice and sent it into the supernatural. The growl itself has roots in the field holler, and its persistent use on single whole notes reflects that relationship. Blues singer Koko Taylor's execution of the growl in the opening sequence of "I'm A Woman" typifies this use. Taylor's "Oh yeah" is an invocation of a supernatural feminine presence.[96] The shock of hearing the growl is in the fact that it is so deeply vibratory it literally shakes the body while carrying a single precise note. Many classical teachers avoid it for fear of damaging vocal chords. To be able to use the growl without such damage is considered a gift.

Amiri Baraka wrote on the structure of these vocal articulations that connect soul desires to sound in his book *Blues People*. Baraka notes the influence of the field holler on the sound and intent of blues music, explaining that "the shouts and hollers were strident laments, more than anything."[97] Shouts and hollers were also markers of individual style. Furthermore, the sound/feelin produced in the shout became the structure by which the blues was created, "as was characteristic of the hollers and shouts, the single line could be repeated again and again and again, either because the singer specially liked it, or because he could not think of another line. The repeated phrase also carries into instrumental jazz as the riff."[98] Yet the riff continues as a vocal sound/feelin by which repetition of notes and words touch on emotional quality as well as musical style.

Karen Clark Sheard, a gospel singer renowned for her use of vocal tricks and developing the "Clark sound" along with her sisters and mother, uses growls specifically to punctuate her iteration of the voice of God in her gospel version of Jill Scott's "He Loves Me (Lyzel in E Flat)."[99] Sheard's version, "You Loved Me (Live)," features her particular vocal ability to create the audial illusion of an echo. By repeating a melodic phrase, diminishing its volume, and altering the pitch, she relates to her audience the sound of "the still voice" of God. She sings, "You're not alone, you're not alone, not alone / I'll hold your hand, I'll hold your hand / I'll hold your hand / I'll help you / I'll help you / I'll help you . . ." and so on.[100] She ends God's melodic monologue with a series of short runs and punctuates this divine voice with a growl, also managing to echo that growl. Karen Clark Sheard's musical talent was honed in the Church of God in Christ, where expressive showmanship and musical expressions of the Holy Spirit are one with God's presence. Sheard takes up anointed authority in her vocal impersonation of God's voice and iterates it through her own full-bodied vocal sound. It is telling that Sheard uses a song most known for its sexual connotations. Jill Scott's original tune is quite explicitly centered on erotic touch. The title "You Love Me" is the first line of the song: "You love me / especial- / ly different / every / time you keep / me on my feet / happily / excited / by your touch . . ."[101] Though Sheard quite expressly states in the song that Jesus is "who [she's] talking about," her use of Scott's sultry tune points not only to the musical connections between secular and sacred Black music but also to a theme within gospel music that features Jesus as an intimate partner.

Another key element of the Sheard version of Scott's song is a performance Karen Clark Sheard and her daughter Kierra Sheard take up as a reference to her first solo album, in which they sang a duet based on call and response. Karen would feed lyrics to her daughter and Kierra would sing in kind. However, there is a turn in which Kierra seemingly goes off script—presumably taken by the Holy Spirit and her own talents—to ad-lib, run, and generally cause a ruckus. The Clarks do this again with the gospel version of Scott's song and the younger, though told by her mother to "behave," goes off to sing more complicated runs, melismata, and a multi-bar growl that ultimately results in her being sent to her room as if to punish her for showing out (and possibly showing her mother up). This vocal showmanship is also performed as the audial and embodied experience of being caught up in the spirit—so much so that one cannot obey mother's orders to sing as (presumably) scripted. While these vocal acrobatics are intentionally used in the context of gospel music and a gospel concert, one cannot forget the song's origins: a love song by an (at the time debut) R&B singer to her first husband whose name is parenthetical to the original title "He Loves Me (Lyzel in E Flat)."

It is a seemingly simple song. However, Scott reveals the depth of her tonal and textual range with layered vocals that begin the song in a sweet head register that is almost a whisper. By the second verse, a little more of her voice is used—still in the head but audially fuller. She goes on to sing along with the synthesized strings that hint at her experience in European classical vocal styles: her palate lifted, with a rounder sound. It is at this point in the song that Scott begins to recite a poem that moves directly into a bridge; she continues in her singing voice with: "Aw when you touch me, I just can't control it . . . I just can't hold it. / The emotion inside of me, I can feel it." After, she continues to ad-lib without words but with vowel sounds that further showcase the range of her voice. The song ends with these vocalizations, one that sounds a bit like a chant produced in the soft palate—in a different scale—and then finally a simple, atonal "la la la" and the sound of raspberries (used by singers to engage the diaphragm and warm up the lips). Technically, Scott is giving us signals that she is a trained and skilled singer who studies her craft. She is also, remarkably, not using the full force of her singing voice in this song at all (as one can hear a bit more of it in the next song on the album, a Go-Go's tune titled "It's Love") but instead communicating the crescendo of ecstatic expression through her slow build that uses slight changes in the texture and tone of her voice to communicate erotic excitement. These subtler vocal stylings, though not as bombastic as the Sheards', do the work of performing ecstasy—perhaps enough for the Sheards to take up the tune for their purposes.

Speaking of a range of ecstatic vocal practice from a whisper to a scream, Rachelle Ferrell's practices of ecstatic vocal work can span many textures, octaves, tones, and genres in one song. For instance, her performance of "I Can Explain" at the 2009 North Sea Jazz Festival included growls, grunts, squalls and more vocal techniques while her recorded performance for the 2002 live album *Live in Montreux* featured a lengthy whistle note and extensive glottal-stop–textured runs. At the end of the tune, you can hear her accessing all of these (and more) techniques and utterances which gives us something we can feel expressed in the lyrics, for sure, but beyond them as well. Here, Ferrell fills the space above the forceful punctuated chords played by her piano, Raymond McKinley's bass, Kenneth Crouch's keys, and William Odum's guitar. Her signature multimodal vocalizations express the plaintive desire within the song. After she has given us melodic lyrics with phrasing and tone that make use of the cathedral of resonant sound that is Rachelle Ferrell's "first instrument," the audience is left on the edge of their seats during an instrumental bridge that gives the audial quality of climax. The listener is sustained in the ecstatic thrall of the sweetness in Ferrell's voice at the close of the song after she chirps the highest notes, growls with no words, elongates, and makes staccato, the song's refrain. She doesn't even complete some of these phrases. She's playing with us. Better thought: she is playing with herself in front of us.[102] Which is to say, Ferrell's vocalizations seem to sound out and resonate for Ferrell first. As her mouth shapes itself to alter and invent new sounds, one might recognize that they are witnessing an artist at (self) play. The tones come at us in different textures and tones all at once on the single lyric, "I love you." Her voice does a lot—too much, and isn't that the state of orgasmic pleasure? Of the excesses Black women's vocality represents? Ferrell finalizes the titillating exposure felt in the song by ending in the middle of a phrase, its conclusion dangling on an inversion and the incomplete lyric, "No one, has ever . . ." Ever what Rachelle? *Ever what?!* The open phrase requires us to resolve—to finish ourselves.

* Poof * Sunshine

Avery*Sunshine's self-titled debut album demonstrates a clear decision to freely traverse the worlds of sacred and secular Black music. My first encounter with the singer was at a backyard party for queer Black women in Washington, DC, where she was the featured performer. She entertained us with the featured tracks on her album, but the most memorable part of her performance was her rendition of the gospel tune, "Safe in His Arms." At this backyard party, which occurs annually during Black Gay Pride in Washington, DC, Avery*Sunshine, who also works as a choir director, led the audience—separating us into soprano, alto, and tenor voices. We harmonized the chorus that would back her up through the song. At a party that wasn't quite intended to be church, she brought church with her. The audience became the choir and the congregation, connected through voice—Sunshine's and our own. Folks sang at the top of their lungs, some shouted (or play-shouted), and some teared up. Imagine this: a space made for queer socializing, a space for those often told that they are not welcome to bring their whole selves into Christian religious space, a space made for open flirtation and communion as Black queer folks was recognized as holy and transformed into a space of ecstatic communion by way of a collective and shared experience with song directed by Avery*Sunshine. During our interview she described her need for spiritual and communal singing at her concerts "[there is] the clear connection between me on the stage with a crowd and me at the church, in the pulpit with the congregation . . . I do have a need for that communal [singing] I do and that's very, very—it's very African. Those are our roots."[103] Sunshine's communal gospel extends into her debut studio album as well.

Sunshine's debut album reflects the influence and importance of gospel, soul, and R&B in her music. It is an overwhelmingly "feel good" album with mostly mid-tempo, upbeat rhythms, like the introductory track, "All in My Head," and playful lyrics, as in her most popular single, "Ugly Part of Me." The track "Blessing Me" is a willful blurring of the sacred and secular; it is an R&B slow groove arrangement of a well-known gospel tune. Self-proclaimed as "Chu'ched" Avery*Sunshine also addresses sensuality and desire.[104] The song "Just Not Tonight" describes forbidden desire, while "Like This" describes a romantic relationship in a guitar-forward, lounge-inspired track. Her first hit, "Stalk You," which is about obsessed sexual desire, is a house tune.

Sunshine's process is deeply spiritual and synergetic. She works with her business partner and spouse, Dana, who plays guitar and co-writes many of her songs. She credits him for pushing her to do her own project. Dana is also embedded in the story of Sunshine's name, a moniker that is, perhaps, the most explicit embodiment of scared experience and sexual desire. When one of Denise White's singles was picked up and it was clear that her music career as a solo artist was beginning, Dana prompted her to rename herself.[105] "Avery" is inspired by the sassy and sexually empowered blues woman, Shug Avery, from Alice Walker's *The Color Purple*, and Sunshine is taken from the character of the same name in the film *Harlem Nights* (Paramount, 2002). In *Harlem Nights*, Sugar Ray (Richard Pryor) asks for a girl who could "turn out" a man. Vera (Della Reese), the resident madam, offers, "I have got a girl whose pussy is so good, if you threw it up in the air it would turn into sunshine." Sunshine (played by Lela Rochon) is a high-priced, exclusive prostitute employed by Vera who manages to seduce a mobster to the point of distraction—an essential element to the scheme cooked up by the protagonists of the film. This mobster promptly decides to leave his wife and children and endangers his life to stay with Sunshine—and thus her radiant pussy. Rochon portrays this character as a soft-spoken, coy, and impeccably dressed seductress who drips with playful sexuality. Avery*Sunshine observes, ". . . well, she was a hooker [or] whatever but it wasn't dirty to me and there was something about her that I admired."[106]

Avery*Sunshine admires Shug Avery from *The Color Purple* for being a "bossy, testosterone-filled woman." It was this "testosterone" that Sunshine identified with in Shug's character. "I've always been told that I have more masculine energy by my ex-husband . . . I do have more masculine energy and I embrace it and I think . . . that masculine energy . . . is nothing but confidence in saying what we [women] want."[107] Confident and self-assured, Shug Avery takes orders from no man and teaches the protagonist, Celie, about her own sexuality, becomes her lover, and gives Celie her greatest theological lesson that "God is more of an it" that wants to be loved.

Sunshine reads Shug Avery as sexually empowered and androgynous despite the narrative of her father in the film which could, arguably, be read as an attempt to reinsert patriarchal power and the desire for male approval in one of the more self-sufficient and empowered female characters. Sunshine reads Shug Avery as especially empowered. Shug Avery is a master teacher of the connectivity of all things, the presence of the Divine in all things, and the oneness of spirituality and sexuality in life and music. Such a character is a fitting frame for Avery*Sunshine's persona and art. Her persona, carefully considered, embraces a self-aware kind of sexuality and spirituality that is also evidenced in her music practice.

Sunshine skillfully uses a blast of vibrato as the central feature of the song "I Need You Now." The song begins with a drum buildup and the refrain, "I need you now / More than I needed you then / It's been a while / But I still need my friend," which is sung with background in harmony. When the refrain ends, drums return to build the momentum and lead us to a blast of the word "I've" in a vibrato-filled C note. The textures of the various vibratos build on the momentum of the song. The first verse continues, "I've really been going through / Beat down caught in a rut." The "I" in "I've" receives the full-throated vibrato. This signals the personal focus of the song. "I Need You Now" is a song about internal struggle directed toward an ambiguous "you." The tone of the song, along with the use of gospel quartet–style background vocals, gives the "feel" of a gospel tune in which the "you" is God.

The second verse continues in this ambiguous vein. Opening with another blast of full-throated vibrato, the beginning of the verse enhances the effect of the growl by using repetition and building, once again, on the anticipation of the drums at the end of the previous refrain. "I've tried I've tried I've tried I've tried" it begins, the blast releasing into a decrescendo that relates the sense of defeat—as if the phrase continues, "I've tried, but I failed." The repetition of words and notes turn the lyrical line into a riff. As the verse continues, Sunshine makes a lyrical allusion to failed attempts to solve deeply spiritual problems in "the world" or in sin. She sings that she's tried, "Hanging out with the crowd / when no one could hear my voice / I guess the music was just too loud." Cut off from needs otherwise unmet, the lyricist's attempt to be understood "in the world" only enhances the sense of isolation in the song and the continued need for this "you." The song's use of this conceit pivots toward gospel styling, yet there continues to be an ambiguity about the "you."

Along with the growl, Sunshine features backup singers who vocalize in the style of the classical gospel quartet. This style encourages every voice in the quartet to harmonize, maintain a distinct timbre, ad-lib, and sustain notes longer than other members or to respond to the soloist in melodic speech. In this style, voices singing in unison seem extremely distinct. This becomes most clear in the bridge.

The bridge transforms and gives new meaning to the song. The ambiguity of the "you" in the song is not resolved but further confounded. Using a conceit common to soul music, Sunshine goes through a list of well-meaning people she has consulted about her dilemma and the various advice they give her, only to be disregarded: doctor, pastor, and finally mother, all of whom entreat her to move on. Sunshine sings, "My doctor said there's nothing wrong / It's all in my head / My pastor said it's time to move on / You know that's the same thing my mama said / But I ain't listening to nobody else / Because I know what I need / and all I need is you."[108]

One famous use of this conceit is by Aretha Franklin in the bridge of Don Covay's composition "Chain of Fools," in which Franklin sings, "My father says leave you alone / my mother says come on home / my doctor says take it easy / but your loving is just too strong."[109] It is also reflected in the spiritual "Jordan River" in which a similar list of family members and friends are unable to "cross the river" with the singer. The drastic decision to cross over is on the speaker alone. By translating this concept in which drastic decisions—drastic enough to allude to death—must come from personal conviction or will, Franklin spoke to the power of lovin in influencing a woman's decision, even to her detriment. Rejecting well-intended advice signals a stronger will beyond logic; in Aretha's case, the will was lovin, and possibly in Sunshine's case too. Sunshine's ambiguous "you" does not allow us to know exactly why she needs this other person or thing, but the need is expressed to be so great it defies logic.

In the bridge, longing turns into erotic desire. Sunshine's bridge alludes to another bridge in Black music where erotic desire is expressed. Sunshine not only signifies on Franklin's conceit lyrically but musically as well. The background vocals during the bridge shift into a doo-wop style similar to Franklin's background vocals on the bridge to "Chain of Fools." This drastic vocal shift mirrors the transitional aspect of the bridge itself. While the bridge further complicates meaning, it does tell us that the "you" in her song may not be God considering Sunshine's pastor is one of the detractors.

In fact, the vamp verifies that the "you" may be a lover. In a sweet tone that is otherwise absent in the rest of the song, Sunshine sings along with background singers in equally sweet harmony: "I need you to come back. See about me." The various points of the song have created a narrative arc where erotic desire is as serious as divine presence and as desirable as sexual ecstasy.

Altering sound to represent and invoke divine presence is common practice in Black music. Returning to Thompson's discussion of the power of àshe, possession of the spirit is affective and embodied. As Thompson states, "To become possessed by the spirit . . . is to 'make the god,' to capture numinous flowing force within one's body."[110] This kind of possession is an embodied experience, which is also witnessed through style and represents àshe—the power to change one's condition. Sunshine alters sound, both vocally and instrumentally, to allude to the desire for God's presence in her desire for sexual attention. Desire itself remains connected to the divine through this sonic force produced within the body. That the difference between her lover and God remains ambiguous throughout the song reflects the ambiguities between sexual and spiritual desire. Singing is the mode by which both sexual and spiritual ecstasy can be experienced, as Sunshine notes, "[singing] releases something very much like sex."[111] In this frame, the divine is sexual partner and singing, or running sound through one's body, is intercourse.

SINGING TO CHANGE YOUR CONDITION

You can't be a good singer and not be vulnerable and I think
being vulnerable allows you to be free. Something about it
allows you to be stress free and at peace. That's that Nirvana.
Do you know what I mean? For me anyway, it's orgasmic.
—AVERY*SUNSHINE

Opening the body's channels to song and allowing the voice to reverberate on the ears of others is an intimate act. I've discussed the extent to which that act mirrors intercourse and divine exhalation. Singing is a tool that some Black women vocalists have used for unlocking their own desires and engaging in this intimate touch. This vulnerability is as strategic as it is powerful. In exposing the vulnerabilities of voice through divine breath, the singer can transform the air through the transmission of feeling made possible by singing a song. Others hear and feel that vibration and are taken up in the opportunity of affective flight and can be changed too.

T. V. Reed began his book *The Art of Protest* with the story of student activists in 1960s Tennessee. In doing so he acknowledged that singing was fundamental and imperative to changing one's condition. During a police raid at the Highlander Folk School, a girl began to sing "We Shall Overcome"; she sings the lyric, "We are not afraid." The act of singing the song while, in fact, being afraid was a mechanism through which the girl sings away "a bit of her fear" and "asserts the . . . right to freedom and justice."[112] These young activists sang to take the air back from the white supremacist presence of the police. Christina Sharpe notes of the "transformative properties of being 'free' to breathe fresh air," and the everpresence of miasma, or bad air that makes it hard to breathe.[113] Ashon Crawley offers an aesthetics for how Black folks took the air and breathed anyhow called *black pneuma*, "the capacity for the plural movement and displacement of inhalation and exhalation to enunciate life, life that is exorbitant, capacious, and fundamentally, social, though it is also life that is structured through and engulfed by brutal violence."[114] While songs were a unifying force, they were also an affective force for activists whose livelihoods, if not their lives, were in constant peril. Bernice Johnson Reagon relates a similar narrative about taking back the air by singing a song.

Sound is a way to extend the territory you can affect, so people can walk into you way before they can get close to your body. And certainly the communal singing that people do together is a way of announcing that we're here, that this is real. And so anybody who comes into that space, as long as you're singing, they cannot change the air in that space. The song will maintain the air as your territory. And I've seen meetings where a sheriff has walked into a mass meeting and established the air because this is a sheriff everybody knows. And they're taking pictures or taking names and you just know your job is in trouble and blah, blah, blah. The only way people could take the space back was by starting a song. And inevitably, when police would walk into mass meetings, somebody would start a song and then people would join in and, as people joined in, the air would change.[115]

While the present circumstances of the group may not change—they may even go to jail—the air would not belong to the policemen who threatened them. They literally took it back through song. The songs themselves had messages, but most importantly they united the activists that sang them, shifting the energy from fear to determination. The energetic importance of the songs is why the songs are simply tools used "To get to the singing."[116] Lyrically they reified the political stance the activists took, carrying a message of freedom to those who sang and heard them. It is ironic that this most vulnerable act was so essential for the civil rights movement, that vulnerability had a certain strength and protection.

These are circumstances in which this practice of running sound through the body was deployed in the moment of an emergency, but what I've explored here is more akin to the everyday necessariness of ecstatic feeling: the practices of pleasure that are made by choice, every day, if one wishes to change their condition. We already know that racism is so quotidian, monotonous. How does one get to feelin in their own skin after that but by practice?

Black women have changed the landscape of popular music by drawing from a musical tradition that incorporates the importance of changing one's condition. Popular artists inherit this aspect of song and performance in their work by using the power of voice, song, and music to articulate sexual desire, spiritual desire, and desire for fundamental change in the conditions of their inner lives. This vibrational change is not relegated to one domain of transcendent experience; here, ecstasy emerges as that fundamental vibrational change that operates on these various planes. Regardless of the song, ecstasy needs practice. It is a practice through which sedulous engagement of the erotic is key as a technical function of running sound through the body and yet is a performance by which the feelin of running sound through the body has potency.

Thinking of the everyday and ecstatic vocal practice, I will end here with a memory of singing in the car with my mother as a child. It seemed like we were always in the car because of her travels, and there, she was always singing. In retrospect, there must have been stress. As I said, we traveled a lot; she'd moved to Los Angeles from Baltimore on her own as s single mother. She's Black in a racist and sexist settler colonial state. There are a lot of pressures she experienced. But she always managed to find a place to sing, so song is all my first memories of her. It is the most cherished thing we share to this day. In that car my mother was my first lesson in song resounding and shaking my whole body. If I dared to join, I'd feel our sound vibrating against the windshield, my little voice and her big voice meeting in a divine place. Hers classical and mine something else—learning, but we'd sing, muddied with a history of sound meant to pierce the heart of God—make God come down and dwell in us.

Figure 13. The waters of the Salish Sea.

Use your mobile device to scan the QR code. You can also navigate to: http://dr.bettinajudd.com /take-me-to-the-water to view the end of this chapter.

Figure 14. Meta Veaux Warrick Fuller, *In Memory of Mary Turner: A Silent Protest against Mob Violence*, 1919. Plaster, paint, 12 inches. Copyright © by the artist. Courtesy of John L. Fuller.

CHAPTER 4

Shame and the Visual Field of Black Motherhood

*There was punishment. Like the way
the body is murdered by its own weight when lynched.*
—BETTINA JUDD, FROM *PATIENT*.

*I*n the sketch, Mary Turner ascends above a violent mob that clutches at her. Her hair is full and crowns her head in a rounded coiffure popular in the 1910s. Her dress is long and her collar is loose. Her solemn expression is discernable by the relaxed and downward pull of her lips but the rest of her expression is less detailed. The faces of the violent mob look to be somewhere between demonic and desperate. They reach for her from the flames of hell as she ascends. Holding the physical weight of Turner's body are billowing clouds that obscure the space between Turner's skirt and the mob. Her head is bowed as she looks down at the clawing crowd with a sleeping infant in her arms. She protectively holds the swaddled baby close and to one side. The sculpture is painted metallic as if to imagine it in bronze.

Meta Veaux Warrick Fuller's sculpture memorializes Mary Turner and protests the mob violence that murdered her. The irony of the sculpture's nominal nod to the large silent protest against lynching that took place in Harlem in July 1917 is clear. Fuller thought this image too incendiary for public view and kept it in her studio.[1] Her visual references to Madonna and child imagery which placed Turner's unborn baby in her arms highlights how the lynching of Mary Turner struck a chord of concern over the conditions of Black motherhood that could still be met with atrocious violence.

The lynching of Mary Turner in 1918 was an event that made clear the ungendered functions of racial violence. That is, that motherhood does not protect Black women from violence, in fact it opens Black women to more pernicious forms of violence. The coming century would further prove the image of Black mothers to be a contested figure. Black feminist thought in the late twentieth and early twenty-first centuries has critiqued this open hatred of Black mothers, notably in the aftermath of the infamous Moynihan report which described the Black family as a "tangle of pathology" and Black mothers as a central dysfunctional figure in that pathology.[2] As Alexis Pauline Gumbs notes, "Black feminists audaciously centered an entire literary movement around the invocation of this criminal act of Black maternity, demanding not only the rights of Black women to reproductive autonomy in the biological sense, but also the imperative to create narratives, theories, contexts, collectives, publications, political ideology and more."[3] Black feminist critique exposes how racialized and gendered hatred of Black motherhood also serves a political function in which Black women's reproductive capacity is cast as a social problem.

In response to ongoing political dramas which invoked figures of Black welfare queens and crack babies, legal scholar Dorothy Roberts declared that, "We are in the midst of an explosion of rhetoric and policies that degrade Black women's reproductive decisions."[4] These decisions are degraded by gutted social programs for poor mothers, coerced contraception, forced and coerced sterilization, the war on drugs, increased carceral practices in schools, child care services, and the foster care system.[5] Legal and social consequences to Black mothers and mothering conjure terrible images of Black mothers in depravity, debasement, and moral contempt. So pervasive is the image of the Black mother as a problem that in the introduction of her book *Killing the Black Body* Roberts demonstrates how every controlling image of Black womanhood—the jezebel, the mammy, the matriarch and on—types itself through ideas of Black motherhood. These stereotypes make visual what Patrick Moynihan, Ronald Reagan (whose political career was amplified by the invention of "the welfare queen") and others proposed as pathological types. The terms "welfare queen" and "mammy" operate both as ideology and images that stick to the Black female body. An image of a Black woman's body cannot remain merely descriptive, it also invokes surplus meaning—what Nicole Fleetwood calls "excess flesh."[6] In chorus with Black feminist thinkers writing in expository propositional prose, Black women visual artists have also taken up issues of Black motherhood as it is visually imagined.

So, I begin with a return to Meta Veaux Warrick Fuller's *Silent Protest* because I think I understand why she created a monument to Mary Turner yet kept it out of public view, opting to keep it close to her in her studio.[7] A close look at the sculpture reveals the fraught issues Fuller had to consider when rendering a Black woman whose body—whose excess flesh was also eviscerated and charred by racial violence. Turner was not, as some might say "a perfect victim." She spoke out of turn in defense of her lynched husband who was accused of murder. She was poor, pregnant, and Black. Her body and the fetus she carried to eight months were made a spectacle during their final moments in life. Everything about her was on grotesque display: her Black and bloody flesh, her intestines—parts of her physical form otherwise understood to be private were available to the white mob that killed her. Her status as a mother to be was not respected, for as Gumbs aptly observes, "motherHOOD is a status granted by patriarchy to white middle-class women [. . .]."[8] Turner could never belong to that sacred and exclusive club and the fault for that was in her very flesh. Fuller wanted, maybe needed, to put Turner's body back together, as the sculpture does afford Mary Turner some dignity: Fuller clothes her here, placed her unborn baby in her arms, coiffed her hair, elevated her above the demonic mob, and even had her look down at them in defiance. But underneath all of that was the image of a woman out of place: a woman speaking out, poor, Black, unprotected, in the shadow of her lynched husband, and *almost* a mother.

Fuller might have found it difficult to render Turner without brushing against the excesses of Black maternal flesh. I am interested in the affective energy that exists around putting Mary Turner's body back together. I call this affective energy shame but I do not contend that it is Meta Fuller or Mary Turner who felt shame. It is the project of racial *shaming* on the Black maternal body that produces the effects of shame—anxious and charged covering or even anxious and charged defiant revealing. This chapter takes up affective negotiations of Black maternal imagery, what I call the visual field of Black motherhood, through the lens of racial, gendered, and maternal shaming. By taking up shame and shaming and its relationship to images of Black mothers, we can parse through the affective modes of racial hatred that are negotiated by Black folks who mother and who have been mothered by Black folks, and further, recover varied modes of being that imagine Black mothering on different terms.

By negotiating shame and shaming, we uncover ways of being that engage the structures of feeling in the public and private sphere that traffic in shame. Defiance, for example, appears repeatedly in Black women's artistic responses to the project of shaming Black motherhood—as in Meta Fuller's monument to Mary Turner and also in Betye Saar's infamous *Aunt Jemima's Revenge*. Saar reimagines the Quaker brand trope of the mammy armed with broom and gun, smiling and unafraid. Shame's twin, pride, serves as another mode of being that diametrically responds to shame. Renee Cox, an artist and photographer known for her bombastic physical presence in her photographs, exemplifies this particular affective response to racial shaming with her avatar "Yo Mama," who appears nude, strong, and always with a defiant gaze. As Cox's photographs exemplify defiance and pride in generally idyllic if not controlled settings, Deana Lawson presents Black motherhood in a complex and conflicted domestic space: a working-class Black home. Each of these artists produce images of Black mothers that negotiate maternal misogynoirist shame(ing) and picture Black maternal figures that exist with and against shame. These figurations stand apart in the visual field of Black motherhood as they attend to new ways of feelin images of maternity in Black. Despite racial shaming and the apparatuses that would seek to end Black maternity altogether, Black mothering is a thing which *be, regardless*, and the Black women artists here negotiate the state of that kind of being through the affective register of shame. The affective encounter of these images radiates through racial shaming as confrontation, sensuality, violence, and mourning. This is what shame conjures and what creative production that seeks otherwise shakes from the visual field of Black motherhood and provokes us to feel too.

I begin this discussion through the field in which Black motherhood is imaged and the feminist critiques of the systems that have devalued Black reproduction and maternal work. Engaged with personal and published interviews with Cox, as well as published interviews with Saar, Lawson, and other visual artists, I tarry with their art that tells us something about how shame(ing) and its relative affects are negotiated in the ongoing discourse of Black motherhood. By wading through this visual field I demonstrate how these visual artists wrestle with the image of the Black mother in an environment in which shame and shaming of Black motherhood are inextricably linked to shaming Black women's sexuality and reproduction. Shame might be the goal of outside forces intent on infiltrating within, yet somehow through these images, and in the world, Black mothers continue to be. How that feel?

Ain't Got Sense Enuf to Be 'Shame(d): Looking at Shame in the Visual Field of Black Motherhood

I have had kids tell me that my hair was so nappy it looked
like a thousand Africans giving the Black Power salute, but
never has anyone said to my face that my whole family—
especially my mama—was "a tangle of pathology."
—ROBIN D. G. KELLEY[9]

I don't have to list the names that politicians, comedians, filmmakers, or the news might call my mama here—it is highly likely that you already know them.[10] The names and the pathologies behind the names have shaped welfare policy, fueled the war on drugs, expanded the prison industrial complex, launched studies by the department of labor, and animated the processed and fast food industry. If the latter is to be clearly understood, you might also be aware of how this imagination of my mama might look—the smiling darky on the pancake box, the debased fiend on the silver screen, the loud-talking flashy diva living conspicuously in inner-city housing projects on your TV—visual symbols of the Black maternal that are maligned by what Patricia Hill Collins names controlling images.[11] If you are reading this as someone familiar with Black feminist thought or parlance you, no doubt, can run through the list of these names off the dome, trace the arc of Black feminist thought that has refuted these assertions about Black motherhood, and name how precisely these notions negatively affect Black folks and Black women specifically.

In her influential essay on the Black woman's role in the community of slaves, Angela Davis describes how the Black mother figure has been used to perpetuate a myth about Black women's complacent role in the conditions of slavery.[12] Her article directly refutes claims made in the US Department of Labor's report on the Negro Family known as the Moynihan Report that the Black family is a "tangle of pathology" due to inherited weak family structures marked by matriarchal rule. Davis argues that the concept of a Black enslaved matriarch is a dangerous misnomer that "implies stable kinship structures within which the mother exercises decisive authority" and further, "ignores the profound traumas the black woman must have experienced when she had to surrender her child-bearing to alien and predatory economic interests."[13] Centrally, the notion of a female-dominated Black household in the era of slavery and carried on to twentieth and twenty-first century understandings of Black family dynamics ignores the oppressive and hardly habitable conditions under which Black mothers mother. It presumes white, middle-class moral structures of cis-heteronormative family life to which Black women in the afterlife of slavery were and are not afforded. Even though the concept of the doomed Black female–headed household is damaging to Black women and Black families, it has been ripe misogynist fodder for androcentric and masculinist discussions on the Black family. As Barbara Ransby and Tracye Matthews note in their article, "Black Popular Culture and the Transcendence of Patriarchal Illusions":

> African American women, especially single mothers, are routinely
> vilified as the culprit [for the "problem with black people"]. For

example, regular attacks on our black women in the media, most often disguised as an attack on the admittedly inadequate welfare system, portray them as lazy, unfit mothers, members of a morally bankrupt underclass, who should be punished for their inability to sustain a middle-class family life-style on a sub-poverty income.[14]

I emphasize this inherent moral code of mothering alongside Davis's intervention because shaming is the affective byproduct of the discourse by which Black mothers are routinely maligned. What do you do after the realization that you or your mama embodies the moral, social, economic, and representational failure of your community? The affective residue of name calling and pathology might be encapsulated in the above quote by Robin D.G. Kelly on Moynihan's report as a gone-too-far snap in a game of dozens.

In the cis-heteronormative construction of reproduction, the public shaming of black motherhood is a form of control directed toward Black women's reproduction and sexuality. Black feminist and queer studies have already taught us that Black motherhood has never quite fit in with cis-heteronormative constructions of reproduction. As Cathy Cohen notes ". . . many of the roots of heteronormativity are in white supremacist ideologies which sought (and continue) to use the state and its regulation of sexuality, in particular through the institution of heterosexual marriage, to designate which individuals were truly 'fit' for full rights and privileges of citizenship."[15] The contested Black maternal figure that Patrick Moynihan centered in his "tangle of pathology" presents a problem because of her relationship to white power structures as Black folks, especially poor Black folks are positioned in opposition to cis-heteronormative ideals.

I discuss here how national discourse and public policy that imagine black motherhood as a perpetual problem have done so by cultivating shaming mechanisms specifically geared toward controlling Black reproduction and motherhood. According to Michelle Wallace, "Cultural shame over black women as mothers is a cultural construction older than we realize."[16] And as Melissa Harris-Perry states, "Black women in their role as mothers and potential mothers are subjugated to surveillance, judgment, and physical invasion. It is not hard to imagine how these experiences produce lasting shame."[17] That cultural shame is particularly placed on the image and embodiment of the mammy, a figure typified by her lack of sexuality and the jezebel/welfare queen, typified for her deviant and insatiable sexuality, reveals something about the sexual implications of racial shame.

A NOTE ON SHAME

Describing it as a "way to intimidate and break the spirit" and a "strategy of colonization," bell hooks directs her study of shame to the auction block, where the body would be the material location for racial shame.[18] This material location is what would make blackness a fact—something obvious, obviously seen, and routinely exposed to scrutiny. As such, racial shaming is not simply a matter of ideas that remain in abstract formations of race, but they are tied intrinsically to the body—to dark skin, size, and hair texture. Frantz Fanon writes of shame through such visual exposure: "Shame. Shame and self-contempt. Nausea. When people like me, they tell me it is in spite of my color. When they dislike me, they point out that it is not because of my color. Either way, I am locked into the infernal circle."[19] The white gaze marks Fanon's belonging to unbelonging by way of his Blackness and overwhelms him. The weight of that gaze enacts Blackness and ·its shame. Perhaps most poignant in what is known as the "Fanonian moment" is the fact that Fanon is blackened by a white child. The white child, though a child, has already inherited the power of their gaze and exercises it in this scene by exclaiming: "Look a Negro!" For Fanon, the experience of being looked at becomes unbearable. "Where shall I hide?" he asks. Shame is enacted here in its protoform of looking, being identified, and being unable to look back.[20]

Looking down or looking away is the bodily reaction to the experience of disconnection between one individual and another. The shamed individual seeks recognition in the eyes of the other, and when that recognition is denied, shame occurs. Subsequently, the shamed one shrinks away from the object by which it was rejected; this physical response is another form of communication. As such, it shapes the identity of the shamed in that moment, an identity of difference. According to Eve Sedgwick, "Shame floods into being as a moment, a disruptive moment in a circuit of identity-constituting identificatory communication."[21] In a moment one thinks of themselves as connected to another; in the next, they are made aware that they are not so connected. Shame, then, is an affect of being disconnected from another and then re-connected, as a perpetual other. Shame makes and unmakes identity and belonging by its mandate of unbelonging. One is exposed in the moment of being identified as not belonging-while-expecting-to-or-desiring-belonging, and in response to such exposure, might duck for cover or avert the eyes in an effort for their own recognition of unbelonging/desire to go on unseen by others. But they cannot, the shamed is always to be looked at, even from within, by the outside—the realm of belonging.

In the shame/ing scene, the inability to look back is a direct challenge to the privileges of masculinity afforded by white cis-heteropatriarchy. For Fanon's masculinist lens on Blackness itself, the denial of this privilege is the psychic drama of anti-Blackness affected within Black people as Black men. As Amber Musser notes, "Fanon's interest in the visual aspects of domination adheres to his articulation of patriarchy as a mode of objectification. To be rendered an object is to be visible, but it is also to be cut off from agency, communication, and volition."[22] For Fanon, the visual field of Black manhood is characterized by the inability for Black men to look while always being available to be seen. To be objectified, seen and unable to look, is characteristically feminine—the condition of woman under patriarchy. Thus the condition of Black men is inherently feminized, touched, as Spillers would say, "by the mother, handed by her in ways that he cannot escape, and in ways that the white American male is allowed to temporize by a fatherly reprieve."[23] The feminizing touch of the mother that Blackness marks on Black men is felt as emasculation in a psychoanalytic Oedipal schema in which patriarchal power is inheritable through the desire to replace the father. As Musser notes, "Fanon's Negro is a non-Oedipal subject because of the historical forces of colonialism. His impotence, however, mires him in shame."[24] Thus the problem of becoming, emerging from the abjection of Blackness, is a concern with the figuration of the Black mother who (in the logics of misogynoir) fails to retain a proper father and remains central to the vision of a Black family unit. Her overarching and singular reach is thus felt in the determinations of Black people as a whole. What does this formation of Blackness and Black gender actually mean for Black mothers? Or, thinking with C. Riley Snorton who asks, "How might one constitute a self from such abjection? . . . What is the function of the black mother as an embodied category and figuration, to a sociogenic process?"[25] The persistent question Du Bois might have asked, "How does it feel to be a problem?"[26] might also be asked, "How does it *feel* to have a Black mother?" If objectification, described as the inability to look but always being available to be looked at, is a condition inherited by the powerless gaze of the mother, and the inability to act—to look or avert from being seen—is the condition of shame, as Musser observes through Fanon, how does one relate to the image of the Black mother?"[27]

Characterized by the ability to look within through the eyes of white patriarchal power, double consciousness is such a description of the objectified's gaze. The objectified might, at the recognition of being looked at, cover themselves in defense, avert their eyes and thus the recognition of having been looked at, and perhaps, seen. Sarah Ahmed describes shame as being characterized by an impulse to cover oneself, as is the etymological root of the term.[28] The shamed looks away, separating themself from the event or object that has shamed them and inverts toward an "individual" response to that event or object, while simultaneously identifying with that event or object in what Tomkins calls "uncontrollable relationality."[29] Exposure by the gaze activates shame and the physical motion to avert one's own eyes or cover oneself so not be seen. This is a gesture made in vain to cover one's exposed self, after having witnessed something that cannot be unseen and to which one is now undeniably linked. Fanon is undeniably linked to his own accused body shamed by the white male gaze:

> And then the occasion arose when I had to meet the white man's eyes. An unfamiliar weight burdened me. The real world challenged my claims. In the white world the man of color encounters difficulties in the development of his bodily schema. Consciousness of the body is solely a negating activity. It is a third-person consciousness. The body is surrounded by an atmosphere of certain uncertainty.[30]

Fanon's dilemma of the outward gaze turned inward invokes the concept of double consciousness, or "two souls," articulated by Du Bois. This double consciousness is predicated on looking, being aware of being looked at, and navigating the difference there made. In identifying his own early understandings of his difference, his being "a problem," Du Bois answers the above question through the protoform of shame once again: looking, rejection, and looking away. He narrates a childhood moment where he was to give a card to a white girl, and she refused. It was then that he realized he was different from his white classmates. Du Bois describes that moment as feeling "shut out from their world"—different somehow but same in "heart and life and longing."[31] Shaming makes cyclical this longing for belonging.

But what if there is another way to see oneself? Another way to choose to be seen? Double consciousness's fundamental orientation to the gaze is, as Kimberly Nichele Brown observes, "intrinsically bound to a Eurocentric paradigm," and as such, "its canonization in African American studies obscures other traditions that do not hold Eurocentric aesthetic values and, by extension, white audiences in such high esteem."[32] Black women writers of the late twentieth and early twenty-first century, Brown argues, do precisely this work and names this period of Black women's writing the "era of the revolutionary diva."[33] Brown characterizes these texts by their unabashed centering of Black female readership—truly

Black women writers centering themselves in what Kevin Quashie would call "self-centered subjectivity" or "oneness," a notion that is opposed to the concept of twoness set forth by the concept of double-consciousness. A Black feminist lens of the visual field of Black motherhood would be another way of seeing that does not begin with a notion of Black motherhood as shameful. That is it does not begin with a white, patriarchal, colonizing gaze. Such a lens could see otherwise and create visions of Black motherhood to see and feel that begins with Black mothers taking up their own way of seeing themselves.

> *It's good news when you reject things as they are. When you lay down the world as it is. And you take on the responsibility of shaping your own way. That's good news.*
> **—BERNICE JOHNSON REAGON WITH SWEET HONEY IN THE ROCK SINGING "GOOD NEWS"**

For Renee Cox, an image maker, taking up the cross of her own life involves taking control of her own image: "For me it's all about: I own it" she says.[34] Taking control over the image and confronting viewers with her own gaze is how Cox makes Black feminist meaning in her work. As Patricia Hill Collins notes, "The insistence on Black women's self-definitions reframes the entire dialogue from one of protesting the technical accuracy of an image—namely, reframing the Black matriarchy thesis—to one stressing the power dynamics underlying the very process of definition itself."[35] Cox's photographs are shameless, dare I say, prideful. Pride, however, is an emotion that operates on the same plane as shame. The logic is based on a shared understanding of good images and deeds and bad images and deeds. Queer studies has long made the near enemy connection between shame and pride. For example, when scholars and activists investigating queer politics question the politics of pride and shame in activism, they discuss the ways in which gay pride adopted assimilationist practices that actually continued to shame non-assimilationist queers. Gay liberal projects picked up the same politics of respectability that formerly shamed and ostracized queers. As Deborah Gould observes, the articulations of gay pride were ostensibly about gay respectability, and "a politics of respectability is almost always deeply ambivalent; concerned above all with social acceptance."[36] By adopting the practices of the culture that shames, one asks for acceptance on that culture's terms.

Sylvia Wynter's discussion of *désêtre*, Fanon's term for the "unbearable wrongness of blackness," articulates this close relationship between shame and pride in reading images of Black peoples. For Wynter, the politics of representation itself is a problem because Blackness is already imposed by *désêtre*.[37] Efforts to understand Blackness on "good" terms fail to dismantle the Western logic by which Blackness is always already maligned. When applying such dichotomous judgments on images, as is the practice of aesthetics, the fallacies of such critique become clear. If aesthetics is, as Wynter observes, the "imperative enactment of each governing code of subject/abject," then the wielding of Eurocentric aesthetics reproduces such dichotomous codes.[38] Shame might be considered an unpleasant feeling because it promises but fails to resolve the problem of Blackness and that failure is also shameful. Here, I am thinking with Sianne Ngai on the matter, placing shame adjacent to her discussion of ugly feelings which are described as the capacity to produce "ironic distance" to oneself through a secondary feeling.[39] For the shaming of Black motherhood, that secondary feeling could be anxiety or shame itself, thus the emergence of the prideful near enemy. Pride and shame then, act as two sides of one ideological coin. In the context of this discussion of Black motherhood, the coin will always come up Black-mother-deviant.

Shame is an unpleasant feeling because its qualities are shaped by perpetual disempowerment and unbelonging. It is designed to keep in place social order through affective structures by which individuals or groups may be compelled to desire citizenship, rights, or protection under the law. Shame is structured as an internal cauterization of interconnectivity and mutual recognition and therefore functions as a tool by which the shamed, in their longing for belonging, might embrace shame's narrative. That is, assimilate oneself in the world as the abject. This negative assimilation might be the only, if not most immediate, opportunity for belonging. The shamed might seek assimilation into the hegemonic order but can only do so through total subordination and obviation of any feelin that would contradict such order. In the circumstance of Black motherhood this poses a limited set of options—perhaps shamed Black mothering would result in understanding Black motherhood to be intolerable and avoided altogether; perhaps it would result in absorbing the controlling images of Black mothers and owning those tropes. Either of these options fix Black motherhood in displeasured feeling.

Shaming as a form of social control in the image of Black motherhood might have some clear intentions—to place in negative light the propagation of Black people through Black female reproduction. We can observe the means by which controlling Black reproduction has been deeply imbedded in US policy, political discourse, and medical practice, but my interest here is in how that is felt by Black folks who continue to mother. If, as Ahmed states, shame is "an intense and painful sensation that is bound up with how the self feels about itself, a self-feeling that is felt by and on the body," how might that affect Black folks' images of our Black mothers or ourselves as Black mothers?[40] How might it shape our attitudes toward ourselves in our bodies? And, if shame is activated by, as Silvan Tomkins observes, "the incomplete reduction of interest or joy" how does a Black mother experience joy and pleasure and still be a mother?[41] Shame would seem to be an instrument that would control Black women's embodied experiences, including that of sexual pleasure. Dubiously, shame "operates only after interest or enjoyment has been activated, and inhibits one or the other or both," meaning that the social shaming of Black motherhood is intended to perpetually inhibit Black women's full and joyful experiences.[42]

At stake here in the visual field of Black motherhood, where shame adheres to Black flesh, is the possibility for retrieval of a Black maternal body. Shame makes Black female reproduction, kinship, and embodiment not only a trope, but a fleshy and flat joke, a snap—as in "Your mother is so fat, she couldn't get section 8, she got section 800."[43] In the visual field, mama's body may be examined, scrutinized, taken apart to further exorcise and/or internalize her pathology from/ to ourselves, our collective shame: her fat, her mouth, her muscle, her womb (or lack thereof), her always available genitalia. At stake here is the symbolic and otherwise matter of maternal kinship. At stake is mama's body—err—flesh "both mother and mother-dispossessed."[44] To fight for mama's body on these terms tends to produce the same results: irredeemable *or* redeemable mamas, shameful *or* proud examples of Black motherhood, acceptable *or* unacceptable Black female sexuality. To fight for mama's body on these terms is to continue to control her.

In this attempt to describe shame, we've covered shame as a relational process in which shame is enacted as verb (to shame, shaming) and is descriptive of being (ashamed, 'shame). Of course there are other forms of the concept by which acts, persons, and conditions are described through shame (i.e., shameful). Black English provides linguistic forms of describing shame and shaming that might reveal the connections between shame as habit, enactment, accusation, or fleeting experience. For example, the US southern phrase, "Ain't got sense enough to be 'shamed," might be used to describe someone freely engaging in activity deemed irreputable. The use of the word "shamed" here can be read as both a shortened affected form of saying "ashamed" as well as a straight ahead use of the word shame.[45] This common phrase highlights the fact that to be ashamed, one must accept an order—a common "sense" that one's actions or being is shameful. Without such sense, shame doesn't have an object on which to stick. This phrase reveals that shame is not an isolated emotion or state of being. It is experienced in relation, even if—or rather because of (dis)communication from others. As such, shame necessitates a shaming agent, real or imagined, in order to produce the affect of shame. The shaming agent in process from shame, shaming, and finally into the stage of being ashamed: *being ashamed, being 'shame*. To be cloaked in shame or to embody shame. Colloquially the phrases merge into one—I am the embodiment of shame by way of being *a*shamed and/or being shamed. What might the embodiment of shame look like? Feel like? To return to the question posed by Du Bois, repurposed by Snorton, and further adjusted to center Black mothers: "How does it feel to be and/or have a Black mother?" If we wade through Black women's visions of Black motherhood along with Black feminist scholarly interventions on the discourses that surround images of Black mothers, we might have some insight.

SHAME AND PUNISHMENT

At work in the scene of shame in which one is shamed, ashamed, and shame is an order of relation and knowledge that valuates belonging, unbelonging, and the qualities of these conditions on people within a scene. For Black mothers the scene is the nation-state. As Tiffany Lethabo King notes, "Black matriarchy has the potential to undo structures of property that undergird the integrity of the nuclear family and the nation."[46] Here, I would like to stay with the function of shaming as an effort of social control that is felt. Nicole Fleetwood anticipates the performances of disciplining and shame when she describes excess flesh as "an enactment of visibility that seizes upon the scopic desires to discipline the black female body through a normative gaze that anticipates its rehearsed performance of abjection."[47] The state's role in the structure of Black maternal shaming is an important consideration for this reading of shame as a form of social control over the excesses of Black female flesh. The state and the public stage are the scenes in which Black motherhood is paraded out for the controlling gaze (e.g., the campaign against welfare queens) and these valuations are publicly and collectively made. Thinking through shame enacted by scenes and performance with the practice of sado-masochism might be helpful here. An example is the case of the central protagonist's scenes of shame and self-punishment in Sapphire's novel *Push*. I redirect the discussion on the visual field of Black motherhood to fiction for two reasons: one is that Sapphire's *Push* is a text that has already done the theoretical work on shaming and Black maternal imagery and so should be read in light of this book's insistence on treating Black women's creative work as theory in the flesh.[48] The second is that even as a novel, *Push* also provides visual reference to the themes in which shame emerges in relation to maternal imagery as excess flesh: fatness, colorism, sexuality, and urban poverty.

Push is narrated from the perspective of Claireece Precious Jones (who goes by Precious), a Black teen mother who lives in the inner city, suffers abuse by both of her parents, and languishes in the cracks of the public school system. Because it is a novel that is written from the perspective of Precious, it manages to narrate her inner life. Many of her thoughts and feelings are imbued with shame. Embodied both as fat and dark-skinned, she is subject to taunting and social disregard in school and in the urban landscape of New York City. A recurring theme in the novel is the trauma-induced flashbacks in which Precious experiences extreme moments of violence and shaming that inflict deep psychic wounds. In order to gain some relief from this conflict, Precious separates from her body.

In her most traumatic moments Precious describes herself as escaping—leaving her body to go into her inner self. She describes that escape while her father is raping her: "I wait for him to get off me. Lay there stare at wall till wall is a movie, *Wizard of Oz*, I can make that one play anytime. Michael Jackson, scarecrow. Then my body take me over again, like shocks after earthquake, shiver me, I come again. My body not mine, I hate it coming."[49] The abuse Precious endures at the hands of her father reifies her contentious relationship with her body. She is both in a scene of suffering and pleasure. Precious learns to hate her orgasms and the mixture of pleasure and pain she is left to make sense of. If we are to take up Musser's engagement with sadomasochism in which sensation "occupies a sphere of multiplicity without being tethered to identity," Precious's orgasm both signifies on her fleshy embodiment and belies her personhood that has not consented.[50] If we understand masochism to be a "diagnostic tool," as Musser suggests, we would have to hold the seemingly oppositional, but nonetheless present facts that Precious is capable of sexual pleasure even as she is in the moment of sexual abuse.[51] Without agency, however, the usefulness of thinking through Precious's trauma through BDSM starts to fall apart, if not for her recuperative act of self-harm and humiliation.

After her father rapes her, Precious goes to the bathroom and smears her own feces on her face—an act among other acts of self-harm that she claims make her feel good. "Don't know why but it do," she says, "I never tell nobody about that before. But I would do that. If I go to insect [*sic*] support group what will I hear from other girls. I bite my fingernails till they look like disease, pull strips of my skin away. Get Daddy's razor out cabinet. Cut cut cut arm wrist, not trying to die, trying to plug myself back in."[52] These acts of self-harm place Precious's traumatized consciousness back into her body.

Precious's survival technique of fleeing her body as she is experiencing trauma is an echo of the survival techniques of Black women. Darlene Clark Hine describes a kind of "fleeing from the body" as a political and survival strategy used by middle-class women at the turn of the century, known in Black feminist thought as the "culture of dissemblance."[53] In her book on Black women's embodiment in art, Lisa Collins describes a desire to flee her body when it is under the scrutiny of her white classmates.[54] In the context of performance studies, Daphne Brooks articulates the ways in which, as a survival mechanism, Black folks have had to disassociate themselves from their bodies. Describing this disassociation as a performance, Brooks calls these strategies "afro-alienation acts." Such acts,

Brooks explains, characterize those in marginal positions as they "seize" on and "reorder" in their self-making process.[55] In other words, for marginalized peoples, escaping one's body allows for opportunities to enter a more whole body of one's own making. For Precious, reentering this body involves a masochistic practice that is both painful and, through pain, pleasurable. Covering herself in her own excrement to effectively "wipe away" and "punish" herself for every aspect of her being which is abject: her fatness, her skin, her illiteracy, and her second pregnancy as a teenager, Precious takes control of what she sees as inevitable—a relentless cycle of shaming. I read this act of sadomasochistic humiliation as stopgap for the scene of shame that is Precious's life. It is not an act that frees Precious for the reader—in fact, the reader may be fully enveloped in the abjection Precious ingests. The act is for Precious alone, who says that it feels good when she performs this scene. It is at this moment where I might depart slightly from Ngai's description of ugly feelings which offer no "therapeutic or purifying release." Enveloped in the feeling as *being* shame becomes more prominent a feelin. Shame here reflects on itself and folds back as a visceral act.

Precious senses this utter abjection and, in her flashback, cloaks herself in the shame meant especially for her. She embodies this shame through the trope of the Black teen mother and is also shamed for her skin, the shape and weight of her body, her presumed mental capacity and that of her disabled child, her race, and poverty. She is also marked by the abjection of her fat and Black mother, Mary, who abuses her sexually, physically, and emotionally. As such, Precious's mark of the mother is through the wounds of abuse and distorted into a relationship of sexual competition for the attention of Precious's father/rapist and enforced control by the state as the face of child services and welfare. As L. H. Stallings notes, "Sapphire demonstrates that Precious and Mary are caught up in a neo-oppressive model of the state in which female agency is consistently denied."[56] In this generational snapshot Precious is rendered as the fleshy embodiment of Spiller's formation of both "mother and mother dispossessed" a few times over. Dispossessed of her own function of motherhood because both of her children are at constant risk of being taken by the state, and dispossessed of being mothered. Her abjection, heightened by corporeal excess—size, dark skin tone, and pregnant belly—makes her presence looming though she remains invisible. Such is the condition of a stigmatized Black mother—hypervisible and somehow falling through the cracks.

Despite what seems like a cultural campaign to curb Black motherhood, Black nurturance and reproduction persist. I propose that while there is clear cultural shame around Black motherhood inscribed by controlling images (imammy, jezebel/welfare queen, matriarch, etc.), there is also a decision to *feel* motherhood. This happens simultaneously as shame is always already entangled with images of Black women. Shame signifies a disjuncture from identifying and being identified *with* another. It marks, puts on grotesque display, another's difference through power of one gaze and the immediate disempowerment of the one who is the object of that gaze. The empowered gaze accuses difference upon the disempowered, and the disempowered's inability to return that gaze can be called shame. We can see, then, how Black maternity is structurally disempowered and shamed. This does not mean, however, that Black women do not respond to these structures that disempower and shame. On the contrary. Through the work of Black women artists, we can observe what happens after Black motherhood finds itself "locked into the infernal circle" and what visions that start from a Black feminist centered oneness see in order to *feel* motherhood regardless of shame(ing).

Liberating Ya Mammy

Mammy might be one of the most contested images of Black mothering in the visual field of Black motherhood. The prototypical image of the mammy is a dark-skinned, corpulent woman, usually seen with a bandana on her head and an apron around her waist. She is the staple of the antebellum mythology of domestic bliss. Her image, perhaps most famously perpetuated by the Quaker Oats brand Aunt Jemima, is recognizable by mere silhouette. While the matriarch and her late twentieth-century little sister, the welfare queen, are vilified as social problems, the mammy is a beloved caricature of Black womanhood in popular culture. As Kimberly Wallace Sanders notes, "The representation of mammy's body is the site where fiction, history, autobiography, memoir, and popular culture meet in battle over the dominant representation of African American womanhood and African American motherhood more specifically."[57] Mammy's connection to the matriarch and the welfare queen is entangled with her perpetual status as servant and her loyalty to white supremacy.

Michelle Wallace describes attitudes toward the stereotypes of the mammy as particularly hostile.[58] Wallace notes that the attention given to the mammy stereotype may reveal some deeply held beliefs about black motherhood in general. Considering the well-documented history of the mammy and matriarch, it is clear that concern for what makes a good black mother is a consistent theme in conversations about the uplift of the Black community as a whole. Mammy's service to the state is an inherent problem for a visual culture of Black freedom. Mammy, as her infamous avatar Aunt Jemima, has been a visual symbol of contention that many Black artists, including Renee Cox, Betye Saar, and others have attempted to revision and liberate.[59]

Renee Cox's *Yo Mama Goes to the Hamptons* features the artist wearing a printed wrap garment.[60] It partially covers one breast, leaving the other engorged breast bare. It holds her crying lighter-skinned child and covers the rest of her body to her ankles. The print of the fabric appears to be polka-dot in some places, flowered in others. She is in the center of the frame, gazing at us through sun-squinted eyes. Her expression is serious and unsmiling. Her thick dreadlocks frame her face, stopping near her chin. The photo appears to be taken outdoors, and bright light reflects on her right side. The backdrop is foliage: bushes, trees, and branches.

The setting is described as the Hamptons, but we are not faced with images of large mansions or beach homes—symbols of the wealth that the Hamptons, an enclave of wealthy villages and towns in New York, are known for. We do see trees, shrubs, grass and this brown-skinned, bare-breasted woman carrying her child. Cox's body in this context, wrapped in this fashion, seems to reference the idealized Afrocentric contexts she often plays with in her images. Cox tells her story of motherhood in the setting of the Hamptons. Here, a very Black mama schmoozes with the wealthy. The image could be glossed over in the company of other images in the *Yo Mama* series where Cox has allowed her Yo Mama persona to travel. It is important to note that the *Yo Mama* series began as a comment on the difficulties of balancing life as a mother and artist—a problem Cox encountered early in her career when she was in the Whitney Museum's Independent Study Program. There, she was pregnant with her first son and was asked if she would continue to work as an artist because of that pregnancy. Yo Mama appeared in many different contexts

Figure 15. Betye Saar, *Liberation of Aunt Jemima*, 1972. Mixed-media assemblage, 11.75 × 8 × 2.75 inches. Collection of Berkeley Art Museum and Pacific Film Archive, Berkeley, California; purchased with the aid of funds from the National Endowment for the Arts (selected by the Committee for the Acquisition of Afro-American Art). Courtesy of the artist and Roberts Projects, Los Angeles, California. Photograph by Benjamin Blackwell. https://www.robertsprojectsla.com/artists/betye-saar.

in her work. This "Yo Mama" who summers in the Hamptons, however, not only takes up residence in new space but references her own presence across time and addresses the meanings of her Black mother self as mother in an otherwise white, wealthy space. In keeping with the intracommunal conversation among Black women artists on the contested image of Black maternal figures, Cox's piece is a direct reference to Betye Saar's *The Liberation of Aunt Jemima* (figure 15).

The Liberation of Aunt Jemima is a three-dimensional piece; a black-skinned corpulent Aunt Jemima figure stands inside of a red cabinet in front of a repetitious background made up of her trademarked image. This smiling figure wears a flower-patterned dress with a polka-dot handkerchief and checkered scarf around her head. In one hand she holds a broom, in the other a rifle. A relief in her skirt (formally a notepad) reveals an image of another mammy, smiling against the backdrop of trees, bushes, and a picket fence—the ultimate symbol of idealized Old South domesticity. One hand is on her hip while a crying light-skinned child is under her other arm. While some critics have identified the child underneath mammy's arm as white, as was intended in the original postcard, Saar intended for the child to be read as mixed race.[61] She made this decision in order to be a "testimony about how black women were 'sexually abused or misused' in the household."[62] Saar punctuates this found image with a black fist, feminized by red paint on the thumbnail. It covers the linen the original advertisement displayed and appears to serve as mammy's skirt.

The pattern in the fabric of Cox's wrap in *Yo Mama Goes to the Hamptons* echoes the fabric in the gun-toting Aunt Jemima of Betye Saar's 1972 cabinet. Her own mixed-race child's crying disposition echoes the crying mixed-race child in Saar's image. The connecting thread through all of this is a disruption of the landscape predicated on the American dream of comfort, wealth, and domesticity that the Hamptons and picket fences symbolize and mammy's servitude secures. The militant fist in Saar's image is implied in Cox's expression, Afrocentric clothing, and hair. That the crying child is Cox's own adds a distinct layer of self-reflectivity and awareness in *Yo Mama Goes to the Hamptons*. Although the child is hers, she does not appear to immediately tend to it as mothers are expected to do; this ambivalence is reflected in other images in the series. Some may decide that this ambivalence is evidence of poor motherly etiquette, but while Saar's mammy may be ambivalent toward her child based on the sexual abuse she alludes to, Cox's mixed-race children were born by choice.

The power in this image is the same power that many of Cox's images exude. Cox's gaze, her center position in the image, and her choice of props (including her child) have appeared in other photographs, each equally, if not more, arresting. The photo's reference to Saar's earlier *Liberation* highlights a thoughtful response to issues of motherhood, domesticity, and belonging that are invoked in the image of a brown-skinned Cox holding a lighter-skinned child in an affluent, white neighborhood. She does not embrace readings of her body as servant in this context but as mother to her own child living her complex life. This photograph serves as a bookmark for Cox's later exploration of navigating the image of the subservient mammy figure *The Liberation of Lady J and UB*.[63] She fits into the category of neither mammy nor housewife, but exists as a mother of her own imagination. Her bare and swollen left breast and the hint of her right breast simultaneously signify the agency she retains to nurse her own children and to own her sexuality. In this photo, she is both: mother and sexual being, a theme that continues in her work.

In her *Rajé* series, Cox creates a mythical heroine who goes about righting racial wrongs, from picking up taxicabs that zip past Black men in New York City with her bare hands, to liberating black caricatures from food packages. In *The Liberation of Lady J and UB* Rajé pulls Aunt Jemima and Uncle Ben from their boxes. She stands center in her trademark leotard in the colors of the Rastafarian and Black Liberation flags. She wears black thigh-high, spiked leather boots, large geometric earrings, smoky makeup, and is crowned with dreadlocks that gather at the top of her head. Rajé is a sexual symbol, as any comic book–inspired superheroine would be. Liberated Aunt Jemima and Uncle Ben stand on each side of Rajé, all three with arms interlocked. Faded replications of Lady J and UB emanate behind them to indicate movement. They have left the confines of their boxes and have been given superhero names. In transforming Aunt Jemima and Uncle Ben into superheroes—Lady J and UB—the physicality of the caricatures also changes dramatically. The elderly Uncle Ben and fat Aunt Jemima become young models. The muscular and shirtless Rodney Charles is UB and leather bikini–clad supermodel Roshumba is Lady J.

Disgust for mammy and her corpulence run deep in academic descriptions of her. In a reading of mammy in Margaret Mitchell's *Gone with the Wind*, Wallace-Sanders takes particular issue with the exaggeration of her features. She states, "She is not just fat, she is grossly obese."[64] She continues, "Her enormous size, her towering strength and endurance, her nonstop nagging often make her seem more monstrous than compassionate. These extraordinary qualities actually detract from her humanity instead of affirming it."[65] Descriptions like these highlight how it is not only the ideology behind mammy's racial allegiances that is problematic but also her physicality.

While She Is at It
For Dolce and Gabbana

Aunt Jemima is in style.
**—NINA SIMONE AT A LIVE PERFORMANCE
OF THE SONG "FOUR WOMEN"**

. . . and while she is at it
on all fours and cleaning your
kitchen, while she is swaying
large hips and hanging breasts
let her dangle from your ears
drip from your children's mouths

while she is at it
hands tied above her head
screaming your fear,
your rage, take her rag
fashion it just so. wear it to parties,
breakfast at tiffany's

while she is at it
multimillionaring your grandfather
looking out, forever tied to your
cupboard wrap her girth
around every black woman you see
tear off her blouse and
suck

Cox's decision to change Aunt Jemima from a corpulent, elderly mammy to a younger, thin supermodel demonstrates how the liberation of Aunt Jemima is contingent upon the transformation of her abject body. The physical changes that have been enacted on Aunt Jemima to dull the racist overtones of the brand since her first appearance in 1893—for example, trading in her notorious handkerchief for a short, curled hairstyle—is not change enough for Cox.[66] In the corpulent and smiling physicality of Aunt Jemima, the historical roots of stereotypical representation run too deep. That the artist transforms and, as the title states, "liberates" Aunt Jemima from these embodied restraints illustrates how she is engaged in this larger discourse on representation and embodiment. Cox liberates Aunt Jemima from her smile, her old age, and her fatness.

Fatness is a particular form of embodiment in which Black women have been racially shamed and critiqued for the embodiment of fleshy excess. As Andrea Elizabeth Shaw notes in her book, *The Embodiment of Disobedience*, "The West has required the ideological erasure of both blackness and fatness as a means of gaining aesthetic acceptability."[67] Cox makes no efforts to challenge this association of blackness, fatness, and shame; rather, she chooses to liberate Aunt Jemima from fatness and age outright. Recasting her in this way does not liberate Aunt Jemima's body but shifts her into a more acceptable body that can be worn with pride but with the original embodiment still present though cast in shadow. The result is a recapitulation of the logics that negatively affect Black women through racial shaming, functioning as a kind of disciplining and respectability.

Attempts to liberate mammy, to sniff out any of her possible contemporary iterations and recast them, are deeply connected to concerns about the matriarch and welfare queen as symbols of Black motherhood. Michelle Wallace notes, "There is a great deal of self-destructive masochistic hostility for the myth of Mammy in the black community as a stereotype, hostility which quite commonly overflows to embrace most contemporary black women, black mothers, and perhaps teenage mothers in particular."[68] Cox's *Rajé* series, in conversation with the *Yo Mama* series, reveals this hostility toward stereotypical images of the Black mother. It also serves as a bookmark in a consistently shifting perspective on Black motherhood as it is experienced and represented in Cox's art, which features her own body.

Cox does not challenge the West's mandate that fatness must be erased in order to be considered acceptable. Instead, the artist identifies with this mandate in her effort to return sexuality and self-efficacy to mammy—a sexuality that is rendered invisible because of her fatness in post–World War II Western readings of fat bodies.[69] Common renderings of mammy as fat are indicative of Westernized standards of beauty from which Black women have been excluded. Mammy's fatness is without sexuality, as much as white women's purported slenderness indicates their sexual availability. If, as Lorraine O'Grady states, "The female body . . . like a coin, . . . has an obverse and a reverse: on the one side, it is white; on the other, non-white or, prototypically, black," then within

143

the construct of the mammy and her white mistress, mammy is fat and without sexuality while the other is slender and sexual.[70] Sabrina Strings also observes the racialization of fatness in disciplining white female bodies as the thin ideal. She states that, "The image of fat black women as 'savage' and 'barbarous' in art, philosophy, and science, and as 'diseased' in medicine has been used to both denigrate black women *and* discipline white women."[71] Cox's decision to cut mammy down in size and reverse time are the methods by which she attempts to give mammy back her sexual agency within the limited visual discourse of Western art and its aesthetics. Though not embodying Aunt Jemima herself, Cox's alter ego ushers in an Aunt Jemima whose body more closely approximates ideals of thinness and youth. Physically, Lady J is a version of the self-contained Rajé. Her smoky makeup, short natural haircut, thigh-high leather boots, and claw rings are shared with her superheroine sister. However, Lady J dares to show even more skin than Rajé. If Aunt Jemima doesn't own her body, the Black woman artist who renders her and takes the form of the superhero who rescues her remakes it.

Does removing Lady J's fatness liberate her? While Andrea Liss observes that, "Cox's remarkable portraits bring into full evidence the denials of slavery brought to bear on the black female body—denials that disallowed women their legitimate motherhood, rightful property, and self-owned sexuality," what remains is the elderly and fat image of Aunt Jemima perpetually incapable of liberation.[72] In a war of good images and bad images, we are still left with the structure of an aesthetic that was never kind to Black women anyway. As Sylvia Wynter observes, aesthetics and counter aesthetics govern and produce the tastes of the same culture.[73] In other words, pre-established aesthetics and aesthetics that seek to counter pre-established aesthetics produce the same moralisms that find Black maternal imagery to be a problem. The aesthetic of a thin ideal that has functioned to render fat bodies as abject and asexual persists in this paradigm.

Full Bodied Woman
For Us after KoKo Taylor

a Full Bodied Woman is a low growl greeting sun
all cocoa butter and hair kink, the soft part of crackling
She who resounds *Oh yeahhhhh* as in: *It is good*
from this we know man's image is in She who covers
all the ground She walks. Moves a boulder with a smile
sweet as pound cake, heart of watermelon.

a Full Bodied Woman's got matrilineage in her hips
lovers remember mothers and aunties without shame
when She enfolds between heavy breasts
hot with sin and a familiar that assures *everything's
'gone be all right* as in: *we walk by faith, not by sight*
from this we know she can feed multitudes.

a Full Bodied Woman can give life in edible chunks.
those who know partake. those who don't
from this we know She will return
for who could reign over a woman who
sings *I'm a Woman* without apology? *As* in:
I am that I am.

Figure 16. Joyce Scott, *No Mommy, Me*, 1991. Leather and beads, 18 × 7 × 5.5 inches. Courtesy of the artist and Goya Contemporary Gallery, Baltimore.

Mammy's fleshy excess is the symbol of the real or perceived instability of Black families and represents the idea of outright rejection of maternal care by Black mothers in lieu of care for white charges. Bead artist Joyce Scott comments on this in her piece *No Mommy, Me* (figure 16). In the sculpture, the beaded brown figure of the child is rendered nearly one-dimensional and clinging to the skirt of their mother who looks at and holds the pink-beaded white child above her head.

The maternal figure's face and hands are darker beads than the child who clings to her and they blend into the black leather that forms the rest of her body. This figure, who holds a white child as mammy and to whom a Black child clings as mommy, represents the tension that the title invokes. This is not an image of a mammy; this is a mommy who is also focused on the white child of her employer.

Her rendering of this Black maternal figure also highlights such tensions between the imagery of a Black mommy and a mammy: her body, formed by rich Black leather is slimmer than mammy's form yet her mouth is shaped by the bright red color reminiscent of late nineteenth-century minstrel imagery. These visual references are intentionally placed on the sculpture as a mask to represent the monolithic idea of Blackness that the figure wears.[74] To whom this body belongs is invoked as a plea in the title, where "mommy" can be read as a verb and a noun. The child could be asking to be mothered "mommied." Or, if mommy is read as proper noun, the child may be asking that her attention be shifted generally to themself. It is the audience's visual reference and the presence of the white child in which mammy might be thought of or invoked.

Representations of Black motherhood in the form of mammy also reveal a sordid and conflicting continuum of shaming around Black women's sexuality and racial fealty. Mammy is often described as being fat and without her own sexual desire, though we know her to be sexually available to her white masters. She is also more loyal to her white enslavers and charges than to her own children or partner. Her fealty is with white power structures and the system of slavery itself. As Snorton notes, "As a matter of labor, the mammy figured a social relation of production that brought surplus value to white families, private property, and the nation."[75] The national attention to her can be witnessed in the visual field through the quotidian imagery of Black mammies as national signs of comfort such as Aunt Jemima on pancake mix and syrup, or as the embodiment of down-home eating at a roadside restaurant in Natchez, Mississippi (figure 17).

Meanwhile, the sexual excesses of the welfare queen and teen mother are characterized by uncontrolled sexuality and poverty, bound to having many children out of wedlock and ultimately, becoming a burden on the state. Cloaked in excess on each end—excessively sexual and excessively fat (and thus in common logic, without sexual appeal)—Black maternal sexual too-much-ness is a problem and a boon for the state. She is an embodiment of a national problem from the problem of the Negro family, to the obesity epidemic in urban centers, or a useful back on which to depend for the nation's errant direction.

In addition to the view of Black motherhood as perpetually troubled, there is another perspective where Black motherhood is revered. As much as the mammy is maligned and rejected, she is also overwhelmingly embraced by those invested in nostalgia for a romanticized Deep South. More deeply, the longing for the Black mother to return home to her Black children both rallies against this mammy image and pulls on the same strings of the selfless, Strong Black Woman archetype.

Sheri Parks makes connections between the strong Black woman trope and the archetype of the sacred dark feminine. She researches the relentless presence of the Black mother, perverted as mammy in American culture, and finds her roots in the archetype of the sacred dark feminine. enmeshed in stereotype and images in popular culture, "Black women automatically inherit the ancient

Figure 17. Mammy's Cupboard restaurant in Natchez, Mississippi. Photograph by the author, October 21, 2018.

myths of the sacred dark feminine."[76] While that inheritance is marred by the legacy of slavery and racism in the United States, Parks sees the importance for women of color, especially Black women, of owning the power of the sacred dark feminine for themselves, rather than having the perversions of the sacred dark feminine define them: "The mythology permeates the secular culture," she states, "and black women have to wrestle with a mythology that arrived before them and will linger long after."[77] According to Parks, the archetype of the sacred dark feminine is so pervasive that Black women will feel and have felt the effects and expectations of it. We might see an example of this in public discourse in the United States regarding civic participation in the 2016 and 2020 elections, where Black women are lauded for saving the nation from itself by voting for the Democratic Party or running for office on Democrat tickets.[78]

This inheritance has its costs, but, according to Parks, it has its own possibilities. She states, "Fierce energy, deep compassion, and often a connection to a holy spirit is a very powerful combination. Black women need to face the image and decide if and how to make use of it."[79] This fierceness, though lauded, reflects the particular postures that mothering as Black folks requires. Novelist Zadie Smith raises an important question in conversation with the maternal imagery of photographer Deana Lawson. She asks "When we call black women queens or lionesses . . . what are we doing? We come to praise. But, at the same time, don't we bury—and implicitly sanction—the idea that a fierceness . . . is the bare minimum needed to raise a black family?"[80] That is, the great amount of planning, defending, and laboring that Black women are praised for is necessary to get to the bare minimum work of nurturance, caring, and children in a world hostile to Black folks.

The elevation of Black maternal figure risks the injurious pedestal that the Combahee River Collective warns of in "A Black Feminist Statement." As they "reject pedestals" the Collective's formative statement centers their experiences as Black lesbians. They state that "the most profound and potentially the most radical politics come directly out of our own identity."[81] Thinking through Parks's discussion of the dark feminine divine and the mythology that has been projected upon Black women in relation to the Combahee River Collective's identity politics which refuses pedestals altogether, we arrive at a crossroads of complex personhood in which Black women's lived experiences circumscribed and imagined by myth. Black feminist thought insists that Black women can assert personhood by exposing the hypocrisy of those myths.

Shame is precisely the emotion in which mythological hypocrisy abounds in the visual field of Black motherhood. Venerated motherhood, divine motherhood, particularly in the context of a Christian vision, is chaste and virginal. Sexuality and the pleasures of sex acts are somehow figured antithetical to motherhood. All the negative controlling images of Black maternal figures magnify this paradoxical relationship to grotesque proportions, perverted by the legacy of imperialist racism. Mammy negates her own progeny for white charges and eschews sexuality altogether; the matriarch's sexuality might oscillate between the sublimated mammy and the oversexed Jezebel, but her maternal capacities are perverted by a pathology of a-maternal if not outright abusive relationships to her children and the men in her family; and the welfare queen and crack mother exemplify the consequences of hyper(hetero)sexuality as a social burden.

We might, at the root of the imagination of motherhood, find where these perversions are made possible and function to control Black women specifically. Cox's photographs address the image of a sexually empowered motherhood through visual cues that respond to white womanhood in Western art and replace these with a pan-African centered counter image that is, in her words, "in your face."[82] Counter messaging is one way to respond to the image of shame, it also risks, to use Sylvia Wynter's words, mistaking "the map for the territory," and leaves certain Black maternal bodies out for irredeemable figuring. To take more seriously the Black feminist mandate to develop a politic that emerges from experience while also considering the effects of the mythology on Black women's lives, the next few pages read Deana Lawson's photography as an example of Black maternal imagery that refutes shame by centering a Black mother figure in the act of mothering, sexual intimacy, and the ways of being that constitute a complex life.

Baby Sleep Mama Creeps: Being Black Motherhood

This is the setting: a nearly bare domestic space (figure 18). Flanked on each end of the photograph are two long burgundy lace curtains covering long windows, against a light ocher wall. The molding framing the windows is a starker white that matches the floorboards. The floor is wooden parquet and in its high gloss sheen are clear reflections of the white framed windows. Between these two windows is a small cross of San Damiano. Below the window to the right of the image is a silver radiator. The figures animate the space's domestic function. A baby sleeps, head tilted upward and to the right of the frame on yellow blankets in a plastic bassinet in front of the radiator. The plastic bassinet suspends the baby about a foot from the ground. In front of the child is a tray that holds plush toys. One toy is in the baby's limp hand. Around the bassinet are more toys: rattles, foam letters and mats, and a soft book titled *Peek-a-Baby*. Just a few inches to the left of the baby is a couple in sensuous embrace. The man, shirtless with blue jeans, leans back in his wooden folding chair. His arm rests on the back of the chair while his head, also tilted away but to the left, leans in to the neck of the nude woman sitting on his lap. His feet flatly meet the ground. Her body faces him, holds the nape of his neck and ear elongating her neck. Her head is tilted upward as she faces the camera.

Her eyes are heavy and her mouth is slightly open, revealing white teeth. Her gaze, the only gaze which extends beyond the internal scene, might be more knowing than inviting. Maybe it is her relaxed and unsmiling mouth, maybe it is the heavy line beneath her eyes—she's exhausted and yet in her erotic power. Her long thick and yaki textured hair falls down her back from a brown-and-gray printed scarf wrapped around her head. The scarf is styled between form and function—it is perfectly placed for laying her edges, but does nothing to protect the longer length of hair that flows down her back.[83] She is between her own sexuality's form and the functions of her life as mother, erotic subject, and partner. Her back is arched, accentuating her round buttocks. Her skin, a few shades darker than her lover's, has a brighter sheen; her feet point downward, and a neatly painted white toenail touches the ground.

A different iteration of photograph in the same setting: The woman on the man's lap wraps her arms around his neck and shoulders so that his face is deep into her chest. They are in front of the radiator. Though her head is slightly bowed, she gazes inward and upward, the whites of her eyes shaped into a crescent. Her hair and headwrap, the same form and function of the above photo. The roundness of her behind accentuated by a deeper arch in her back as her man rests his hands on each cheek. Her feet are lifted from the ground and he is flat footed. The baby in the bassinet is asleep and facing slightly to the middle right of the frame. Toys are strewn about the floor. A red rattle with the face of a man, foam shaped in the numbers eight, three, and the letter Z, or perhaps an N and a clear toy ball.

Figure 18. Deana Lawson, *Baby Sleep*, 2009. Inkjet print photograph, 20 × 25 inches. Artwork copyright © Deana Lawson, courtesy of Sikkema Jenkins & Co., New York; David Kordansky Gallery, Los Angeles.

These two images titled *Baby Sleep* by Deana Lawson are both documentary and symbolic.[84] The flash that nearly obscures the cross of San Damiano puts one in the mind of family flash photography—exposing and high contrast. The cross's small but prominent space in the frame of the picture also integrates the complexity of domestic existence that enforces considerations of sexuality, parental duty, and religion within the context of Black working-class life. The couple steals time to be intimate while the baby sleeps and is in close proximity. The sacrilege of engaging in sexual acts with an infant nearby is further highlighted by the presence of the cross which depicts the birth, life, crucifixion, and resurrection of Christ. Mirroring the multiplicity of the telling of the story of Christ, Lawson's

Baby Sleep tells a multilayered story of domestic Black working class life. In particular, the mother figure takes prominence in the frame as the only nude in the image. In addition, her position is the most dynamic in both photographs. Her position signifies feminine sexuality and control in the erotic life of the domestic space. Her eyes are raised in ecstasy, perhaps giving visual reference to the figure of Christ in this depiction of the cross as his eyes are lifted to the heavens in ecstatic transfiguration. The body of the Black mother here is dynamically posed as the space in between erotic desire and parental duty. She is both.

As for the symbology, the San Damiano cross has significant meaning in the Franciscan order of the Roman Catholic religion. According to legend, Saint Francis is instructed to rebuild Christ's church during "a time of contemplation and ecstasy."[85] In his ecstatic state, Jesus inhabits the cross of San Damiano and Saint Francis receives this message from the mouth of the crucified Jesus on the painted cross.[86] In representational community with Saint Francis, this mother's ecstatic work builds her domestic space—sexual and sacred nurturance. We can see her cradling her man while mounting him an act of erotic preform to sex and nurturing embrace. She is figured as natural and divine—her functional head wrap a halo; her upward and outward gaze are gazes of ecstatic experience like the upward gaze of the crucified Jesus, divine preoccupation and direct viewer confrontation. She is in her sacred-sexual-maternal element and in control of that element.

Baby Sleep depicts a complex experience of Black motherhood: Black motherhood as a historically and socially contested position in the social imagination and Black motherhood in the act and being as contested in everyday life. In her dissertation on the poetics of bafflement, Sarah Stefana Smith advises readers of this image that to decipher *Baby Sleep* requires "multiple encounters with spectatorship, which function simultaneously as a wound to the black body and as recovery of the black body from an infliction."[87] In this reading of the image, we encounter Black motherhood and its historical injuries meeting Black motherhood's daily lived realities—or *being* despite and perhaps in light of these historical injuries.

Lawson describes *Baby Sleep* as a depiction of simply *being* a working mother. As she states of her own experience in an interview in 2011:

> Artists can get caught up in life, whether it be work or anything that takes them away from making their own art. I really need sustained time. I do a lot of things, you know. I'm a mother. I have to get my son ready for school in the morning. I gotta cook. I do need that time to just dedicate to my work and that's important. I also think—you know you were asking before about if I felt the presence of my female-ness in my work and so forth—I never really had the luxury of being in a studio environment and when I think of traditional philosophers, you know, sitting with a pipe thinking for a long time about these theories and sh*t . . . I mean, girl, I don't have that kind of quietude! I don't think a lot of women do. Even that mess though can be used for material for your work. Which is what I do. For example the image *Baby Sleep*—that is directly drawn from real sh*t![88]

Lawson wrestles with the work of motherhood and the work of an artist, and engages these issues through her creative practice. In doing so, she confronts much more than motherhood itself but the injuries against Black motherhood and maternal work. Like Cox's reference to the particular conditions of Black motherhood through her Yo Mama persona, Lawson's title *Baby Sleep* gives a nod to Black English's multilayered meanings. *Baby Sleep* is titled without indefinite articles, and the lack of a comma between "baby" and "sleep" allows for grammatical slippage between noun and verb. Upon first reading the title of the work, a Black English reading of the title can also be a declarative statement as in, "The baby *is* asleep," as in "The baby is asleep, let's get it on." Another reading of the title could be that the title describes the image as circumstances in which the baby is center, regardless of the viewer's electric gaze at the nude woman in the image. This whole scene is the encounter of what might be called "baby sleep."

As we view this mother in the act of sensuous embrace just inches from her sleeping child, the viewer might be confronted with a sense of sacrilegious boundary crossing. The baby is asleep, but what if they wake up and get a peek (as the children's book *Peek-a-Baby* playfully suggests) at the act in which these adults are engaged? The viewer might be confronted with their own misogyny as it is the woman here who dominates the man sexually—acting on her desire so close to the infant. *How could she? She is a mother!* And then we might think of what the cross signifies in our discomfort: the worship of a figure who is known for being born of a virgin. The woman in the figure is no virgin maiden, this child is no Christ, and this man is not Joseph if he is thought of at all. How do we come to understand domestic life through the idea of an impossible Christo-centric domestic circumstance?

The image is documentary in that it depicts a reality that working parents might well know: parents of young children have sex on borrowed time—when the baby sleeps might be that chance. In depicting such a matter-of-fact experience, Lawson challenges viewers to consider the value in which we hold sex acts—the extent to which shaming structures the values by which mothers might live the reality of their lives. The consequence of sacrilege is shame and shaming—and yet this mother is simply doing the work of living a complex life.

Lawson's attention to the erotic as a mother and as an artist who often depicts the domestic setting in her work stems from her own interest in engaging the erotic as the essential material of the bodies she photographs; in that same interview previously cited she states, "What I imagine to be eternally erotic involves a spiritual aura that resides in the physical body, and informs how one moves, thinks, and loves in the world. I use this idea as psychic material when thinking about photographs, and working with subjects."[89] Lawson attends to the sexual and the sacred in her work regularly, an issue she admits may have something to do with her relationship to her own conservative mother.[90] Her creative practice not only gives opportunity to feel an otherwise possibility for Black maternal imagery but is also described her as her own work toward self-mothering.

Her intention to push boundaries by focusing on the domestic setting is certainly felt. As one critic noted of the show in which the original *Baby Sleep* was shown, "Lawson's photographs play on our moral nodes beyond gender and the body . . ." and finally concludes, "It seems that something is not right in the work of Deana Lawson. Not, 'not right,' as in the obviously wrong. But, it just ain't right, and that is what makes it so compelling."[91] I would argue that it is that play with moral nodes by virtue of centering a nude Black woman that feels not quite right—it is the viewer's confrontation with competing and conflicting ideas about Black motherhood and at a larger extension, the Black family, which sets us in dis-ease.

Smith aptly interrogates what dis-ease *Baby Sleep* signals through a reading of Black studies, queer-of-color critique and Black feminist thought's critique of psychoanalysis. Through what she calls a poetics of bafflement, Smith deciphers the image through a "visual deciphering practice located within interdisciplinary archives [which] moves beyond the formalistic qualities of a visual text [and] mobilizes resources and references to express a more dynamic set of interpretations of meaning."[92] Such a reading directs us to the functions of race and its (un) gendering that have shaped Black family life and mandated Black gender and family as functionally and already queer.[93] Guided by the work of Roderick Ferguson and Cathy Cohen, Smith observes the function of excess flesh in the visual framing of Black life that may have heteronormativity as a referent, if not a goal, but will always be outside of such a normative frame, as is the condition of the afterlife of slavery. The Black mother's fleshy excess in *Baby Sleep* existed before her nudity or this picture was taken. If we aren't careful, we might not see her in this image at all—missing the opportunity to hold Black maternal complexity in reverent regard. To acknowledge the capacity for Black mothers to be sacred and sexual, nurturing and strong, vulnerable and confrontational. What is "not quite right" is our encounter with our own vision that has perverted this scene. We ought to be 'shamed.

AIN'T NO SHAME IN MY GAME: FORMING AN INSURGENT MATERNAL SUBJECT

I began this chapter with a Black mother artist who attempted to piece back together the body of another Black mother. Meta Fuller envisioned a Mary Turner who was not harmed, could not be harmed, whose motherhood ascended into the divine. This was an act of personal recovery, focused on the process and possibility of honoring Turner. Renee Cox, inspired by events in her own life that revealed to her that her motherhood was a liability, refashioned a vision of her own bombastic motherhood and engaged troubling discourse around the Black maternal body in her work. Deana Lawson engages issues of the troubled discourse around Black motherhood and situates her photographs in forms that challenge the viewer. In their engagements with discourse on the visual field of Black motherhood, these artists traverse problems related to class, respectability, sexuality, violence, and moral codes which shape the troubled visual field of Black motherhood that has worked to shame Black women's reproductive and maternal capacities. Their visions reveal that there is always and already a paradoxical problem in representing Black mothers because of the anti-Black and sexist visions of the viewers and even themselves as artists.

The discourse in which these artists engage reveal the trouble of attempting to retrieve the Black maternal body, to save mama from the grammars that "will most certainly *kill* us."[94] What I hope has been demonstrated here is that these artists' engagement with the visual field of Black motherhood addresses how shame and shaming function as an overarching affective structure for representations of Black motherhood and presses toward an otherwise mode of visually seeing and affectively knowing, feelin, Black motherhood. Divinity, pride, recovery, and the erotic make way for another kind of visual rendering of the Black maternal. In their discourse that intervenes in the visual field, these artists may not have definitive answers, but they might image(ine) for us a Black maternal figure that does, and perhaps, *must* function without hegemonic notions of family. Or as Tiffany King notes, "There are other ways to name each other as our relations."[95] These artists and Black feminist scholars have certainly told us as much—that cisheteropatriarchal notions of family have not worked for Black folks in the New World, and warring over how closely we can adhere to those ideals does not make for us a more stable future but it just might break momma's back.

CHAPTER 5

Toward a Methodology of Anger

Ritual of Anger: In Special Collections Reading *The Negro a Beast*
October 28, 2008

The Negro is a beast but created with
articulate speech, and hands, that he may be
of service to his master—the White man.
—Title page of *The Negro a Beast, or In the Image of*
God by Charles Carroll, "Revelator of the Century"

What I am uncovering is the scalpel deep in flesh. Another
finding becomes a feeling: a medium between the "Revelator
of the Century" and my mother's anger. To see the present
absences is an unfortunate gift. It is understanding science
and the ghost's exhale. Another finding becomes a feeling:
God and the idea of God's Absence. There is a spiral here, a sadness. Who would lay hands? Why would they if God is dead?
Whom would they be in service to? Another finding becomes a
feeling: Perhaps, there is no Negro. No White man. Then what
would hold us here—returning to checkout? To know if our
skin is still ablaze? Another finding becomes feeling: She is in
the page. I am turning myself.

—BETTINA JUDD, FROM *PATIENT.*

I begin with my mother and her ritual of anger because our intimacy
refuses the overwhelming and ready-made myth. Otherwise, the angry
Black woman meets me before I have a chance to get properly riled up.
Sapphire, the angry Black woman, explains me to myself through television,
everyday interactions, and my adult inner life as a caricature animated by white
supremacist fears and patriarchal mores. The mental image of her: hands on
hips, rolling eyes, wagging finger, stops me from being heard for she has already
spoken as white noise. She is my shame before I am allowed anger or any feeling

adjacent. My shame is also shameful as my feminist politics knows and loves her for her power. She is, for many Black women, "our heroine,"[1] and yet her antics make her our adversary. With this figure and her baggage ahead of and within me, can I *be* angry? What do I have to do with that feeling, with her, my unwanted avatar speaking over and within me, questioning whether I, truly, am feeling at all? Could I—should I repress feeling in an effort to escape her projection? Eat anger's bile two times over to escape my shame? All options seem to be in favor of my obliteration, so I return to her.

I wrote the poem that leads this chapter while reflecting on a visit I took to the University of Maryland's special collections. I was looking for *The Negro a Beast*, a book my mother repeatedly checked out when she attended the University of Maryland, Baltimore County, in the early 1970s. Throughout my childhood, she recounted to me her practice of going to the library, borrowing this book, and fueling her own anger at the convergence of religion and science to support anti-Black racism. My visit to special collections in 2008 was to research my mother's anger. To feel what she felt, to experience what she repeatedly visited and actively researched. I went to special collections to understand the legacy. Why so many years later, she would recount this ritual of anger to me, her daughter who would eventually attend the University of Maryland as a graduate student. Our interests have some parallels: My mother would get her degree in psychology and African American studies. I would study women and gender, focusing my research in emotion as knowledge, Black feminism, and Black women's art. These interests were impacted by our experiences with racism and sexism—including our angry responses to them. Creating a ritual of anger seems to be apropos of understanding anger to be informative, to be fuel, but ritualizing it also means that anger was not a thing that would consume us without our consent.

Reflecting on my mother's anger, I can acknowledge the ways that she has put it to practical use. I can identify the hatred that ignites her anger and a whole other world of knowing: my mother's youthful and developing racial consciousness, her activist spirit, not to mention the long-lasting effects of the history of science and religion in the devaluation of Black folks. My recording it in this poem is a step in tracing anger, finding anger to be, to use Lorde's words, "loaded with information and energy."[2] It was anger that put me in the place of inquiry, anger that tied me to the academic endeavor.

This chapter is about angry Black women and Black women's anger. It demonstrates how the angry Black woman trope is a distortion of Black women's knowledge. This distortion makes apparent the immediate threat that Black women experience by speaking and being. I argue that tracing anger in Black women's creative work and speech is a way of reading Black feminist thought otherwise disregarded and I propose that creative production makes legible Black women's articulations of anger. By asking you to consider Black women's anger, I have invited you into recognition of how Black women *be* through emotional labors enacted for our own survival. A seemingly simple step—to acknowledge that Black women have rich inner lives, that we work for them, that they are ours. But when we come to the subject of anger and Black women, the stereotype of Sapphire signals that there must be something about our inner lives that is dangerous. Why else has such an emotion been so surveilled? Our utterances cut short at the root of experiencing this particular feeling. By thinking seriously about Black women's inner lives, we can shift the focus from the modes of knowledge by which the angry Black woman trope is meaningful to engage with Black women's selfhood and contribution to knowledge. We start with Sapphire in order to reveal what is beneath her mask—and to differentiate Black women's speech from her distortions.

To be clear, I am not interested in negotiating whether or not Black women are human and how we can prove it to be so. I am interested in how Black women's peculiar anger demonstrates that the idea of the human is troubled by Black women's knowledge. I am interested in Black women's anger in order to sharpen a lens on the experience of racism, sexism, and misogynoir and examine how knowledge is produced through these experiences.[3] I am interested in the constellation of these matters because it seems as though the very idea of angry Black women as a type of any kind suggests that: Black women are inherently angrier than other group, therefore less capable of reason as anger is understood to be an irrational emotion, and consequently Black women are regarded as being further from human. In addition, I am dubious of any claim that Black women's anger is a *particular* enhancement of our abilities to know. The prefixes of the human, whether super- or sub-, do us no service here. If we are gifted with a special power that is anger, it is only because misogynoir demands we have no power at all. To continue, I have to make this point perfectly clear: Black women are no angrier than any other group of people.[4] I'm pissed that I even have to tell you this.

By initiating with Sapphire, I choose feeling anyway. She is the backlit image and sound of the angry Black woman stereotype. A fictional character from the radio and television show *Amos 'n' Andy*, Sapphire was the comic foil to her husband, Kingfish.[5] Her quick tongue and mean disposition allowed audiences to feel loving sympathy for her bumbling buffoon of a husband, while painting her as emasculating. The name for her over time and circumstance has shifted. In service to others she is a strong Black woman, in service to herself and no one else, she is a Black bitch.[6] Her media image continues to titillate and delight in the form of reality TV show characters such as Omarosa and her attributes of no-nonsense, telling truth to power, attributed to public figures such as Michelle Obama and Maxine Waters. This type is but one of those controlling images of Black women that are used "to justify oppression"[7] and suppress Black feminist thought.

Constructed through the system of knowledge that is dependent on the idea of the human through difference/sameness, Sapphire produces a paradox by which Black women's knowledge and feeling is sequestered into chaotic impulse rather than controlled reason. To become angry is to become Sapphire, to become Sapphire is to confirm the negative relationship to humanity for which Sapphire is constructed. Yet, to resist feeling anger is self-destructive and also does nothing to disrupt the system of knowledge that produces Sapphire. To express anger places everyday Black women in danger by the apparatus readied for law and order. By consequence, the order prevails—a Black woman silences herself, is silenced. Tracing Black women's anger troubles this and invokes rites that Black women engage by *being* anyhow. It is a means of scoping the fractal image from the chaos Western thought projects on Black women's anger. These rites constitute the rituals of anger that manifest in what I call texts of rage—texts made to obliterate knowledge as we know it. A methodology equipped to analyze these texts would recover that knowledge suppressed by (the creators of) Sapphire's shadow. To trace Black women's anger is to take seriously the paradox that Sapphire and Black women's real and experienced anger entwines:

Sapphire Paradox

After Tyehimba Jess

When I said that I was angry, I meant I am angry
called that, called outside of myself daily
Sapphire, a provocation to witness anger
gleefully wrest the possibility that I be
who I be: Swift tongued and imaginary, angry
but only enough to set into place theythoughts
in stone. Cured in hate, theyask *why you so angry?*
when I am divinely mad. My splintered speech
shake beehives from trees. Yes, I am Angry
a Black Woman who obliterates at a whim

No longer asking to be seen, but every day, being
I name the peace in my heart *girl*, she that is lost
dissolved into matter, not on the verge but *being*
today, like I would any day. There is no verb for
what I am other than *is*. Imagine me being
sweet for once, nurtured, feeling through hunger
and laugh at the absurdity of questioning my being.
kiss me, speak with me, feed me, tuck me into bed
love me anyway. Dear soul I am levelly being
human, as any other Black woman[8]

The central features of a methodology of anger involve acute recognition of the invocation of Sapphire in describing a Black woman as a harbinger of critique. In addition, close attention to the tone and style of Black women's speech would enable many methods of reading such a text. A methodology of anger would ask: What is at stake? Why wouldn't this Black woman be silent, knowing the risks of displaying anger? Such a methodology would have in its arsenal a literacy for the craft of communication that texts of rage deploy: that "simultaneity of discourse" that has the capacity to convey clearly, and obscure, adroitly.[9] As Wynter notes, it is the gravity of language in poetry, the expansive and emotive possibilities of art that bridge the gap between the natural and philosophical human.[10] Poetry—for its weighted language dependent on rhythm, cadence, and tone that has the capacity to signify multiple meanings at once—conveyed appropriately, has the capacity to reveal the complexities of the *context* of its utterance. Tone can communicate that which accompanies anger: fear of death, haughtiness at the absurdity of racism, the pleasure of emotive release. Just as Stallings argues for awareness and decipherability of "pitch, tone and mood" for discussions about rights, sexuality, and the legibility of Black female pleasure, attention to tonal semantics makes legible what Geneva Smitherman calls "the 'deep structure' of life, that common level of shared human experience that words alone cannot convey."[11] The deep structures of life that are misread in regards to Black women.

Anger as ritual and practice signifies, too, the fact of anger as a choice as well as a birthright. Julia Jordan-Zachary invokes Black feminist hauntology as a framework for understanding her own anger and the Black feminist uses of anger she wields in the wake of police murders of Black folks. By using this framework, she signifies on Sheri Parks's figure of the dark feminine divine and makes the angry Black woman an ever-present ghost that fuels her desire to turn anger into action. Anger here is a way to connect the living and non-living in a mutual desire for social justice. She states that "Anger as an emotion is 'in-between' in the sense that its ontology is neither present nor fixed. Anger can exist between worlds and can give voice to the dead; thereby fostering a relationship with those existing in the now."[12] The transmission of anger across living and non-living beings makes way for understanding anger as a form of knowledge, being, and doing that challenges notions of self-contained humans. I would argue that the transmission of anger as knowledge by Black women who are structurally vulnerable to anger's effects defies any such constructs of the human and highlights Black women's practice of *being*. Anger moves through this paradox of being—shapeshifts as chaotic feeling through the absurd conditions of racism, capitalism, imperialism, and colonialism. For Black women, anger must be so flexible if it is, if we are, to exist at all. A ritual—a practice of anger invokes *that what must be felt* in order to survive. My mother's very real and living presence ushered me into a ritual of anger: it is something worth conjuring so as not to forget my odds.

Art makes it possible to trace the contours of anger, to unveil the thing that fuels it—and thus land on steadier ground. Ritual situates the rites within ceremony into meaningful place—the methodology to a method. A ritual of anger convenes physiological response with the object of rage. The hybridity of the two comes into formation and is practiced as knowledge. A methodology of anger demonstrates how Black women's affective labor is productive work toward *being*. That Black women are no different from others who *be angry* for anger's sake, and that the practice of anger is a practice of being that operates outside of the logics of the current order.[13] To demonstrate this methodology behind many methods, I produce and analyze texts of rage and offer creativity as a ritual by which anger is practiced under duress and misnaming.

First, I analyze a text of rage, Nina Simone's "Mississippi Goddam," with close attention to the song's context, content, tone, and style.[14] "Mississippi Goddam" is a text of rage that points to the injustices Simone faced as an artist in the music industry as much as it protests the apartheid US South. It addresses the very raced and gendered struggle of owning anger as a Black woman and foreshadows Simone's decision to defect from the United States. Next, I discuss the process of the creation of my book *patient.* as a text of rage. The autobiographic thread of the book traces anger and results in a recount of the legacy of medical experimentation on Black women. Through poetry, anger unveils the connections between the histories of medical abuse in the past to those of the present.

The final text of rage engages the methodology as a creative tool for analyzing Black women's speech. In this instance, Sandra Bland's violent encounter with the Texas state trooper Brian Encinia. This section applies a methodology of anger to Bland's speech, deploying the methods of close reading for tone and content, and through creative process, revealing the antagonism and hatred harbored by Encinia. In addition, creative methods of retraction, annotation, song, and repetition produce a text of rage that highlights the hatred to which Bland was responding.

These three applications of a methodology of anger demonstrate how tracing anger within our approaches to Black women's expression directs us to more information about Black women's experiences. It centers Black women's knowledge production as interrogative of what it means to be human and challenges the silencing effects of Sapphire. Anger tells us that there is more to know and is able to do so because it is an aspect of human experience for which Black women are uniquely silenced. Only by reinforcing the idea that Black women must prove their humanity in order to *be human* does the myth of Sapphire work. Taking up Sapphire as a stance by which Black women are able to express critique resituates the discourse around Black women's humanity to center Black women, ourselves.

Black Women's Inner Lives and the Luxury of Anger

I know that I tread on some seriously dangerous ground by talking about angry Black women. To talk about Sapphire is to take seriously those damaging stereotypes and cement them into demonstrable reality. If I am treading on dangerous ground it is only because I was already in danger, already the trope itself. Sapphire is so totalizing that it does not take any real anger on the part of a Black woman to be accused of being angry. Anger can merely be a descriptor of Black women's speech and creative work. For example, when Robert Staples wanted to delegitimize the creative works of Michelle Wallace and Ntozake Shange, he did so by naming them "Angry Black Feminists."[15] In a response to his essay, Audre Lorde noted that the descriptor of the "Angry Black Woman" is a silencing tool, made to center Black men's rage over the feelings of Black women.[16]

Anger must have stayed on Lorde's mind because she continued her thoughts on anger as a response to racism in her keynote address for the National Women's Studies Association in 1981.[17] She argued that anger is an informative response to racism, and to respond to anger as the problem and not racism itself, is to collude with forces that would have a vested interest in silencing critiques of racism.[18] She addresses anger and racism again in 1983, imploring Black women to self-reflect on our anger in order to discern and expel from our inner lives the hatred to which anger is a response. In order to do so, Black women would have to luxuriate in self-reflection—for the sake of ourselves and each other.[19] Many of us since and before have done so under the threat of being associated with Sapphire's destructive behavior.

As a stereotype, the angry Black woman delegitimizes Black women's speech. To characterize Black women as having a natural disposition to anger invokes the binary of logic/chaos and places us on the side of chaotic irrational feeling, which justifies oppression according to a "common sense" understanding of Black women as hostile and therefore pathologically unreliable. Without the banner of white womanhood that would render us proper victims, Black women have had to become tactical in order to "gain a rhetorical foothold" for what Rebecca Wanzo calls "mobilizing affect."[20] In their article on Black women's speech in legal testimony, Marilyn Yarborough and Christina Bennett recount a litany of popular examples of incredulous reactions to Black women's testimony, including the testimony of Anita Hill and the rape accusations of Tawana Brawley and Desiree Washington.[21] All of these cases compound lack of trustworthiness with other well-known stereotypes of Black women in order to produce uniquely situated sites of vulnerability. For example, because Black women are perceived as sexually promiscuous (e.g., the jezebel stereotype) our accusations of sexual harassment are often deemed unreliable even when others corroborate our stories.[22]

Distorting Black women's anger through stereotype flattens the truly complex emotional experiences of Black women. It is a tactic to diffuse what would otherwise be an incredibly powerful force. In her recasting of the strong Black woman stereotype into the archetype of the Great Mother/Dark Feminine Divine, Sheri Parks recounts the conservative media campaign against Michelle Obama, which cast her as an unpatriotic angry Black woman unfit for the role of first lady after she stated that for the first time in her life she was "proud of her country."[23] While the Obama administration's objective and outcome was far from what many of us would consider radical change, the possibility for the incoming White House to engage in anything other than US exceptionalism seemed at the time, quite exceptional. The angry Black woman trope was deftly used to silence any critique from the woman who would be the first African American First Lady. No doubt, the angry Black woman trope continued to be used as Michelle Obama's punishment and fee for her entry into the apex of national cisheteronormative positions.

To consistently cast Black women as angry is invariably a practice of disregard and an allegiance to willful ignorance. When it comes to Black women, we are more compelled to ignore than struggle through particular forms of knowledge *because* they are complex, loaded, difficult and often hard to hear. Anger is a circular energetic force, an appropriate response to injustice fueled by repetitive forces of injustice. It is also reenergized by the willful disregard and distortion of a legitimate response to injustice, anger itself. Anger's energetic force is a demand to shift these affective paradigms or, as Lorde described, "Anger is the grief of distortions between peers and its object is change."[24] Anger is anger's response to its own abjection. To disregard, distort, and further pathologize Black women's anger does not render it silent.

So, let us luxuriate in the richness of Black women's emotional lives. I mean this in the most home way of saying it: luxuriate, as in, to rest without resisting what is, to reflect on the work and windows Black women have given into our inner worlds without the intent to destroy or dispute. The experience may be vexed, uncomfortable, the politics might not be right, fair, or well thought out. In luxuriating, we can address those things, we must address all of it without denying every ugly, vexed, or pleasureable feeling. Let us listen for the valuable information held there amid Sapphire's din as her presence, like any presence codified by misogynoir, flags the possibilities to know more.

Darlene Clark Hine's intervention on historical narratives of migration showed us how Black women's uniquely situated and often secret knowledge reveals more complex dimensions of class, sexuality, and the inward experiences of racism and sexism. This secret knowledge, particularly the culture of dissemblance, has raised questions among Black feminist thinkers about Black women's self-silencing, class-based respectability politics, Black women's pleasure politics, and the like. However, an important point of Black women negotiating our own silences must not be overlooked: if luxuriating in the richness and complexity of Black women's inner lives allows us to understand migration patterns, the history of sexual violence and labor practices in the United States, and the class-based complexities of Black women's sexuality what else could it tell us?[25] What does it mean to find use in Black women's emotional labor useful, and for the benefit of whom?

The trope of Sapphire and how she proves herself to be real when Black women do get angry only operates within a set of logics that already count us out. Sapphire belongs to that "nigger chaos" that predetermines Black existence as devalued.[26] "The nicknames by which African-American women have been called, or regarded," as Hortense Spillers notes, "demonstrate the powers of distortion that the dominant community seizes as its unlawful prerogative."[27] Sapphire, matriarch, black bitch, are ideas of Black womanhood that become more pervasive for those who are Black and female than for womanhood generally. The ability to be named rather than self-name is the condition of the human's lesser cousin.

Because of the pervasiveness of this logic, it is not enough to attempt to "reclaim" Black women's humanity through already faulty logics around emotion and knowledge that deliberately reject us. I propose we interrogate why and

161

when there is a doubling-down of the presumption of Black women as less than human through a feeling such as anger. Sapphire pops up when Black women speak, are expected to speak, emote, are expected to emote and de-legitimizes Black women's speech and emotions whether we are angry or not. It marks anger as a symptom of our pathology, our natural state of being, and not a feature of human experience shared by many. Black women's anger is surveilled to this extent while conversely the anger of others goes on unchecked.[28] In a flash, these logics do this co-constitutive work: define humanity as the ability to experience rational cognition, mark anger as an emotional response that hampers rational cognition, and characterize Black women as predisposed to habitual anger. A methodology of anger challenges these logics by looking at how Black women *be angry* even as these ideas about anger persist. Why, under constant surveillance by the stereotype, Black women go ahead and *be angry* anyway and do so in practice of deliberate selfhood.

When I say that Black women *be angry* I invoke the polyglossal modes of Black women's speech and literacies through the use of "standard" English and Black American Language (BAL) or African American Vernacular English (AAVE). The standard English use of the verb *be* means, "to exist in the world," and the BAL use of the verb *be* means to exist constantly, habitually, in the past, and into the future.[29] Therefore, to *be angry*, to lean into our anger in art, texts, or everyday speech is a practice of being that challenges clock time. Here, I take up Black women's anger as readable text—texts of rage—to understand how Black women *be*, anyway.

Black women's expressions of anger, whether through quietude, yelling, what some may call sass, the production of music, writing, speech, or other art forms is best understood by those who engage with the particular sets of literacies involved in their production. Here, I follow Elaine Richardson's description of Black women's literacies, which include "storytelling, conscious manipulation of silence and speech, code/styleshifting, and signifying, among other verbal and non-verbal practices."[30] To read Black women's texts of rage requires an effort in such forms of literacy that understand these manipulations of silence and speech, the uses of tone, and misdirection which may otherwise be misread.

A methodology of anger would require us to make the less effable but felt experiences of hatred (racism, sexism, homophobia, transphobia, and so on) more legible. There are three different but deeply connected ways of using Black women's anger as methodology, and all of them require flagging and tracing. The first is naming anger as it used as a weapon against Black women. That is, to acknowledge when, where, and how the trope of Sapphire is deployed. The second requires luxuriating in the examination of Black women's inner life experiences, our emotional lives. Such reflection has two productive sub-elements: a) it provides the opportunity for us to learn more about Black women's selfhood outside the expectation of ducking hatred and silencing; b) it allows for an acknowledgment of the particulars of selfhood that are entangled with hatred. It could, perhaps, bring one's self into sharper view. Third, a methodology of anger requires new approaches to producing knowledge: new art, new texts, new ways of knowing what it means to *be*.

There are levels to this: I am talking about Black women's engagements with the world that may spark anger in us as moments in which texts of rage are produced, I am also asking that we take the time to read Black women's art, research, and everyday speech for its expressions of anger as meaningful texts of rage. In addition, I am asking that Black women as knowledge creators take our own experiences with anger seriously, as it tells us something about the hatred that we encounter in our lives and work. What a methodology of anger assumes is that regardless of which texts are read, anger is a signal that there is more to know and a process by which we can see the pattern for the so-called chaos.

In the texts of rage included here, I signal where anger emerges as a critique of anti-Black woman violence. Nina Simone's "Mississippi Goddam" does that through the song's exceptionable refrain "everybody knows about Mississippi, goddam!" Simone's rendering of anger draws attention to the absurdity of what is considered objectionable in the United States. Her words are more likely to draw backlash by mainstream white America than the murder of Medgar Evers—the event to which the song initially responds. Further, she creates through her unique position of a Black woman artist whose art and anger were policed. Simone situates herself within rage and performs that rage as an act of self-making.

By evaluating anger's role in the creative process of the next text of rage, *patient.*, I demonstrate how anger can be generative knowledge. By tracing my feeling of anger that began with a personal medical encounter, I discuss how a creative and intellectual project developed from asking myself the question: "Why am I angry?" The result is a series of poems that take up the history of racist medicine and the Black women who endured its experiments, the inherited memory of such abuses, and the possibilities for healing in the present.

Lastly, I demonstrate how we might find anger to be a useful means of developing work that examines fully the hatred to which anger is response. Borrowing from the practice of redaction in erasure poetry and inspired by Christina Sharpe's intervention of redaction and annotation, I produce a poem and sound in the context of writing this article as a method of reading an excerpt of the interaction between Sandra Bland and Brian Encinia before her arrest.[31] I redact Encinia's antagonisms and center Bland's responses that news pundits read as anger. This forces us to enter a space in which Sandra Bland's critique is centered. The multidimensional function of anger as methodology reveals another thing: collective mourning by those of us who identify with Sandra Bland because we too, feel the targeted aim of the hatred of the police represented by Brian Encinia. While this collective feeling is an issue that could be interrogated further, what I found in the processes of anger, close reading, redaction, and re-rendering through creative production is that when we view the dash cam footage and read transcripts of the event, we are observing her death happen while she is still alive. Close reading of Bland's responses reveal that she is observing a violent script *happen to her* and she is able to disrupt that narrative by naming it as it is happening. "She watched the sea," is a refrain in the audiovisual component of the poem. *She watched the sea* could imply that she watched herself drown in the overwhelming wash of police violence. Black women watch Sandra drown in the overwhelming wash of state violence. We watch as we too float away and toward each other, in the waters of our oceanic past and present. As we float away and to each other, so does our feeling. Like grief that travels, so does anger, passed down and on like a rite of passage transforms who we are and what we know. By luxuriating in anger in this way, I hope to connect the notion of feelin to spiritual, affective registers of inheritance. That is, the modes of emotional experience that are learned and carried by relations of blood and spirit between and among living and non-living beings.

Text of Rage: "Mississippi Goddam"

Oh, but this whole country is full of lies
You're all gonna die and die like flies
I don't trust you anymore
you keep on saying, "Go slow."
— NINA SIMONE, "MISSISSIPPI GODDAM"

I have a right to be angry. If you're a black person
and you're not angry, you're damned mad.
— NINA SIMONE IN CONVERSATION WITH LASHONDA BARNETT[32]

Dr. Simone said the United States of America was a lie. That no amount of respectable suit-wearing marching would cease the murders of Black folks. She was spitting mad, laughing mad, and creatively frustrated. Although she was a classical musician by training, she was rejected by that world at every turn. And when Medgar Evers was killed in his own home in Mississippi in the summer of 1963 by white supremacists, she was angry enough to get a gun.[33] Instead of getting that gun, she composed a show tune that nods to the legacy of Black entertainers in vaudeville, and she damned Mississippi, no, the whole country to hell.[34]

Nina Simone is a woman whose autobiography reads like a chronology of the civil rights movement as much as a self-story. It is clear that she understood her story to be intertwined with the struggle of Black folks. She talks about being uncomfortable with being pegged as a protest singer yet could not stop herself from protest.[35] Embittered by an industry that pigeonholed her as a popular musician, Simone felt distant from her work and stuck in a cliché. Making meaning out of her music as an artist-activist elevated her craft and sharpened her purpose. Reflecting on the years after "Mississippi Goddam" was released, she said, "My music was dedicated to a purpose more important than classical music's pursuit of excellence; it was dedicated to the fight for freedom and the historical destiny of my people."[36] "Mississippi Goddam" would be her debut as an artist of her own making, angry as it was.

Beyond the shock of hearing a Black woman say "Goddam" on wax, let's examine the information that shock provides. Her incendiary language was met with more ire in the white run music industry than the murder of Medgar Evers itself. For example, a record dealer returned the recording to the record label, broken in half.[37] This irony was not lost on Simone and made it clear to her that her position as a musician would have the capacity to affect change.

When Simone damns Mississippi in God's name, her approach is no different from that of activists and theologians in her era, before it, and after. Martin Luther King made a similar statement in the notes of his undelivered final sermon, "Why America May Go to Hell," and he did so in the tradition of his Black Christian theologian predecessor Richard Allen, and later, James Cone.[38] If there is a difference in Nina Simone's utterance, it is because she is a Black woman who is the daughter of an evangelical woman preacher. But it is precisely this difference that sharpened Simone's critique: it would be unseemly for a Black woman to speak with such conviction and vitriol. When she sings, "Yes, you lied to me all these years / you told me to wash and clean my ears / and talk real fine just like a lady / and you'd stop calling me Sister Sadie," she is naming the lie that there are rewards for Black women's respectability. Her career showed that there were no such rewards for Black respectability, as did the death of Medgar Evers.

In the first and second bridges of the song, Simone articulates her frustration with the pace of the movement and how that pace was dictated by liberal politics. As she sings about the conditions of Black folks, her band shouts "too slow" in refrain. For Simone, the slow pace of progress is a chance for the lying country to renege on its promises. The song demanded self-actualization rather than asking for white American acceptance when she sings, "Don't tell me, I'll tell you / me and my people just about due," and warned that a slow movement would only lead to more suffering.

With as much fire and brimstone as any evangelical preacher, "Mississippi Goddam" promises eternal death for America's sin—more lasting punishment than would come from her gun. Unpatriotic and blasphemous, "Mississippi Goddam" articulates an ethical position carved out of righteous anger. Perhaps in this moment of creative self-actualization, we might also see into Simone's future, when she defected from the United States until her death in 2003. Her anger on wax, in interviews, shocks. Sure. But the context is clear: Mississippi, the United States, all of y'all are too hateful for God's blessings, the blessings being Black people and at the very least, Nina Simone herself. So, she left. Simone's angry song tells us about her particular position as a Black woman and musician in the movement. It also reports the radical notion, well within Black prophetic traditions, that liberation means that one must be unpatriotic—and in the United States that is blasphemy. It laughs at the absurdity of racism in this country through tone: a classically trained musician who is a Black woman may only write show tunes in the United States because she is a Black woman—goddam. A man who advocated for the lives of Black people in peaceful protest was murdered in front of his own home—goddam. By speaking her anger about these issues Simone would be made out to be inappropriate. Never to fit the trappings of idealized womanhood in the classical music world, or even the world of popular music—goddam. Goddam.

Text of Rage: *patient.*

Every Black woman in America lives her life somewhere
along a wide curve of ancient and unexpressed angers.
—AUDRE LORDE, "EYE TO EYE"

In the next few pages I discuss *patient.*, a collection of my poems that tells the story synthesized below. Interspersed are poems and excerpts from the book. Although the story as narrated here might anger, and contains anger, it is not the object of anger. The object of anger is hatred: the legacy of medical mistreatment and experimentation on Black women. The methodology is anger. My book *patient.* is produced from that methodology; poetry is the primary method.

> I must have been found guilty of something. I don't feel innocent
> here lurking with ghosts. See it happens like that. I start at a thought
> that is quite benign and end up peccant, debased.[39]

In 2006, I had an ordeal with medicine. This ordeal led me through courses of experience that manifested as spiritual, bodily, and intellectual knowledge about race, medicine, memory and trauma. I had an ovarian torsion, a relatively benign circumstance if not for the immense pain involved. I visited three hospitals before being accurately diagnosed and having my ovary removed. I spent a week in acute pain, subjected to diagnoses as condescending as menstrual cramps, a bladder infection, appendicitis, and ectopic pregnancy (despite my professed sexual history devoid of contact with non-trans men). After fifteen hours at Johns Hopkins Hospital, I was diagnosed with an ovarian torsion and scheduled for immediate surgery to remove the dead organ. Johns Hopkins is the nearest hospital to my grandparents' home in East Baltimore, where my late uncle took me to be in their care. (This geography becomes more important later.) I was diagnosed with the torsion after numerous tests, questions about my sexual history, pelvic exams, more questions about my sexual history, and finally, an ultrasound of my pelvis.

When the doctor informed me that I would be subject to yet another pelvic exam, the third exam in one day, I had a break from patient decorum. Through a fog of morphine, I told her, "Fine, do whatever you have to. Gynecology was built on the backs of Black women anyway." There was silence. The younger doctors shadowing her nervously giggled while she asked, "Has anyone here done something to offend you?" My late grandmother intervened, saying that the day had been exhausting, that I was in a lot of pain and there had been no solutions to my problem as of yet. Thank God for her wisdom because I was no longer able to parse words with people who would, in a few hours, cut me open on the operating table. After this outburst, for the first time at this hospital, a Black nurse administered my pelvic exam:

You Be Lucy, I'll Be Betsey
February 17, 2006

> The nurse with the natural compliments me on my locs. We begin in that nappy-hair banter, *when did you start yours?* All of this happening between my thighs. Between speculum and cotton swab, *I just had to stop running to the salon.* Between the manual test in the vagina, *You're going to feel a pinch*, and the manual test in the anus, *It's so much easier to manage this way.* Nothing said of my outburst. Nothing about the angry patient on this floor, *Yours look so healthy*, nothing about why she tends to me after that. *Almost done.* Just two black women and a speculum, each asking the other *When did you get free?*[40]

I've tried to come to terms with how three enslaved women from Alabama came to me on that hospital bed. Anger propelled me into another way of knowing—one in which spirits, frightening coincidences, and racist legacies haunt me. Another way I might describe what happened to me that evening was that I got in my feelins. I took some personal things politically, and some political things personally. An army of Black women who knew too well the shenanigans of medical racism crowded my bed.

During the healing process, I went to an article by Terri Kapsalis that connected the legacies of the "father" of gynecology in the United States, J. Marion

Sims, to the "father" of US popular culture, P. T. Barnum. Influenced by the connection that Kapsalis observes—both of these men began their careers via the exploitation of the bodies of enslaved Black women—I tried to make sense of what happened to me by painting.[41] A few revelations came, but then there was silence.

At a weeklong poetry workshop in Greensburg, Pennsylvania, in 2007, where I was required to write a poem a day, I carried with me Benjamin Reiss's *The Showman and the Slave.* The book ends with a speculative biography of Joice Heth, the woman P. T. Barnum publicly displayed as the 161-year-old former wet nurse to George Washington.[42] My final day there, I heard a clear voice announce, "And for my last trick, I will release the ghost!"

AND FOR MY LAST TRICK
I WILL RELEASE THE GHOST
Hover over my corpse
and escape.
        —"JOICE HETH PRESENTS: HERSELF!"[43]

I have never been one for persona poems. In fact, this is the first persona poem I had ever penned. Writing in her voice was so frightening that it felt unlike me, but it *was* my voice. It was angry, lucid, and useful.

After Heth's death on February 25, 1836, P. T. Barnum would continue to profit from her body by engaging in the spectacle of her public dissection, and subsequently, what we would call today, a "media circus" surrounding the authenticity of her death and the possibility that she might have been an automaton.[44] In the persona poems that followed, Heth's voice played with the absurdity of the circus. From this poem on, I wrote in the voices of all the women I felt would let me. When I couldn't, I wrote in the voice of my researcher/patient self, searching for meaning and understanding about my outburst and those rememories I was experiencing. Heth, and the intervention of her voice in the realm of the spiritual and creative, made possible a new way for me to engage these harrowing stories.

But that was not the end of my haunting or the experiences of inhabiting anger, and writing with it. Henrietta Lacks's story—a story that was already embedded in Baltimore narratives about the untrustworthiness of Johns Hopkins—was gaining popularity because of a best-selling book about her life.[45] Henrietta Lacks is more than a ghost. She is the very structure of scientific research. Her cells, known in the scientific community as HeLa, facilitate new discoveries including lifesaving vaccines. In 1951, these same cells obliterated her body.[46] Lacks was treated for a severe form of cervical cancer at Johns Hopkins. Johns Hopkins was her care provider of choice, no doubt, because she too, lived in East Baltimore, where Hopkins would be the nearest hospital. East Baltimore was increasingly a haven for Black folks who, like my family, migrated from the tobacco fields of Virginia and North Carolina in the mid-twentieth century.

Lacks's story, the means of its proliferation amid a communal knowing about Johns Hopkins in the city of Baltimore, and the story of her family being shut out of the wealth of medical discovery found from her cells, creates an ocean of unspeakable anger for me. Anger, because it is a truth Black folks in the United States already know. We know stories like the Tuskegee syphilis experiments. We know the horrors behind terms like "Mississippi appendectomy."[47] We know stories like those documented in Marilyn Nelson's *Fortune's Bones*—the bones of enslaved people and Indigenous people who were subjects of research in the name of discovery.[48] The same teaching hospital that harvested Henrietta's cells also owns my dead ovary. Despite my requests to retrieve it, to see it, they told me that my ovary was now a smear of cells on a plate. However, when I ordered my medical files from Johns Hopkins a year later:

```
The specimen was received fresh labeled with the patient's name,
████████████, and is designated "left ovary." The specimen consists
of an enlarged and hemorrhagic ovary, weighing 160 grams and
measuring 9 x 6 x 3 cm.  The surface of the ovary is smooth with
areas of hemorrhage and hyperemia.  The ovary is received with
several cut surfaces.  Serial sectioning reveals mainly multiple
areas of confluent hemorrhage.  There are intervening areas of
fibrous white stroma.  Representative sections are submitted.
Approximately 50% of the specimen is submitted.
```

Figure 19. Bettina Judd, *How Much Does It Hurt on a Scale from One to Ten? #2*, 2013 (detail). Kraft paper, gouache, collage, 72 × 36 inches.

They lied.

I was searching for meaning amid the fury in creative expression and the research process. I had anger, haunts, voices, points of entry into a research project, and yet all of it felt like a problem. This research practice and its disembodied methods were a problem for the work I was *actually* doing. Work that seemed more feasible through the creative process, whether poetry or paint. Meeting these women meant meeting a part of myself that was not innocent in the practice of their erasure. As a researcher, I could do them little justice, as research had done them no justice. As a Black woman, I had different, if uncomfortable, investments. My work as researcher and writer had to shift to accommodate the spiritual and affective plane on which these women's stories reverberated in me:

At first I thought I feared your eye, Mrs. Lacks. But now I realize it
is the gaze of your loved ones. I should make monument to you.
Instead, it is as if I am figuring my life through your death.[49]

I was entangled with the work that I do as it threatens to pathologize. If I went through the accepted routes of academic research, I could only see these women through the lenses of the men who enslaved them and owned their cells and bodies. What I was writing in poetry was intimate knowledge. Things were not neat. Things were layered, complicated, and hard. Through creative process, my understanding of knowing and telling shifted and came alive. I was certain about art as knowledge because I was able to see and understand through concurrent projects in which inquiry and mind/body/spirit experience collided. Everything seemed to gather and launch from one thing: anger. It was anger that made itself known despite morphine drips, Oxycodone, patient forms, and academic projects. Between my own ordeal and the ordeals of Black women that haunted me there was a large network of sensation and knowing, and anger was its cue.

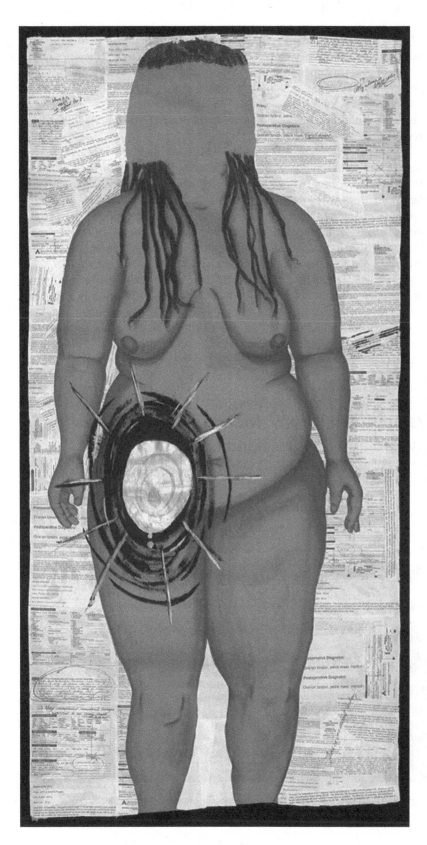

Figure 20. Bettina Judd, *How Much Does It Hurt on a Scale from One to Ten? #2*, 2013. Kraft paper, gouache, collage, 72 × 36 inches.

Perhaps what I was experiencing in those hospitals could be explained through Black feminist hauntology.[50] My critique lodged through morphine drips and in the face of being cut open would, as Viviane Saleh-Hanna says, "produce a more appropriate critique of them, their colonizing ways, their moral bankruptcy and their varying systems of enslavement."[51] With anger running a current between these ghosts and me, I was able to articulate precisely the problem that I was experiencing.

What needs to be known does not end with anger alone. There is always something else to examine, more questions from which to seek answers. Anger is "an incomplete form of knowledge" that signals the presence of hatred.[52] Why Black women are on the receiving end of hatred requires another set of questions beyond the scope of this chapter, but they too are important questions to ask. Above, I discussed how tracing anger may be used to write ourselves into being, but there are often costs for expressing anger. Because anger is a response to what Lorde calls, a "societal death wish" and that wish is likely to come true.[53]

In the final pages of this chapter, I will use the methodology of anger to trace the fatal incident between Sandra Bland and officer Brian Encinia, using poetry as a creative mechanism to re-render the transcript of that incident and, most importantly, to highlight the otherwise knowledge that it is not Sandra Bland who caused her own incarceration and subsequent death—as the angry Black woman trope would confirm—but white supremacist and sexist hatred.

"Is Anything Wrong, Ma'am?" Brian Encinia's Hatred and Sandra Bland

> *In a landscape drawn from an ocean bed, you can't drive yourself*
> *sane—so angry you are crying. You can't drive yourself sane.*
> —CLAUDIA RANKINE IN *CITIZEN*

Figure 21. Hover your mobile device over this QR code to navigate to the video at http://dr.bettinajudd.com/on-or-about-july-10-2015.

On or about July 10, 2015

You are plowing through heartbreak, a cigarette between your fingers, the radio's bass beating into your sternum, a song in your throat.

You feel watched, you pull over to avert and the eyes pull over with you.

You know that this happens. You know how this happens and why. You know that it has no name, cannot be named without a price, to call the officer out, to call the officer the po-leese, to say a thing like *my rights*, you will be naming that which will invite your death. It will be you.

It is not funny how he asked a question to which he knew the answer and yet didn't understand his own damned question.

It is an old question.

Discount your memory (and they will) but his answer to his question was: *It feels like you will die very soon.*

On or about July 10, 2015, you lived.

Heartbreak, whether you like it or not makes you woefully aware that you have a heart. That it is beating, that it beats in a chorus and it is yours. You can live for the heart even if, perhaps because, it is breaking. But you cannot live for him. So . . .

On or about July 10, 2015, you chose to live.

Which invited a very certain and undeniable death. So very certain, that three days later they called it suicide, called you crazy, invoked a trope to make it fall into sense:

Arrogant, uncooperative, belligerent, angry black woman.

And we knew, Sandra, that whatever your choices were, whatever hand wrapped a thing around your neck (we know that thing), whomever witnessed your last breath (we know them as well), however you moved about your sadness (who would we be without sadness?), we knew that you did not merely, so happen to, in this particular instance, even though you may have any number of reasons to implode.

That is never how it works.

On or about July 10 to July 13, 2015, at various points in time you lived as electronic reverb, yourself surrounded by your fading self in the vacuum of silence that is Black womanhood.[54]

On July 10, 2015, Sandra Bland, a twenty-eight-year-old woman from Chicago, is pulled over by a state trooper, Brian Encinia, in Waller, Texas. During the stop, she smokes a cigarette inside of her car. According to the dash cam video Encinia asks her to put out her cigarette. She refuses, noting her right to smoke inside of her car.[55] Encinia orders Bland out of her car and threatens her with a Taser gun. Then, Encinia forces her out of the car, beats and arrests her. The Waller county police detain her for three days. During this time, Bland attempts to post bail. On the third day, she is found dead, hanging in her cell and her death is deemed a suicide.[56] I am moving quickly through these events as they have been reported because it is difficult to write. Because I want to get to the point, which is not about reproducing this event as social media has done ad nauseum, but because I am more interested in a brief moment between Bland and the police and its devastating effects. This moment appears to be benign yet encapsulates the threat of racism and sexism to Black women's speech. It is a moment about tone—its misreading, or perhaps its perfect reading. It is the moment in which Bland's annoyance and frustration articulated through speech and silence are read as a threat, and Brian Encinia exerts force in order to put *an angry Black woman* in place. It is Encinia's hatred of Sandra Bland to which she responds. The dialogue unredacted and in redaction:

> **E:** You okay?
>
> **B:** I'm waiting on you. You—this is your job. I'm waiting on you. What do you want me to say?
>
> **E:** I don't know—you seem very irritated.
>
> **B:** I am. I really am. [Unclear] what I am getting a ticket for. I was getting out of your way. You were speeding up, tailing me, so I move over, and you stop me. So, yeah, I am a little irritated. But that doesn't stop you from giving me a ticket, so . . . [unclear].
>
> **E:** Are you done?
>
> **B:** You asked me what was wrong, then I told you. So now I'm done, yeah.
>
> **E:** Okay. Do you mind putting out your cigarette please?
>
> **B:** I'm in my car. Why do I have to put out my cigarette?
>
> **E:** Well you can step on out now.
>
> **B:** I don't have to step out of my car.
>
> **E:** Step out of the car.
>
> _____
>
> **E:** ▬▬▬▬▬
>
> **B:** I'm waiting on you. You—this is your job. I'm waiting on you. What do you want me to say?
>
> **E:** ▬▬▬▬▬▬▬▬▬▬▬▬▬▬▬
>
> **B:** I am. I really am. [Unclear] what I am getting a ticket for. I was getting out of your way. You were speeding up, tailing me, so I move

over, and you stop me. So, yeah, I am a little irritated. But that doesn't stop you from giving me a ticket, so . . . [unclear].

E: ▮▮▮▮▮▮▮▮

B: You asked me what was wrong, then I told you. So now I'm done, yeah.

E: ▮▮▮▮▮▮▮▮▮▮▮▮▮▮▮▮▮▮▮▮

B: I'm in my car. Why do I have to put out my cigarette?

E: ▮▮▮▮▮▮▮▮▮▮▮

B: I don't have to step out of my car.

E: ▮▮▮▮▮▮

The encounter escalates and he opens the door. He threatens to remove her physically and punches her or attempts to punch her. She gets out of the car and lets him know that she plans to sue. She tries to document the incident with her phone. He orders her to put the phone down. I can stop here because the moment that I want to highlight has already passed. The moment in question is when he returns to the car and asks what seems to be a benign question, marked here in italics:

You okay?

Encinia likely wanted her to reply, "Yes, I am fine," an answer that would acknowledge his power—her obeisance to his power. His ability to control her is *fine*. If Bland had responded in such a manner, he would not have to hear her testimony. Bland was a problem to his/the official narrative of benevolent policing, and force was the solution. When she does not give him his desired response, *he* becomes irritated. Encinia wants to remind Bland of his ability to do what he wants with her body, to which she replies: "I'm in my car. Why do I have to put out my cigarette?" Note that she doesn't answer his question, "Yes, I mind" or, "No, I will not put out my cigarette." She asks about what is beneath his question. She is asking why he's engaging her with aggression. This doesn't solve the issue at hand: Encinia needs to make Bland aware of his ability to use force, by telling her to get out of her car. Yet, another attempt to control what Bland does with her body, despite the fact that he has no reason to assume that she is a physical threat to him. And here, for the third time, Sandra invokes her rights and speaks directly to the conversation of power and violence that Encinia is attempting to mask: "I don't have to step out of the car." It is at this moment when Encinia starts to threaten brute force. Encinia's hatred looks like this:

You okay? / I dare you to say what is wrong about this interaction.

Has anyone here done anything to offend you? / I dare you to say that I have offended you.

Is there a problem? / You are the problem

All of these seemingly benign questions are not questions but dares—tests to see whether the one asked knows her place. To go off script is to be out of place—to be "arrogant" as one pundit described Bland.[57] All of these questions are perhaps another more menacing version of the question Du Bois recounts in *The Souls of Black Folk*:

> *How does it feel to be a problem?*
> *You won't be a problem now, will you?*
> *Don't be*
> *a problem.*[58]

It would be easy to surmise that Bland's speech is what put her in danger, but that doesn't explain why she was followed in the first place or what transpired in the days after her arrest. Bland insisted on drawing attention to the script being handed to her. She cited the pattern, saw the fractal of hatred where Encinia insisted that *she* was violent chaos. She insisted on letting Encinia know she had an awareness of her rights. In public discussions of this series of events, she was cast as angry and arrogant and thus responsible for her own death. I want to acknowledge this kind of reading of Black women's anger because it highlights the function of the trope, which is to justify oppression and, in this case, murder. Bland may have been angry but it was not *her feeling* that put her in danger. It was Encinia's hatred, his desire to exert power over her.[59]

Sandra Bland's death is the result of Black women's vulnerability in their interactions with law enforcement.[60] The destructive force, or at least the specter of it here, is embedded in the speculation of her death as suicide. Her death, whether ultimately by her hand or not, was orchestrated and facilitated by the state embodied in Encinia's hatred, and it is the invisible hand of white supremacist ideology which created a narrative by which her death would seem to be a natural course of events. Such a logic would assume that Sandra Bland failed herself multiple times. That she was headed toward death even before she was pulled over. This logic is gruesome. It is clear to me that the appropriate response to Bland's death is anger. It is the white imagination of our rage that justifies violence before it has occurred.[61] Black women have been particularly vocal about this vulnerability, about our anger, its feeling, its effects, and its consequences. By engaging Black women's anger and texts of rage, we can better understand how Black women are in effect providing ample material for understanding the contours of hatred: racism, sexism, homophobia, transphobia, and on. Let us put all of this to final rest, Sandra Bland was murdered by the hatred of Brian Encinia and the Waller County Police Department, and she told us as much during the stop.

Coda: "I'm Still Here"

As knowledge subjugated by stereotype, Black women's anger holds within it details of the function of hatred launched at us in the form of anti-Black sexism. Here, I have demonstrated how a methodology of anger can facilitate a reading of the events at the end of Bland's life that seem to be a mystery to some but are quite clear to so many Black folks and Black women for certain. In recounting the development of *patient.* and its uses of anger, I demonstrated how interrogating the source of my own anger unfolded felt knowledge of the legacy of medical experimentation. A methodology of anger also has the capacity to give Black woman–centered insights into creative texts, particularly when they are self-conscious about anger. Applying anger as a trackable object in Nina Simone's "Mississippi Goddam" reveals the many layers of meaning the song may encompass: the stymied position of Simone as an artist, the stymied position of her people, and the inevitability of premature death for even the most gracious of Black leaders.

Luxuriating in the richness of Black women's inner lives provides so many possibilities for understanding the practice of being human. If we are to restructure knowledge in order to repair the grave rupture in the formulation of what it means to be human, the value by which felt experience is graded must, too, be restructured. Here, I draw attention to the usefulness of anger because of the particular ways that connotations of anger warp when inhabited by or projected on the bodies of Black women. This warping, made evident in the Sapphire stereotype, signals the function of feeling and emotion in producing difference. Beginning with Sapphire as a critical site of silencing and navigating such silences, we inevitably make ourselves available to otherwise ways of knowing. A byproduct of a methodology of anger is the revelation that anger is accompanied by many felt experiences answering to hatred. Pain, joy, shame, pleasure—all of these felt experiences provide information about the experience of hatred.

While anger in its many manifestations adds much needed dimension to the ways that we look at Black feminist intellectual, activist, and creative work, the expansiveness of the concept of anger itself has yet to be explored, particularly in relation to its more amenable cousin, pleasure. Anger, and all of the ways in which anger manifests, or is misread, is a practice of being human, but what other rituals of knowing do we have to share with one another? What other ways of being?

I do not forget bell hooks's warning about the ability for anger to consume. She warns that, "it must be tempered by an engagement with a full range of emotional responses to black struggle for self-determination."[62] Such is the threat with any pleasures—any feeling and the structures thereof. But I am compelled by the reverberations, the touchstone quality of the feeling that is anger because of how the logics around that feeling called anger are cast on the bodies of Black women. The fact of anger's existence continued for generations through practice and careful conjure tells me something about structures of feeling as they relate to Black women. It is as if a note was handed to me. Not through death, but by birthright as in, "You have a right to the tree of life." Always pushing toward that insurgent subject.

I think about that last phone call Sandra Bland made to her friend from the Waller County jail—the sadness and frustration in her voice. One could hear it in the sighs between, "How did switching lanes with no signal turn into all of this? I don't even know," "But I'm still here," and "So I guess call me back when you can."[63] Breath as exasperation, breath as resilience ("But I'm still here"), breath as hopefulness. Sandra Bland's sighs were breath in an era of "I can't breathe." The phrase was uttered by Eric Garner just a year before on July 13, 2014, and once again by George Floyd on May 25, 2020. (And yet, who else?) As Crawley notes of the dying plea turned abolitionist announcement, " 'I can't breathe' charges us . . . to produce abolition against the episteme that produced for us current iterations of categorical designations of racial hierarchies, class stratifications, gender binaries, mind-body splits."[64] Let it be known that at every turn on or about July 10, 2015, Sandra Bland *was* breathing. She embodied otherwise knowledge with each breath, and spoke from there. She spoke directly to the hatred that wanted her dead, she spoke to her own frustration and sadness, her resilience. *But I'm still here*, she said. Then when she finally could not breathe, they told us it was suicide.

Bland's expressions were complex and inclusive of anger but the Waller County police department claimed that a past suicide attempt was proof that her emotional state had the capacity to take her over the edge of life and would explain the outcome of her encounter with police. Her anger was cast as her instability and her instability would be blamed for her death. With such a reality, no wonder anger was something handed to me like a secret. No wonder as Black feminist scholarship critiques knowledge it examines feelins—that which is considered chaos by a hateful and violent order. But Bland's sighs speak to knowledge otherwise, knowledge discounted. Knowledge signaled by Bland's righteous anger and Sapphire's emergence.

The End: Everything in the Ocean

everything in the ocean

porpoises
some swimming humans
some drowning ones
fish
birds that swim
them dog looking fellas
funny looking plants (edible)
funny looking plants (not edible, quite poisonous)
also funny looking fish and some
beautiful and unfriendly
things that are both plant and animal
things that will kill you by exhaling
panties, plastic, and condoms
shipwrecks
black people
some bones
treasure?
volcanoes
otherwise dormant mountains
valleys
dinosaurs
ancient city ruins
things within
beyond my imagination
unthinkable amounts of
salt
water

What do we not know that we don't know? It is a frightening thing if one thinks about it too long—the vastness and un-livability of the ocean to us as beings unaccustomed to living under water. I am asking about the technical possibilities of knowing and knowing that one knows something as vast. I'd offer that this kind of questioning is the larger contribution of Black feminist critique. That is—the language and our thoughts have failed us, will fail us, and so we must find other ways of feelin each other and thus, knowing anything at all. Black feminist thought has already taught us about engaging what it means to always be in the apocalypse—to be at the juncture of history and knowledge characterized by non-being as in *All the Women are White all the Blacks are men but. . . .*

Scholar and media artist Tiffany Lethabo King takes up the metaphor of the shoal as a gathering and deliberate space for the meeting of Black and Indigenous thought. It is at the shoal where colonial logics of conquest are marginal, where Black and Indigenous movement building and critiques of the human bump up and blend as a total critique of the vectors of conquest upon which slavery and genocide depend. "As a process," she states, "it is the movement of the ocean from greater to shallower depths," as space in which the ocean and land gather.[1] It is "an analytical and a methodological location [that] constitutes a moment of convergence, gathering, reassembling, and coming together (or apart)."[2] This Black feminist oceanographic intervention confronts the over-determining oceanic metaphor of Blackness in Black studies and the metaphors of land in Indigenous studies to uncover an apparent depth of meeting between the two that trips up, slows down, confounds Western narratives of benign conquest, objective scientific and humanist ideology, and even the presumptions of coalitional politics. At the shoal, critique of critique moves over any attest to natural assumption.

The Black shoals finds us at Junot Diaz's *Brief and Wonderful Life of Oscar Wao*, and his use of the concept of *fúku* which describes the curse of conquest on those in the Dominican diaspora. King considers how Diaz's incorporation of this concept enacts itself through the performance of *fúku* on the page. That is, in an attempt to exorcise, to explain the reaching effects of *fúku* through writing practice in this novel and others, Diaz also enacts the violence of conquest in life as he has been outed as an abuser by women colleagues. She states, "Diaz's quest for the language and courage to speak his trauma, as well as his own transgressions as an abuser, is an unending labor, like the work of finding a grammar for conquest. He must now contour the ways that the horrors of conquest made him a predator, and he must linger in the process of healing the individuals he has harmed. This healing and accountability is also a grammar of conquest that Native and Black artistic and intellectual endeavors continue to birth."[3] In taking up Diaz's work on and off the page through the metaphor of the shoal, we can appreciate the incisiveness of Diaz's invocation of the persistence of conquest in his award-winning work and also in his life's working. No one is off the hook in this approach, not even Diaz, in his attempt to explain his own positioning and participation in sexual violence. What readers take up as pleasure and insight on the page and his acclaim is also the function of that colonial violence. All of this to say, what the ocean offers is not utopia but our complex mess.

Black feminist oceanographics take these concerns into deeper depths—to a politics of care in which our being forever cursed by conquest is neither the end nor the beginning of our existence—entangled, yes, but not totalizing. Christina Sharpe invokes wake work as a politics of care by which we continually acknowledge the ongoing and never-ending violence of colonization and enslavement and make each other accountable and seen in the process. The modes of tending to ourselves, our own, our dead, and yet to be born, jut against a hedonist positionality that would end in *fúku*. A Black feminist oceanographic politics of care does not find pleasure, or even pleasure *as* freedom, to be an ultimate good and above critique. The work we do, the ways that we move about this world, must be revisited, our intentions and impacts shoaled. Where and how our feet land and paddle must be considerately placed.

I find this concept of the Black shoal useful in its necessary slowing down of thought *as* movement. It is movement that resists impositions of Western clock time, as in *colored people's time*, as conquest itself moves quickly across land and psychic space. The work of naming, of producing grammars to critique conquest, is never complete as we are always in the process of recovering from that which is ongoing. As King notes, ". . . the relations of conquest continue right through this very moment, shaping these very thoughts. Conquest must be perpetually elaborated and interrogated with all of our existing faculties, as well as the ones that have yet to be developed."[4] To resist clock time would make way for new ways of knowing, of being, and of making being known. It would change the tenor of the processes, compulsions, and means of production by which knowledge is engaged, understood, shared, and received. It would challenge the vectors by which this very book is urgently written. It would slow us down just enough, just maybe, to read the word *being*

and never look for its modifiers.

To *be* because, quite simply, there are no other options, and if we are brave enough, to bear witness to that new emergent subject. There are no other options because existing in, through, and in response to the molds hammered out through conquest and enslavement have produced the same conditions by which sea waters rise and whole species and people are extinguished. To be because the modes by which we understand development, progress, and expansion, have deteriorated the possibilities for existence of many, if not all species.

We have been called chaos—resistant to order and the embodiment of disorder—compelled toward emotion rather than reason. This project has taken seriously that which has been considered chaotic and disordered, not to redress chaos as order but to highlight how chaos is constructed as such and to expose how order might not make much *sense*. This project has taken seriously both Black women's creative work that performs a curiosity, a deep engagement with the chaos of feelin, and the projection of that chaos as well. Here we have discussed how the practice of *joy!* is manifest as an orientation toward life and its complexities—how it makes us marvel at our capacity for mourning and feeling at all. This project's meditation on grief dives into engagement with cross-species grief and its relationship with nonhuman species. This meditation on grief, located at the Salish Sea, bookmarked an orientation toward grief in Black studies—one which considers grief as the feelin of Black studies. Blackness itself within Black studies has been marked by racial shame, and creative responses to the image of Black motherhood might tell us something about the experience of that shame, and possibilities beyond it. For a people who have come to be associated with anger as an inherent way of being, anger both real and imagined might be a signpost to otherwise disregarded knowledge. Though Black female vocalists have become an icon of erotic transmutability, this study's engagement drinks in what the erotic in vocal practice does for the singer, and its powers to change one's condition. Each of these cases reveal how deep engagement with the chaos of feelin orients us to objects of study quite differently than we may have initially expected. The mismappings are relentless, though Black women's creative response to these mismappings and the traps of our very language are too, relentless.

What we don't know that we don't know exists on a horizon of an unknown future and an unknowable past. All around us, endless ocean meeting sky. In her collection *What the Water Knows*, Jacqueline Jones Lamon writes in the aftermath of many apocalypses and asks what the water can tell us. After Hurricane Sandy, Hurricane Katrina, after the transatlantic slave trade, after Flint, Lamon traces how modernity functions to estrange us from living with water. From the way that we might choose not a glass of water but wine, to the trauma and survival after the flood, to the amniotic fluid of the womb:

> How deep can we plunge and still discern
> the finest shades of difference? Today,
>
> the sea presents us with waves worthy
> of riding, shoving us away on the surface,
> while reeling us home with its fierce
>
> undertow. The surfers will need this,
> but maybe not us.[5]

Indeed water is seen as that which has the capacity to kill us, to cradle us. Aracelis Girmay teaches us in *The Black Maria* that scientists have misnamed large craters on the surface of the moon, naming them oceans—black maria. In this misnaming, blackness marks distance, not of the unknowable, but the mis-known, though the most powerful telescopes, the greatest technologies of modern are at our disposal. What is in the sea is more elusive than our most careful observations can grasp:

> Inside the sea, there is more
> than sea . . .
>
> though it seems, from this distance
> a flat blue line—actually, a purling there:
>
> the dead move mammalian through
> its buried light
>
> & a graveyard is built
> out of history & time[6]

The distances between persons, the living and the dead, and the earth and moon, are all a matter of our willingness to know—to see with new eyes. In this titular poem, Girmay turns toward a story told by Neil deGrasse Tyson. In his youth, Tyson hauled a large telescope to the roof of his apartment building. A suspicious white neighbor of whom, Girmay notes, "(it is important to mention that she is white)"[7] calls the police—misidentifying his telescope as something more sinister. Girmay is with us on the grave danger Tyson is faced with here: "you might be holding / your breath for him right now / because you know this story."[8] It is, frightening to think about—a black boy in the dark, police on their way to him. But this is a story about distance, curiosity, and the tools by which we choose to see. Tyson's instrument—a telescope—in his hands could mean mortal danger though he:

> [lugged] it up to the roof
> to better see the leopard body of
>   space speckled with stars & the moon far off,
> much farther than (since I am spelling *The Thing*
>   out) the distance between
> the white neighbor who cannot see the boy
>   who is her neighbor, who,
> in fact, is much nearer
>   to her than the moon . . .

The ocean and space here are matched in their vastness, and in our constant misnamings, but what of our curiosity? Our willingness to go deeper? To know anew? We might have to reorient ourselves to the planet, other species, and thus ourselves. Or as poet and self-named post-colonial ethnobotanist Adjua Gargi Nzinga Greaves writes, "We live on Earth where sex is fuel, and I have longed to spend my time here in the body of a wild creature. Longed for every part of this figure to declare my soul's connection to our corner of the cosmos."[9] In this orientation to life, we are reminded that,

> Falling in love with nature means falling in love with sex.
> Means falling in love with the ubiquity of creation.
> And admitting your comfort at the orgy.[10]

This orientation feels sacred sex work in the process of creation—the product of which is life force. *The erotic as power.*

"Water is another country" and the ocean is another cosmos.[11] Different orientations toward the ocean and its inhabitants might tell us something about what is in the ocean and thus ourselves. Alexis Pauline Gumbs, reflecting and speculating on the end of the world, excavates an archive of the ocean and recounts, this is what it takes to cool the planet. hold the world together. protect the mysteries (despite the surface violence. and the pollution you try to bury in your heart).

this is what it takes. the strength of no separation. the bravery of flow. The audacity of never saying this is me, this is not you. this is mine, this is not yours. this is now, this was not ever before.[12]

And after having to imagine the end of the world, and what happens after, Gumbs turns to our oceans of now to acquaint us with sea mammals who are and will be our family (we hope, as they will be more well adapted to this ocean living). She invites us to listen to the witness of living of ocean-dwelling mammals. In her book *Undrowned* Gumbs is a "marine mammal apprentice" who listens closely to the possibilities of relation and living *within* the ocean.[13] A Black feminist oceanographic would expect the apocalypse, prepare for its coming—its inevitability a promise and the tools of the study, that is the practice, that would make living possible. As Denise Ferreira da Silva says, "Toward the end of the World produced by the tools of reason, the Black Feminist Poet peers beyond the horizon of thought, where historicity (temporality/interiority), framed by the tools of universal reason, cannot but yield violence."[14]

Figure 22. "Where U From?" Use your mobile device to hover over this QR code to experience the video poem at http://dr.bettinajudd.com/where-you-from. The video uses lines from the poem "indigenous to no land," previously published in *Meridians: Feminism, Race, Transnationalism* 11, no. 2. 2013.

Tourmaline's experimental film *Atlantic Is a Sea of Bones* enacts Black feminist oceanographic analysis through the arc of Black trans resilience and generational nurturance floating above the oceans that hold the remnants of so many apocalypses. Named for the Lucille Clifton poem of the same name, the film explores geographies of violence and erasure along with the capacities for Black trans thriving in Manhattan. In the film, the spirit of water, which Tourmaline notes "is not something that can be contained," emerges as a character in the telling of Black trans self-actualization.[15] As the film opens, Egyptt Labeija points to her old home, a "hut" on the piers where she lived in otherwise homelessness until "one day [she] just snapped out" she says, "this can't work no more. And just I began reaching for better things." She takes a breath, on the verge of tears, realizing that she is looking down from above this particular spot of struggle. She collects herself, gazes directly into the camera and says, "The times of the village, from Fourteenth Street to Christopher Street, the memories. People should never forget where they came from." After the watery and marbled title card, we see Egyptt in a red gown and sandy blonde curls in performance mode against a modern cement building—the new location of the Whitney Museum. The camera pans out from her French manicured hands in feminine performance to an even wider shot of her, a tiny but somehow larger than life form atop the building that overlooks the piers. In her artist statement, Tourmaline notes the violence of the placement of the new Whitney upon the queer geography of the piers: "Because of its new location," she says, "it is one of the places implicated in what feels so fundamentally part of a very violent cleansing. The Meatpacking District and the Piers were spaces for HIV+ people, for Black and trans life, and these spaces still exist; they are not completely gone."[16] Egyptt Labeija's story—living as a Black trans woman in the earlier days of the HIV/AIDS pandemic, the criminalization of HIV/AIDS, and gentrification in queer communities in Manhattan, as well as her activism for trans people—enfolds into the fantasy world of the film as metanarrative to the possibilities of Black trans living and thriving *with* life giving waters.

The water in the piers becomes a milky bath, and we are met again with Labeija's hands caressing her own thighs. A hand emerges through what sounds like ocean waves. The shot moves below her. The electronic soundscape created by Geo Wyeth invigorates the tension and interiority from each shot to the next. Heavy bass and synthesizers give nods to the sounds of the '80s and early '90s while electronic strings and electronic vocalizations propel us into the science-fiction interiority of the latter scenes in the film. The bath covers Labeija's midsection so that her body emerges from the water as three separate islands: her torso, head and one arm raised to her temple; one hand lightly holding the side of the standing tub, and two legs bent and leaning. Her expression is thoughtful—the lighting is a deep indigo that illuminates her brown skin. Her eyes close and we are drawn into the interiority of the moment along with the synthesizers and bass. Purple water transports us to a moment of care, Labeija carefully fluffing and smoothing out the edges of a younger figure's hair. The scene returns to the indigo tub where Labeija holds her neck in her hands in introspection and immerses herself in the milky water that transforms into the marbled liquid seen in the title shot. A ghostly face, the "Plutonian, Scorpio ghost figure" Jamal, emerges from the waters.

A scene later in the film depicts an intimate party. A couple makes out on a leather couch. People mill about. Labeija looks around, a little alienated but looking intent and curious. Jamal appears again, fully made up here and dancing. They reach out their hand to Labeija in invitation and they dance. They dance through the night in the blue and pink lights. The music becomes more bass heavy and she is taken by the music. She is smiling and dancing. Then we are brought back into the reality of the initial bath. Egyptt emerges from the deep and milky, as if newly reborn. We are back at the rooftop of the Whitney overlooking the piers. Egyptt Labeija's hand raised as if to fashion herself victorious. A new beacon over the waters of the Atlantic. A more whole Liberty. The credits roll.

Tourmaline's film wades through everpresent modes of Black trans bodily extraction and exploitation—to a watery interior of otherwise possibility and becoming in which elders enliven and support new generations and new generations return in kind in that diasporic knowing of circular time. It takes up moments of alienation and deep intimacy to reflect what it means to be in constant unfolding. To begin at the memory of destruction and ending of worlds that the Atlantic represents—a sea of the bones of Africans meant to be enslaved—to the temporary refuge of Egyptt Labeija on the piers where she presently in the film overlooks, or as Lucille Clifton writes, "my elegant afrikans / connecting whydah and new york, / a bridge of ivory"[17] to the artist Tourmaline herself filming Egyptt Labeija with this futuristic story that really tells of a vibrant present and a subjugated past of Black trans becoming is to document the circularity of Black diasporic time and self-centered (in the Quashian sense) subjectivity/oneness which crosses status of elder and younger, past and present, now and forever.

I hope that you realize by now that the weight of considering the ocean in this manner is not lost on me. It is an existential body that continues to confound but it is that confounding in which affective sedulity finds something to sink into. As if to attempt to map the way back home through the ocean as Dionne Brand does in *A Map to the Door of No Return*—a sedulous look into the feeling of belonging. "Too much has been made of origins," she repeats, finding the Door of No Return as illusive as its name—and thus the way of getting there is an existential quest for belonging anywhere in diaspora. The map which depicts and makes sense of oceans and the existential quest "is only a life of conversations about a forgotten list of irretrievable selves."[18] And so to travel without a map is to "travel without a way." The map so often failing us, "a set of impossibilities, a set of changing locations." Brand reminds us that this way making without the map has been done before—"misdirection became the way."

Your, methods, your questions, the answers they invite. How that feel?

Perhaps these interventions on knowledge will find special use as we experience the effects of climate catastrophe, the increasing damage to our environment, the seemingly limitless privatization of natural resources that enriches the very few. I don't find it hyperbolic to say that perhaps we need another system—another way of knowing and yet another way of knowing what we know. Here, I am talking about methods, forms, processes, and yes, rituals. Ways of knowing that try other senses. If rising sea levels are upon us, then Black feminist oceanographics might just assist us since it grapples with the paradox of being forced to live where we cannot breathe.

Notes

INTRODUCTION

1 Ntozake Shange, *The Lizard Series*, 67/100 of a limited-edition, self-published chapbook, 2007, 12.

2 Nina Simone, "Why? (The King of Love Is Dead)," *'Nuff Said*, RCA Victor LSP-4065, 1968, compact disc.

3 Ellen Brown, "Writing Is Third Career for Morrison," *Cincinnati Enquirer*, September 27, 1981, sec. F-11.

4 Lisa Gail Collins, "'The Evidence of the Process,'" *Transition*, no. 109 (2012): 57, https://doi.org/10.2979/transition.109.45.

5 Roy DeCarava, *Edna Smith*, 1955. The photograph may be viewed at https://www.moma.org/collection/works/50486 or https://www.phillips.com/detail /roy-decarava/NY040317/38. The photograph is also included in a MOMA catalog. Peter Galassi, *Roy DeCarava: A Retrospective* (New York: Museum of Modern Art, 1996), 107.

6 D. Antoinette Handy, *Black Women in American Bands and Orchestras* (Lanham, MD: Scarecrow Press, 1998), 108.

7 A more in-depth comparative reading of these two images and how they fashion Fuller as a member of the so-called Talented Tenth is availble in Renée Ater's book on Fuller's ouevre, *Remaking Race and History: The Sculpture of Meta Warrick Fuller* (Berkeley: University of California Press, 2011), 29.

8 Audre Lorde, *Sister Outsider: Essays and Speeches* (Berkeley, CA: Crossing Press, 1984), 39.

9 Patricia Ticineto Clough, introduction to *The Affective Turn: Theorizing the Social*, ed. Jean O'Malley Halley and Patricia Ticineto Clough (Durham, NC: Duke University Press, 2007), 1.

10 Clough, 3.

11 Lorde, *Sister Outsider*, 37.

12 Angela Y. Davis, *Blues Legacies and Black Feminism: Gertrude "Ma" Rainey, Bessie Smith, and Billie Holiday* (New York: Pantheon Books, 1998), xiii.

13 Dian Million, "Felt Theory: An Indigenous Feminist Approach to Affect and History," *Wicazo Sa Review* 24, no. 2 (October 8, 2009): 54, https://doi.org/10.1353/wic.0.0043.

14 Lorde, *Sister Outsider*, 53.

15 Barbara Christian, "The Race for Theory," *Cultural Critique*, no. 6 (1987): 51, https://doi.org/10.2307/1354255.

16 Christian, 52.

17 bell hooks, *Teaching to Transgress* (New York: Routledge, 1994), 61.

18 hooks, 75.

19 Geneva Smitherman, *Black Talk: Words and Phrases from the Hood to the Amen Corner* (Boston: Houghton Mifflin, 2000), 222.

20 Geneva Smitherman, *Talkin and Testifyin: The Language of Black America* (Detroit: Wayne State University Press, 1986), 19.

21 Kevin Quashie, "To Be (a) One: Notes on Coupling and Black Female Audacity," *Differences: A Journal of Feminist Cultural Studies* 29, no. 2 (2018): 72, https://doi.org /10.1215/10407391-6999774.

22 "Feel, v.," in *OED Online* (Oxford University Press), accessed March 3, 2020, http://www.oed.com/view/Entry/68977; "Feeling, n.," in *OED Online* (Oxford University Press), accessed March 3, 2020, http://www.oed.com/view/Entry/68981; "Feeling, adj.," in *OED Online* (Oxford University Press), accessed March 3, 2020, http://www.oed.com /view/Entry/68982.

23 As Smitherman would say, "The African cultural set persists, that is, a predisposition to imbue the English word with the same sense of value and commitment—'propers,' as we would say—accorded to Nommo [Malian ancestral spirits] in African culture." Smitherman, *Talkin and Testifyin*, 79.

24 Claude Brown, "The Language of Soul," in *Mother Wit from the Laughing Barrel: Readings in the Interpretation of Afro-American Folklore*, ed. Alan Dundes (Englewood Cliffs, NJ: Prentice-Hall, 1973), 230.

25 Brown, 234.

26 Avery Gordon, *Ghostly Matters: Haunting and the Sociological Imagination* (Minneapolis: University of Minnesota Press, 1997), 8.

27 M. Jacqui Alexander, *Pedagogies of Crossing: Meditations on Feminism, Sexual Politics, Memory, and the Sacred* (Durham, NC: Duke University Press, 2005), 299.

28 Alexander, 309.

29 Alexander, 310.

30 Alexander, 311.

31 Nikky Finney, "The Clitoris," in *Head Off & Split: Poems* (Northwestern University Press, Evanston, IL: 2011), 56.

32 Evelynn Hammonds, "Black (w)Holes and the Geometry of Black Female Sexuality," *Differences* 6, no. 2–3 (Summer 1994): 138; Darlene Clark Hine, "Rape and the Inner Lives of Black Women in the Middle West," *Signs* 14, no. 4 (1989): 192; Hortense J. Spillers, "Intersticies: A Small Drama of Words," in *Black, White, and in Color: Essays on American Literature and Culture* (Chicago: University of Chicago Press, 2003), 153.

33 Take for instance Hammond's assertion, "Rather than assuming that black female sexualities are structured along an axis of normal and perverse paralleling that of white women, we might find that for black women a different geometry operates." Hammonds, "Black (w)Holes and the Geometry of Black Female Sexuality," 139.

34 L. H. Stallings describes funky erotixxx as "unknowable and immeasurable, with transgenerational, affective, and psychic modalities that problematize the erotic and what it means to be human, and it can be made legible in sexual cultures rather than the biopolitics or necropolitics of asexual cultures." L. H. Stallings, *Funk the Erotic: Transaesthetics and Black Sexual Cultures* (Urbana: University of Illinois Press, 2015), xv.

35 Hammonds, "Black (w)Holes and the Geometry of Black Female Sexuality," 141.

36 "Pleasure, n.," in *OED Online* (Oxford University Press, 2017), https://www.oed.com /view/Entry/145578 (emphasis mine).

37 Amber Jamilla Musser, *Sensational Flesh: Race, Power, and Masochism* (New York: New York University Press, 2014), 156, http://muse.jhu.edu/book/36064.

38 Debra Walker King, *African Americans and the Culture of Pain* (Charlottesville: University of Virginia Press, 2008), 17.

39 Sara Ahmed argues that feminists identify pain and thus the way one would move away from physical pain is to create move(ment) away from it. Sara Ahmed, *The Cultural Politics of Emotion* (New York: Routledge, 2013), 173.

40 Rebecca Wanzo, *The Suffering Will Not Be Televised: African American Women and Sentimental Political Storytelling* (Albany: State University of New York Press, 2009), 2.

41 Bettina Judd, *patient.* (New York: Black Lawrence Press, 2014).

42 Hine, "Rape and the Inner Lives of Black Women in the Middle West," 912.

43 Jennifer C. Nash, *The Black Body in Ecstasy: Reading Race, Reading Pornography* (Durham, NC: Duke University Press, 2014), 149.

44 Musser, *Sensational Flesh*, 1.

45 Stallings, *Funk the Erotic*, 2015, xv.

46 Black studies has long illuminated the role of the Enlightenment in producing the European human as the universal human and thus, the black African as oppositional to this human subject. As Sylvia Wynter notes, the production of genres of man fictively constructs Black peoples as the "embodiment of ultimate Human Otherness to Man(2)." Rational thought would be so defined by the supremacy of the mind, and rational thought as it related to the human would be in opposition to the body or what Hortense Spillers would observe: flesh. As Alexander Weheliye notes, ". . . black subjectivity appears as the antithesis to the Enlightenment subject by virtue of not only having a body but by being the body—within Enlightenment discourses blackness is the body and nothing else." The issue to which Stallings attends is the way that the body and its sensualities would come to define Black folks/human otherness and Black folks' otherwise knowledge and experience of sexual pleasure. Sylvia Wynter, "The Ceremony Found: Towards the Autopoetic Turn/ Overturn, Its Autonomy of Human Agency and Extraterritoriality of (Self-)Cognition," in *Black Knowledges/Black Struggles: Essays in Critical Epistemology*, 196; Hortense J. Spillers, "Mama's Baby, Papa's Maybe: An American Grammar Book," *Diacritics* 17, no. 2 (1987): 67; Alexander Weheliye, "'Feenin: Posthuman Voices in Contemporary Black Popular Music," *Social Text* 20, no. 2 (June 1, 2002): 28.

47 Stallings, 19.

48 Stallings, 10.

49 Stallings, 6.

50 Patricia Hill Collins, "Comment on Hekman's 'Truth and Method: Feminist Standpoint Theory Revisited': Where's the Power?," *Signs* 22, no. 2 (1997): 381.

51 Sandra Harding, "Comment on Hekman's 'Truth and Method: Feminist Standpoint Theory Revisited': Whose Standpoint Needs the Regimes of Truth and Reality?," *Signs* 22, no. 2 (1997): 383.

52 Patricia Hill Collins, *Black Feminist Thought: Knowledge, Consciousness, and the Politics of Empowerment* (New York: Routledge, 2008), 14.

53 Collins, 9.

54 Collins, 98.

55 Barbara Smith, *The Truth That Never Hurts* (New Brunswick, NJ: Rutgers University Press, 1999), 4.

56 Smith, 6.

57 Daphne Brooks, *Liner Notes for the Revolution: The Intellectual Life of Black Feminist Sound* (Cambridge, MA: The Belknap Press of Harvard University Press, 2021), 3.

58 Marjorie Pryse, "Introduction: Zora Neale Hurston, Alice Walker, and the 'Ancient Power' of Black Women," in *Conjuring: Black Women, Fiction, and Literary Tradition*, ed. Marjorie Pryse and Hortense Spillers (Bloomington: Indiana University Press, 1985), 3.

59 Farah Jasmine Griffin, "That the Mothers May Soar and the Daughters May Know Their Names: A Retrospective of Black Feminist Literary Criticism," *Signs* 32, no. 2 (2007): 483, https://doi.org/10.1086/508377; Alice Walker, *In Search of Our Mother's Gardens: Womanist Prose* (San Diego, CA: Harcourt Brace Jovanovich, 1983).

60 Mary Helen Washington, *Invented Lives: Narratives of Black Women, 1860–1960* (New York: Doubleday, 1987), xxi.

61 Washington, xxi.

62 Deborah McDowell, *"The Changing Same": Black Women's Literature, Criticism, and Theory* (Bloomington: Indiana University Press, 1995), 23.

63 Hortense J. Spillers, "A Hateful Passion, a Lost Love," *Feminist Studies* 9, no. 2 (1983): 294, https://doi.org/10.2307/3177494.

64 Spillers, 295.

65 Quoted in Teresa Brevard, "'Will the Circle Be Unbroken': African-American Women's Spirituality in Sacred Song Traditions.," in *My Soul Is a Witness: African-American Women's Spirituality*, ed. Gloria Wade-Gayles (Boston: Beacon Press, 1995), 36.

66 Marsha Houston and Olga Idriss Davis, *Centering Ourselves: African American Feminist and Womanist Studies of Discourse* (Cresskill, NJ: Hampton Press, 2002), 92.

67 In the last lines of her posthumously published *To Be Young, Gifted, and Black*, Lorraine Hansberry writes: "If anything should happen—before 'tis done—may I trust that all commas and periods will be placed and someone will complete my thoughts—This last should be the least difficult—since there are so many who think as I do." Lorraine Hansberry, *To Be Young, Gifted, and Black: A Portrait of Lorraine Hansberry in Her Own Words*, ed. Robert Nemiroff (New York: Signet, 1970), 265.

68 Notably, liner notes are scarcer now that music is often purchased and downloaded over the internet. The National Academy of Recording Arts and Sciences has noticed this trend and has launched a campaign called "Give Fans the Credit" that allows fans to see liner notes.

69 Musser, *Sensational Flesh*, 22.

70 Germán Toro-Pérez, "On the Difference Between Artistic Research and Artistic Practice," in *Art and Artistic Research. Music, Visual Art, Design, Literature, Dance*, ed. Corina Caduff, Fiona Siegenthaler, and Tan Wälchli (Zurich: Zurich University of the Arts, 2010), 34.

71 Audre Lorde, "Poetry Is Not a Luxury," in *Sister Outsider*, 39.

72 Graeme Sullivan, *Art Practice as Research: Inquiry in Visual Arts*, 2nd ed. (Thousand Oaks, CA: Sage Publications, 2010), 174.

73 Gloria Anzaldúa, *Borderlands/La Frontera: The New Mestiza* (San Francisco: Aunt Lute Books, 1987), 101.

74 I am grateful for this insight into the structure of Bridgeforth's "scriptwriting by experience." In the fall of 2012 at Hampshire College, I was able to participate in a performance reading of her play *Bloodpudding*. Bearing witness to her creative process as director allowed me to see how varied text and text shape on the page may represent multiple characters on the stage. Nothing, not even the number of characters presented in the text, was fixed. The performance took the shape of the actors and singers who came to participate. Here, in my placement of text and invocation of myriad voices and modes of writing, I find that instructive.

75 Lucille Clifton, "I'd Like Not to Be a Stranger in the World: A Conversation/Interview with Lucille Clifton," interview by Michael S. Glaser, *Antioch Review* 58, no. 3 (Summer 2000): 325.

76 Gail Pellett, dir., *The Songs Are Free: Bernice Johnson Reagon and African American Music*, with Bill D. Moyers, Sweet Honey in the Rock, and Freedom Singers; Public Affairs Television, aired on PBS, 1991. Distributed by Films for the Humanities and Sciences, Princeton, NJ, 1997.

77 Denise Ferreira da Silva, "Toward a Black Feminist Poethics: The Quest(ion) of Blackness Toward the End of the World," *Black Scholar* 44, no. 2 (2014): 84.

78 June Jordan, "Some of Us Did Not Die," in *Some of Us Did Not Die: New and Selected Essays* (New York: Basic Books, 2003), 8.

79 Angela Y. Davis, *Freedom Is a Constant Struggle: Ferguson, Palestine, and the Foundations of a Movement* (Chicago: Haymarket Books, 2016), 147.

80 Nikky Finney, "The Making of Paper," in *The World Is Round* (Atlanta, GA: InnerLight Publishing, 2003), 98.

81 Finney, 100.

82 Audre Lorde, "Uses of the Erotic, the Erotic as Power," in *Sister Outsider*, 56.

CHAPTER 1

1 Claudia Rankine titles an essay on racial violence with a quote from a friend, "The condition of Black life is one of mourning." Claudia Rankine, "The Condition of Black Life Is One of Mourning," *New York Times*, June 22, 2015, sec. Magazine, https://www.nytimes.com /2015/06/22/magazine/the-condition-of-black-life-is-one-of-mourning.html.

2 Barbara Christian, "The Race for Theory," *Cultural Critique*, no. 6 (1987): 52. https://doi .org/10.2307/1354255.

3 Sharpe describes "wake work" as new ways of "plotting, mapping, and collecting the archives of the everyday of Black immanent and imminent death" as well as "tracking the ways we resist, rupture, and disrupt that immanence and imminence aesthetically and materially." In that spirit, this chapter does not "seek to explain or resolve" the structure of grief for a Black collective, but simply grieves and tarries with other studies of grief and grieving. Christina Sharpe, *In the Wake: On Blackness and Being* (Durham, NC: Duke University Press, 2016), 13, 14.

4 Saidiya V. Hartman, *Wayward Lives, Beautiful Experiments: Intimate Histories of Social Upheaval* (New York: W. W. Norton, 2019); Alexis Pauline Gumbs, *M Archive: After the End of the World* (Durham, NC: Duke University Press, 2018).

5 Leroi Jones [Amiri Baraka], *Blues People: Negro Music in White America* (New York: Harper Perennial, 1999), 28, 60.

6 George Clinton and Ben Greenman, *Brothas Be, Yo Like George, Ain't That Funkin' Kinda Hard on You?: A Memoir* (New York: Simon and Schuster, 2017), 103; italics mine.

7 Raymond Williams, "Structures of Feeling," in *Marxism and Literature* (Oxford: Oxford University Press, 1977), 132.

8 Mamie Till-Mobley and Christopher Benson, *Death of Innocence: The Story of the Hate Crime That Changed America* (New York: Random House, 2011), 247.

9 Saidiya Hartman, *Lose Your Mother: A Journey Along the Atlantic Slave Route* (New York: Macmillan, 2008), 155.

10 Hartman, 155.

11 See also Rae Paris's poetic collection that takes up the site-specific aspect of rememory. Rae Paris, *The Forgetting Tree: A Rememory* (Detroit: Wayne State University Press, 2017).

12 Toni Morrison, *Beloved* (New York: Knopf, 2007), 43.

13 Alexander, *Pedagogies of Crossing: Meditations on Feminism, Sexual Politics, Memory, and the Sacred*, 309.

14 Karla FC Holloway, *Passed On: African American Mourning Stories, A Memorial* (Durham, NC: Duke University Press, 2003), 9.

15 Holloway, 70.

16 Anne Anlin Cheng, *The Melancholy of Race: Psychoanalysis, Assimilation, and Hidden Grief* (Oxford: Oxford University Press, 2001), 170.

17 Cheng, 174.

18 Cheng states: "A fundamental relationship has been set up between identification and the compensation of loss. As such, identification may in fact be said to be, literally, an *expression* of grief." Cheng, 178.

19 Rhaisa Kameelah Williams, "Toward a Theorization of Black Maternal Grief as Analytic," *Transforming Anthropology* 24, no. 1 (2016): 19, https://doi.org/10.1111/traa.12057.

20 Williams, 22.

21 Tina M. Campt, *Listening to Images* (Durham, NC: Duke University Press, 2017), 114.

22 Gumbs, *M Archive*, 100.

23 Jared Sexton, "Afro-Pessimism: The Unclear Word," *Rhizomes: Cultural Studies in Emerging Knowlege*, no. 29 (2016): 18, http://www.rhizomes.net/issue29/sexton.html.

24 Harriet Ann Jacobs, *Incidents in the Life of a Slave Girl* (New York: Skyhorse Publishing, 1861), 129.

25 C. Riley Snorton, *Black on Both Sides: A Racial History of Trans Identity* (Minneapolis: University of Minnesota Press, 2017), xiv.

26 Toni Morrison, *Song of Solomon* (New York: Vintage International, 2004), 319.

27 Sharpe, *In the Wake*; Jericho Brown, *The Tradition* (Port Townsend, WA: Copper Canyon Press, 2019); Claudia Rankine, *Citizen: An American Lyric* (Minneapolis: Graywolf, 2014).

28 Sharon Patricia Holland, *Raising the Dead: Readings of Death and (Black) Subjectivity* (Durham, NC: Duke University Press, 2000), 181.

29 Layli Maparyan, *The Womanist Idea* (New York: Routledge, 2012), 291.

30 Dagmawi Woubshet, *The Calendar of Loss: Race, Sexuality, and Mourning in the Early Era of AIDS* (Baltimore: Johns Hopkins University Press, 2015), 3, 34, http://ebookcentral .proquest.com/lib/washington/detail.action?docID=3318887.

31 Tiffany Austin et al., *Revisiting the Elegy in the Black Lives Matter Era* (New York: Routledge, 2019).

32 William Edward Burghardt Du Bois, *The Souls of Black Folk: Essays and Sketches* (Chicago: A. C. McClurg & Company, 1903), 207.

33 From Nell's moments while thinking of her friend, Sula. Toni Morrison, *Sula* (New York: Knopf, 2007), 155.

34 Woubshet, *The Calendar of Loss*, 3.

35 Katherine McKittrick, "Mathematics Black Life," *Black Scholar* 44, no. 2 (2014): 17.

36 Sharpe, *In the Wake*, 13.

37 Alexander, *Pedagogies of Crossing*, 289.

38 Saidiya V. Hartman, "The Time of Slavery," *South Atlantic Quarterly* 101, no. 4 (2002): 758.

39 Holland, *Raising the Dead*, 34.

40 Holland, 35.

41 Sharpe, *In the Wake*, 7.

42 Holloway, *Passed On*, 212.

43 Christina Sharpe describes weather as "antiblackness as total climate." Sharpe, *In the Wake*, 105.

44 Solimar Otero and Toyin Falola, *Yemoja: Gender, Sexuality, and Creativity in the Latina/o and Afro-Atlantic Diasporas* (Albany: State University of New York Press, 2013), xix, http://ebookcentral.proquest.com/lib/washington/detail.action?docID=3408785.

45 Olive Senior, "Yemoja: Mother of Waters," *Conjunctions*, no. 27 (1996): 58.

46 Ella E. Clark, *Indian Legends of the Pacific Northwest* (Berkeley: University of California Press, 2003), 199, https://doi.org/10.1525/9780520350960.

47 There are various versions of this legend. I was first introduced to the story through a 2015 film by Longhouse Media in conjunction with the tribute to Kʷʔkwálʔlwʔt erected at Rosario Beach in Anacortes, Washington, Coast Salish lands (Longhouse Media, *Maiden of Deception Pass: Guardian of Her Samish People*, https://vimeo.com/130576433). See also Brent Douglas Galloway, *Phonology, Morphology, and Classified Word List for the Samish Dialect of Straits Salish* (Ottawa: University of Ottawa Press, 1990), 100–115, http://muse.jhu.edu/book/65590; Kenneth C. Hansen, *The Maiden of Deception Pass: A Spirit in Cedar* (Anacortes, WA: Samish Experience Productions, 1983); Clark, *Indian Legends of the Pacific Northwest*, 199–201.

CHAPTER 2

1 This passage is an excerpt from my remembrances of Clifton, given at a community gathering in her honor at the Enoch Pratt Library in Baltimore in June 2010. When the master of ceremonies, poet Reginald Harris, welcomed guests and introduced the poets, he began with his own reflection on Clifton's "joy!" It was fortuitous (but not coincidental) that my own reflection, my biggest lesson from Ms. Clifton, was this very concept.

2 Lucille Clifton, "in the mirror," in *Mercy* (Rochester, NY: BOA Editions Ltd., 2004), 27.

3 Clifton, 27.

4 This chapter references the King James Version of the Bible for literary purposes and the New Revised Standard Version for the purposes of interpreting biblical text alongside theological discourse here cited. I use the KJV here in line with Clifton's own writing, which references this version of the Bible. See James 1:2.

5 Lucille Clifton, "prayer," in *Good News About the Earth: New Poems* (New York: Random House, 1972), 14.

6 Ashon T. Crawley, *Blackpentecostal Breath: The Aesthetics of Possibility*, Commonalities (New York: Fordham University Press, 2016), 7.

7 Lucille Clifton, "I'd Like Not to Be a Stranger in the World: A Conversation/Interview with Lucille Clifton," *Antioch Review* 58, no. 3 (Summer 2000): 310–28.

8 Avery Gordon, *Ghostly Matters: Haunting and the Sociological Imagination* (Minneapolis: University of Minnesota Press, 2008), 4, http://muse.jhu.edu/book/27669; Patricia J. Williams, *The Alchemy of Race and Rights* (Cambridge, MA: Harvard University Press, 1991), 10, http://hdl.handle.net/2027/mdp.49015001280453.

9 This line is from Lucille Clifton, "won't you celebrate with me," in *The Book of Light* (Port Townsend, WA: Copper Canyon Press, 1993), 25.

10 Yes, even though she was raised Baptist. Crawley, *Blackpentecostal Breath*, 7.

11 Clifton, "won't you celebrate with me," 25.

12 In a video that is part of the Lannan Literary Series, featuring readings and a discussion with Quincy Troupe, Clifton prefaces her reading of this poem by saying, "I would like to close this reading part of the evening with this poem, which is something of a celebration poem for me, something of a signature poem. I wrote it for myself but then I discovered that it applied to so many people. To even places. It applied on a large scale as well as an individual, personal one." Dan Griggs (Media Revolution), dir., *Lannan Foundation: Lucille Clifton* (Los Angeles, 1996).

13 While I recognize all facets of her work are important to understanding Clifton's atheology of joy, this chapter does exclude some important texts that make up the entirety of her life's work but beg for further research and study. These include her children's books—particularly the Everett Anderson series—and her Emmy Award–winning writing for television. While the absence of this aspect of her creative work can be seen as a shortcoming of this particular study, I consider it a call to other scholars in literature and visual culture to take up the important writings that Lucille Clifton has left for us to consider.

14 Crawley, *Blackpentecostal Breath*, 12.

15 Clifton describes her spiritual practice and herself as a natural channel in conversation with Akasha Hull. I write more about Clifton's spiritual practice later in this chapter. Gloria T. Hull, *Soul Talk: The New Spirituality of African American Women* (Rochester, VT: Inner Traditions, 2001), 58; Crawley goes on to characterize theological and philosophical thought in these terms. Crawley, *Blackpentecostal Breath*, 12.

16 Tiffany Lethabo King identifies the required violence of "genocide, mutilation, displacement, and the negation of Black and Indigenous peoples and their ways of living" that maintain the idea of the human in her pivotal book *The Black Shoals*. Tiffany Lethabo King, *The Black Shoals: Offshore Formations of Black and Native Studies* (Durham, NC: Duke University Press, 2019), 53.

17 James Haba, David Grubin, and Bill D. Moyers, *The Language of Life : A Festival of Poets* (New York: Doubleday, 1995), 84.

18 Kelly Brown Douglas, *The Black Christ* (Maryknoll, NY: Orbis Books, 1993), 109.

19 Lucille Clifton, "An Interview with Lucille Clifton," by Charles H. Rowell, *Callaloo* 22, no. 1 (Winter 1999), 61. Hereafter, "An Interview with Lucille Clifton."

20 In a conversation about her book *Thomas and Beulah*, Dove discusses the factual differences between her poems and the biographical history of her grandparents—beginning with her grandmother's name. She says the following: "There were lesser challenges—a challenge, for instance, to decide how much was going to be strictly autobiographical and at what point to begin to invent, and I began to invent very early. And once that barrier was over, it was fine. I mean invent in a sense that, for instance, my grandmother's name was not Beulah, it was Georgianna. That was a decision I made—an aesthetic decision, actually—because Georgianna, though it's a wonderful name, was first of all too male-based for me, and second of all didn't have the Biblical connotations that I wanted for the book. Also, it's a long name, and a very difficult name to fit on a line. So once I broke through that, I didn't have to be absolutely faithful according to biographical truth. I could go after an inner truth. That freed me." Grace Cavalieri, "Rita Dove: An Interview," *American Poetry Review* 24, no. 2 (1995): 11.

21 The editors of *This Bridge Called My Back*, Gloria Anzaldúa and Cherríe Moraga, describe "theory in the flesh" as the contradictions of their existence made manifest in the writing of radical women of color. They state: "A theory in the flesh means one where the physical realities of our lives—our skin color, the land or concrete we grew up on, our sexual longings—all fuse to create a politic born out of necessity." Gloria Anzaldúa and Cherríe Moraga, eds., *This Bridge Called My Back :Writings by Radical Women of Color* (Albany: State University of New York Press, 2015), 19, http://hdl.handle.net/2027/hvd.32044133774174.

22 "An Interview with Lucille Clifton," 61.

23 Clifton makes this comment about the antecedent to her poetry in conversation with Quincy Troupe in *Lannan Foundation: Lucille Clifton*.

24 In numerous interviews Clifton discusses that she is a very spiritual person but not religious, as she did not attend any church. See Lucille Clifton, "Between Starshine and Clay: An Interview with Lucille Clifton and Remica Bingham," *Writers Chronicle* 43, no. 4 (February 2011): 12; Lucille Clifton, "Her Last Interview, with Chard DeNiord," *American Poetry Review* 39, no. 3 (June 2010): 6; "An Interview with Lucille Clifton," 67.

25 Clifton, "Her Last Interview, with Chard DeNiord," 5.

26 I write at length about Clifton's automatic writing process evidenced in her papers. See Bettina Judd, "GLOSSOLALIA: Lucille Clifton's Creative Technologies of Becoming," in *Black Bodies and Transhuman Realities: Scientifically Modifying the Black Body in Posthuman Literature and Culture*, ed. Melvin G. Hill (Lanham: Lexington Books, 2019), 133–49. Further, a history of automatic writing may be found in Diane Dearmont, "Automatic Writing: A History from Mesmer to Breton" (PhD diss., University of Washington, 2004), http://search.proquest.com.proxy.wm.edu/docview/305106649/abstract.

27 I use brackets to note when the writing is barely legible or undecipherable. Lucille Clifton, "Spirit Writing, 1977," Stuart A. Rose Manuscript, Archives, and Rare Book Library, Emory University. Box 30, Folder 1.

28 Clifton, "Spirit Writing, 1977."

29 Remica Bingham, "Finding the Myth in the Human and the Human in the Myth: Midrash and Mythos in the Work of Lucille Clifton," *Langston Hughes Review* 22 (Fall 2008): 27.

30 Gen. 3:17, NRSV.

31 As Sylvia Wynter notes, this new formulation of the human relies on the logic of medieval Christianity as counternarrative; the concept of the man of the flesh that is mythologized in Adam's fall morphs into a man whose flesh is second to the innate power of his mind. Sylvia Wynter, "The Ceremony Must Be Found: After Humanism," *Boundary 2* 12/13 [vol. 12, no. 3 and vol. 13, no. 1] (Spring–Autumn 1984): 29, https://doi.org/10.2307/302808.

32 As Nyasha Junior discusses, there is a legacy of intepretations of the mark of Cain being the darkening of skin. Such interpretations, she argues, have been used to legitimize slavery. However, Junior argues for a counternarrative of this history among Black interpreters that purported that the mark of Cain was the whitnening of skin, and moreover, a sign of white violence. Nyasha Junior, "The Mark of Cain and White Violence," *Journal of Biblical Literature* 139, no. 4 (2020): 661, http://dx.doi.org/10.15699/jbl.1394.2020.2.

33 James Weldon Johnson, *God's Trombones: Seven Negro Sermons in Verse*, electronic edition (Chapel Hill: University of North Carolina at Chapel Hill Libraries, 2004), 17, http://docsouth.unc.edu/southlit/johnson/menu.html.

34 Johnson, 20.

35 I use they/he pronouns interchangeably for Lucifer, due to their shapeshifting qualities and to honor the way that he merges with Clifton as the "Lucifer in Lucille."

36 Lucille Clifton, "oh lucifer where have you fallen to," in *Quilting: Poems, 1987–1990* (Rochester, NY: BOA Editions, Ltd., 1991), 71.

37 Lucifer is referred to as the son of the dawn or the day star in Isaiah 14:12.

38 Clifton, "oh where have you fallen to," 71.

39 Isa. 14:3-27, NRSV.

40 Clifton, "oh where have you fallen to," 71.

41 Clifton, 71.

42 Clifton, 71.

43 Lucille Clifton, "remembering the birth of lucifer," in *Quilting*, 72.

44 Clifton, 72.

45 Lucille Clifton, "whispered to lucifer," in *Quilting*, 73.

46 Clifton, 73.

47 Clifton, 73.

48 Lucille Clifton, "lucifer understanding at last," in *Quilting*, 75.

49 Clifton, 75.

50 Lucille Clifton, "the garden of delight," in *Quilting*, 76.

51 Lucille Clifton, "eve thinking," in *Quilting*, 78.

52 Lucille Clifton, "eve's version," in *Quilting*, 74.

53 Clifton, 74.

54 Lucille Clifton, "the story thus far," in *Quilting*, 79.

55 Clifton, 79.

56 Lucille Clifton, "the road led from delight," in *The Book of Light* (Port Townsend, WA: Copper Canyon Press, 1993), 73.

57 Toni Morrison, *The Bluest Eye* (New York: Alfred A. Knopf, 1993), 83; Susan Willis describes "eruptions of funk" in Toni Morrison's work as markers in which alternative social worlds come into being. Susan Willis, "Eruptions of Funk: Historicizing Toni Morrison," *African American Review* 50, no. 4 (Winter 2017): 689.

58 Lucille Clifton, "lucifer speaks in his own voice," in *Quilting*, 80.

59 Clifton, 80.

60 Clifton, 80.

61 James H Cone, *God of the Oppressed* (New York: Seabury Press, 1975), 177.

62 Delores S. Williams, "Black Women's Surrogacy Experience and the Christian Notion of Redemption," in *After Patriarchy: Feminist Transformations of the World Religions*, ed. Paula M. Cooey, William R. Eakin, and Jay B. McDaniel (Maryknoll, NY: Orbis Books, 1991), 13.

63 Douglas, *The Black Christ*, 114.

64 Douglas, 98.

65 William R. Jones, *Is God a White Racist? A Preamble to Black Theology* (Boston: Beacon Press, 1998), 187; Anthony B. Pinn, *Why, Lord? Suffering and Evil in Black Theology* (New York: Continuum, 1995), 157.

66 Lucille Clifton, "invitation," in *The Book of Light*, 69.

67 This is in reference to the original version found in *The Book of Light*.

68 Clifton, "invitation," 69.

69 Lucille Clifton, "how great thou art," in *The Book of Light*, 70.

70 Clifton, 70.

71 Clifton, 70.

72 Clifton, 70.

73 Cheryl A. Kirk-Duggan, *Exorcizing Evil: A Womanist Perspective on the Spirituals*, Vol. 14, Bishop Henry McNeal Turner/Sojourner Truth Series in Black Religion (Maryknoll, NY: Orbis Books, 1997), 39.

74 Kirk-Duggan, 41.

75 Lucille Clifton, "as for myself," in *The Book of Light*, 71.

76 Clifton, 71.

77 Clifton, 71.

78 Clifton, 71.

79 Clifton, 71.

80 C. Riley Snorton, *Black on Both Sides: A Racial History of Trans Identity* (Minneapolis: University of Minnesota Press, 2017), 53. Snorton begins this chapter on the history of gynecology with J. Marion Sims's claim that suffering is inherent and inevitable for women.

81 Clifton, "the story thus far," 79.

82 Lucille Clifton, "in my own defense," in *The Book of Light*, 72.

83 Clifton, 72.

84 Clifton, 72.

85 Lucille Clifton, "the silence of God is God," in *The Book of Light*, 74.

86 Gen. 1:3, NRSV.

87 Carolyn Forché, "The Angel of History," in *The Angel of History* (New York: HarperCollins, 1994), 5, http://hdl.handle.net/2027/mdp.39015028871021.

88 Gen. 2:10–15, NRSV.

89 June Jordan says "To be honest, I expect apocalypse . . . But life itself compels optimism. It does not seem reasonable that the majority of the peoples of the world should, finally, lose joy, and rational justice, as a global experiment to be pursued and fiercely protected. It seems unreasonable that more than 400 million people, right now, struggle against hunger and starvation, even while there is arable earth aplenty to feed and nourish every one of us." June Jordan, *Some of Us Did Not Die: New and Selected Essays* (New York: Basic Books, 2003), 4.

90 Lucille Clifton, "the beginning of the end of the world," in *Quilting*, 43.

91 Clifton writes of her own capacity for cruelty: "when i wanted the roaches dead i wanted them dead / and i killed them. i took a broom to their country" in the poem that begins with "cruelty. don't talk to me about cruelty" Lucille Clifton, *Next: New Poems* (Brockport, NY: BOA Editions, Ltd., 1987), 27.

92 Clifton, "as for myself," 71.

93 Alexis Pauline Gumbs beautifully and rigorously considers the aftermath of the ending of this world through the work of M. Jacqui Alexander in her book *M Archive*. Pointing to the narrative of the beginning of the world at the time of the Fall, Gumbs postulates, "after tigris and euphrates got names it [so-called civilization, civilizing, those who would eventually call themselves human] became crass and territorial." Alexis Pauline Gumbs, *M Archive: After the End of the World*, 42.

94 Friedrich Wilhelm Nietzsche, *The Joyful Wisdom* ("La Gaya Scienza"), in *Complete Works, Volume Ten*, ed. Oscar Levy, trans. Paul V. Cohn and Thomas Common (Project Gutenberg, 2016), 168.

95 Charles H. Long, *Significations: Signs, Symbols, and Images in the Interpretation of Religion* (Philadelphia: Fortress Press, 1986), 58.

96 Wynter, "The Ceremony Must Be Found," 36.

97 Long, *Significations*, 61.

98 Long, 59.

99 See figure 10.

100 Kevin Quashie, *The Sovereignty of Quiet: Beyond Resistance in Black Culture* (New Brunswick, NJ: Rutgers University Press, 2012), 129.

101 Lucille Clifton, "still there is mercy, there is grace," in *The Book of Light*, 75.

102 Lucille Clifton, ". . . . . is God," in *The Book of Light*, 76.

103 Clifton, 76.

104 Clifton, 76.

105 Clifton, 76.

106 Psalms 46:10, NRSV.

107 Long, *Significations*, 62.

108 The poem says, "will i begin to cry?// if you do, you will cry forever." She also uses this line in an earlier version of the poem "grief," and in the Lannan reading of "in the meantime" says, "And I do understand that if one began to grieve for all of the possible one would . . . it would be overwhelming." Lucille Clifton, "Consulting the Book of Changes: Radiation," in *The Terrible Stories* (Rochester, NY: BOA Editions, Ltd., 1996), 23; *Lannan Foundation: Lucille Clifton* (1996).

109 Clifton talks to Rowell about wholeness and the capacity to be evil as well as good. The full quote is, "So as long as we don't see in ourselves the possibility of great good as well as great evil, as long as we think that bad stuff is done by some people who are sort of isolated and wear bad stuff T-shirts or something, we can't fight against it." "An Interview with Lucille Clifton," 62. See the section epigraph ("there's Lucifer in Lucille"). Hilary Holladay, *Wild Blessings: The Poetry of Lucille Clifton* (Baton Rouge : Louisiana State University Press, 2004), 188.

110 Kai M. Green and Treva Ellison, "Tranifest," *TSQ: Transgender Studies Quarterly* 1, no. 1–2 (May 2014): 223, https://doi.org/10.1215/23289252-2400082.

111 Calvin Warren, "Calling into Being: Tranifestation, Black Trans, and the Problem of Ontology," *TSQ: Transgender Studies Quarterly* 4, no. 2 (May 1, 2017): 270, https://doi.org /10.1215/23289252-3815057.

112 Clifton, "won't you celebrate with me," 25.

113 Erica Hunt and Dawn Lundy Martin, eds., *Letters to the Future: Black Women/Radical Writing* (Tucson, AZ: Kore Press, 2018), 17.

114 Alice Walker, *Possessing the Secret of Joy* (New York: Harcourt Brace Jovanovich, 1992), 279, http://hdl.handle.net/2027/mdp.39015025166359.

115 Drawn from the above quote by Dawn Lundy Martin. Martin reflects on Black women writing a future which requires a similar work around self-making and personhood. One in which Black women must imagine and create in the present when "disaster is the convention of the present state." Dawn Lundy Martin, "Introduction: Destructions of [The Yoke of It All]," in *Letters to the Future: Black Women/Radical Writing*, ed. Erica Hunt and Dawn Lundy Martin (Tucson, AZ: Kore Press, 2018), 17.

116 Clifton, "won't you celebrate with me," 25.

117 Clifton, 25.

118 Sylvia Wynter, "The Ceremony Found: Towards the Autopoetic Turn/Overturn, Its Autonomy of Human Agency and Extraterritoriality of (Self-)Cognition," in *Black Knowledges/Black Struggles, Essays in Critical Epistemology* (Liverpool, Eng.: Liverpool University Press, 2015), 193, http://www.jstor.org/stable/j.ctt1gn6bfp.12.

119 Alexander G. Weheliye, *Habeas Viscus: Racializing Assemblages, Biopolitics, and Black Feminist Theories of the Human* (Durham, NC: Duke University Press, 2014), 8.

120 Hortense J. Spillers, "Mama's Baby, Papa's Maybe: An American Grammar Book," *Diacritics* 17, no. 2 (1987): 80, https://doi.org/10.2307/464747.

121 Clifton, "won't you celebrate with me," 25.

122 Audre Lorde, "Litany for Survival," in *The Collected Poems of Audre Lorde* (New York: W. W. Norton, 2000), 256.

123 Clifton, "I'd Like Not to Be a Stranger in the World," 325.

124 Clifton, "Between Starshine and Clay," 11; "An Interview with Lucille Clifton," 67.

125 Lucille Clifton, "grief," in *Blessing the Boats: New and Selected Poems* (Rochester, NY: BOA Editions, Ltd., 2000), 30.

126 Clifton, 30.

127 Much could possibly be said in consideration of the biblical figure invoked here, Joseph as a metaphor for Black people abused by their siblings. Joseph, who has a coat of many colors, is rejected by his brothers—yet retains his divine birthright even after he is sold into slavery and becomes a prophet. Gen. 37–45, NRSV.

128 Clifton, "grief," 31.

129 "An Interview with Lucille Clifton," 61.

130 Clifton, "Between Starshine and Clay," *Lucille Clifton* (Lannam Foundation, 1996).

131 Clifton, "won't you celebrate with me," *The Book of Light*, 25.

CHAPTER 3

1 In this narrative, the voices of various vocal instructors I have had are in bold.

2 In her autobiography, Aretha Franklin makes note of the phrase "you peed" to extol someone for singing hard and well. The idea being that one sings so hard that they do, in fact, pee on themselves. "Singing far too hard, I also peed here and there in the early days; I quickly realized no one should sing that hard." Aretha Franklin and David Ritz, *From These Roots* (New York: Crown, 1999), 51.

3 Farah Jasmine Griffin, "When Malindy Sings: A Meditation on Black Women's Vocality," in *Uptown Conversation: The New Jazz Studies*, ed. Robert G. O'Meally, Brent Hayes Edwards, and Farah Jasmine Griffin (New York: Columbia University Press, 2004), 107, http://www.degruyter.com/doi/book/10.7312/omea12350.

4 Bernice Johnson Reagon, in Pellett, Gail, dir., *The Songs Are Free*.

5 Reagon, in *The Songs Are Free*.

6 Lorde, "Uses of the Erotic, the Erotic as Power," 53; Stallings, *Funk the Erotic*, 2015, 10.

7 Avery*Sunshine, interview by the author, Skype, November 4, 2012.

8 Lorde, "Uses of the Erotic, the Erotic as Power," 53.

9 Weheliye asks the question, "What new modes of thinking, being, listening, and becoming . . . are set in motion" by the sonic and the discourses of the sonic reproduced through technologies? "The answer," he intones, "sonic Afro-modernity." Alexander G Weheliye, *Phonographies: Grooves in Sonic Afro-Modernity* (Durham, NC: Duke University Press, 2005), 10, https://doi.org/10.2307/j.ctv125jh4w.

10 Phyl Garland, *The Sound of Soul* (Chicago: Henry Regnery Co, 1969), ii.

11 Garland, *The Sound of Soul*, iii.

12 Emily J. Lordi, *Black Resonance: Iconic Women Singers and African American Literature* (New Brunswick, NJ: Rutgers University Press, 2013), 7.

13 Lordi, 10.

14 Ed Pavlic notes that the album is a product of the live performance as well as a studio recording. Ed Pavlic, keynote address to *Aretha Franklin's Amazing Grace: From Watts to Detroit: A Two-Day Symposium Celebrating the Life of the Queen of Soul*. University of California Los Angeles, March 24 and 25, 2019, https://youtu.be/HV7X3rTXFfI; Aretha Franklin, *Amazing Grace*, Atlantic SD-2-906, 1972, vinyl LP 12″, 33 1/3 rpm; *Amazing Grace: Aretha Franklin*, Al's Records & Tapes Production, 2019, streaming audio, https://play.google.com/store/movies/details/Amazing_Grace.

15 Margo Perkins, "The Church of Aretha," in *My Soul Is a Witness: African-American Women's Spirituality; A Sourcebook*, ed. Gloria Jean Wade-Gayles (Boston: Beacon Press, 1995), 129.

16 What might be more accurate is that "Dr. Feelgood," as it appears on the album, is a mix of the performances between March 5 and 7, 1971. Aretha Franklin, *Aretha Franklin—Full Concert—03/07/71—Fillmore West (OFFICIAL)*, 2014, https://www.youtube.com/watch?v=Vyx34kgHGng; Aretha Franklin, *Aretha Franklin—Full Concert—03/06/71—Fillmore West (OFFICIAL)*, 2014, https://www.youtube.com/watch?v=bzOKVInJ8vc.

17 While there is an aspect of improvisation that likely did happen with this performance, the idiom of the trilling soprano as an accent for joyous celebration is consistent in gospel music and Baptist and Pentecostal styles of worship.

18 Emily J. Lordi, *The Meaning of Soul: Black Music and Resilience since the 1960s* (Durham, NC: Duke University Press, 2020), 89.

19 Ashon T. Crawley, *Blackpentecostal Breath: The Aesthetics of Possibility* (New York: Fordham University Press, 2016), 163.

20 Dennis Wiley, "Spirit in the Dark: Sexuality and Spirituality in the Black Church," in *Walk Together Children: Black and Womanist Theologies, Church, and Theological Education*, ed. Dwight N. Hopkins and Linda E. Thomas (Eugene, OR: Cascade Books, 2010), 213.

21 Rufus Thomas, "Little Sally Walker," Stax 45-167, 1965, vinyl 7″, 45 rpm; Eva Grace Boone, "Little Sally Walker," *Field Recordings Vol. 4: Mississippi & Alabama (1934–1942)*, 1998, streaming audio, Music Online: American Music database, https://search.alexanderstreet.com/view/work/bibliographic_entity%7Crecorded_cd%7C74522; Nettie Mae, Alenda Turner, and Sid Hemphill's Band, "Little Sally Walker," *Afro-American Folk Music from Tate and Panola Counties, Mississippi*, Rounder Records, 2000.

22 Aretha Franklin, "Spirit in the Dark," *Aretha: Live at Fillmore West*, Atlantic, SD 7205, 1971, vinyl LP 12″33 1/3 rpm.

23 E. Patrick Johnson, "Feeling the Spirit in the Dark: Expanding Notions of the Sacred in the African-American Gay Community," *Callaloo* 21, no. 2 (1998): 399.

24 In his essay on sexuality and spirituality in the Black church, Rev. Dr. Dennis Wiley notes the song's drive toward ecstatic worship. He states, "The ad-libbing, the improvisation, the repetition, the call-and-response, and the heightened anticipation, as one level of ecstasy surpasses the former, are all reminiscent of the expressive praise, unspeakable joy, and spiritual possession that characterize innumerable Black worship experiences." Wiley, "Spirit in the Dark: Sexuality and Spirituality in the Black Church," 213.

25 Garland, *The Sound of Soul*, 191.

26 Garland, 198.

27 Garland, 194.

28 "To state the problem metaphorically, the black woman must translate the female vocalist's gestures into an apposite structure of terms that will articulate both her kinship to other women and the particular nuances of her own experience." Spillers, "Intersticies: A Small Drama of Words," 167.

29 Farah Jasmine Griffin, "When Malindy Sings: A Meditation on Black Women's Vocality," 119.

30 Fredara Hadley, "Remarks on Black Feminine Genius," *Aretha Franklin's Amazing Grace: From Watts to Detroit: A Two-Day Symposium Celebrating the Life of the Queen of Soul.* University of California Los Angeles, March 24 and 25, 2019, https://youtu.be/HV7X3rTXFfI.

31 Griffin, "When Malindy Sings," 119.

32 Hadley observes the powerful moment in which we see how Black feminine genius is passed down during Aretha Franklin's taping of *Amazing Grace* where Clara Ward, who once taught Franklin, sits down, enwrapped in the spirit during Franklin's performance of "Old Landmark." Hadley, "Remarks on Black Feminine Genius."

33 Pellett, Gail, dir., *The Songs Are Free.*

34 Crawley's formulation of Blackpentacostal breath is an aesthetic drive toward what he calls"otherwise possibility," ways of being and thinking that counter Enlightenment notions of subjectivity. Crawley, *Blackpentecostal Breath*, 2.

35 Weheliye analyzes a literary moment of singing as challenging notions of singular subjectivity in Ralph Ellison's *Invisible Man*. In the scene, the protagonist of the book is surrounded by a cacophony of sound, first through a preacher pontificating toward ambivalence of what Black is and what Black is not and then to a woman spiritual singer who bemoans the death of her master. He observes, "Were we to place this haze of multiple times and spaces into the psychoanalytic paradigm, this scene would provide an 'oceanic fantasy' par excellence wherein the protagonist's coherent self gives way to an anterior subjectivity in which the borders between self and other blur." Alexander G Weheliye, *Phonographies*, 61.

36 Lordi, *The Meaning of Soul*, 75.

37 Stallings, *Funk the Erotic*, 236.

38 Maureen Mahon, *Black Diamond Queens: African American Women and Rock and Roll* (Durham, NC: Duke University Press, 2020), 7, https://doi.org/10.1215/9781478012771.

39 Mahon, 232.

40 Crawley, *Blackpentecostal Breath*, 30.

41 Stallings, *Funk the Erotic*, 60.

42 Brooks, *Liner Notes for the Revolution*, 3.

43 Brooks, 107.

44 Brooks, 89.

45 David Evans, "Blues: Chronological Overview," in *African American Music: An Introduction*, ed. Portia K. Maultsby and Mellonee V. Burnim (New York: Routledge, 2006), 85.

46 Although these names—the devil, Lucifer, and Satan—are often used interchangeably, they aren't necesarily interchangeable. Lucille Clifton explicitly differentiates Satan from Lucifer, for example. "I don't ever talk about Satan," she says, "I do talk about Lucifer." Clifton, "I'd Like Not to Be a Stranger in the World," 323.

47 Avery Sunshine, "A Conversation with Avery Sunshine," interview by Tamara Harris, *Kick Mag*, August 13, 2010, http://www.kickmag.net/2010/08/13/a-conversation-with-avery-sunshine/.

48 Ayodele Ogundipe decribes how Esu Elegbara came to be associated with Lucifer through missionary colonization. Ayodele Ogundipe, "Esu Elegbara, the Yoruba God of Chance and Uncertainty: A Study in Yoruba Mythology" (PhD diss., Indiana University, 1978), 177, https://www.proquest.com/docview/288436194.

49 Evans, "Blues: Chronological Overview," 87.

50 1 John 2:27, NRSV.

51 2 Cor. 4:7, NRSV.

52 Acts 10:38, NRSV.

53 1 Sam. 10:1, Luke 4:16, NRSV.

54 Sunshine, interview with the author, November 4, 2012.

55 Trineice Robinson-Martin, "Developing a Pedagogy for Gospel Singing: Understanding the Cultural Aesthetics and Performance Components of a Vocal Performance in Gospel Music" (PhD diss., Columbia University, 2010), 18, http://search.proquest.com /docview/756254736/.

56 Sunshine, interview with the author, November 4, 2012.

57 Pellett, Gail, dir., *The Songs Are Free*.

58 Robert Farris Thompson, *Flash of the Spirit: African & Afro-American Art & Philosophy* (New York: Knopf, 2010), 5.

59 Thompson, 16 (italics mine).

60 Hazel V. Carby, "It Jus Be's Dat Way Sometime: The Sexual Politics of Women's Blues," *Radical America* 20, no. 4 (1987): 9; Davis, *Blues Legacies and Black Feminism: Gertrude "Ma" Rainey, Bessie Smith, and Billie Holiday*; LaMonda Horton-Stallings, *Mutha' Is Half a Word : Intersections of Folklore, Vernacular, Myth, and Queerness in Black Female Culture* (Columbus: Ohio State University Press, 2007).

61 Kelly Brown Douglas, "Black and Blues: God-Talk/Body-Talk for the Black Church," in *Sexuality and the Sacred: Sources for Theological Reflection*, ed. Marvin Mahan Ellison and Kelly Brown Douglas (Louisville, KY: Westminster John Knox Press, 2010), 50.

62 Douglas, 51.

63 Douglas, 53.

64 Christine Dall, dir., *Wild Women Don't Have the Blues*, DVD (California Newsreel, 2007).

65 "In the News: COGIC Music Dept. Issues Statement about Kim Burrell," *GospelPundit.com* (blog), February 18, 2010, https://web.archive.org/web/20160803005216/http://www .gospelpundit.com/2010/02/in-the-news-cogic-music-dept-issues-statement-about-kim -burrell/.

66 Troy Lilly, "She Said: Exclusive Interview with Kim Burrell," *GospelPundit.com* (blog), May 20, 2011, http://www.gospelpundit.com/2011/05/she-said-exclusive-interview -with-kim-burrell/.

67 The lyrics of "I Believe in You in Me" are religiously ambiguous. Ambiguous in the sense that they are about a love relationship, however, the song's refrain alludes to the hymn "Amazing Grace" by adopting the lyrics, "I was lost, now I'm free." It is also one of the few secular songs on Houston's only gospel album—the soundtrack to *The Preacher's Wife*.

68 Sunshine, "A Conversation with Avery Sunshine."

69 Moriba Cummings, "Oh, Word? Kim Burrell Disrespectfully Slams 'Perverted' Homosexuals in Sermon." *Celebrity News and Media*. BET (blog), December 31, 2016. https:// www.bet.com/article/j85pv8/kim-burrell-disrespectfully-slams-homosexuals-in-sermon.

70 An example of this theme in Black women's preaching is Juanita Bynum's breakout sermon "No More Sheets," which launched her high-profile preaching career. Terrion Williamson discusses spiritual ecstasy at the scene of this sermon in Terrion L. Williamson, *Scandalize My Name: Black Feminist Practice and the Making of Black Social Life* (New York: Fordham University Press, 2016), 55.

71 C. Riley Snorton, *Nobody Is Supposed to Know: Black Sexuality on the Down Low* (Minneapolis: University of Minnesota Press, 2014), 6.

72 Amaryah Shaye, "Kim Burrell and the Power and Pleasure of Authority: On Sexuality and Transformative Justice in the Black Church," *Women in Theology* (blog), January 9, 2017, https://womenintheology.org/2017/01/09/kim-burrell-and-the-power-and-pleasure -of-authority-on-sexuality-and-transformative-justice-in-the-black-church/.

73 Williamson, *Scandalize My Name*, 52.

74 Much of Burrell's sermon is a direct comment on controversies around Bishop Eddie Long and internet sensation Andrew Caldwell, who made waves with a video circulated from the 2016 COGIC convention in which he declared that he was "Delivered!" from homosexuality. Burrell read his persistent feminine behavior as a mockery to the church despite the continued claims by Caldwell that he no longer engages in homosexual sex acts or cross dressing (described as carrying a purse). Caldwell's performance of being delivered from homosexual sin in an apparent moment of ecstatic worship at the COGIC's largest annual function serves as a reminder that it is not only (or at all) homosexual sex acts that trouble churchgoers; it is the very suspicion of queerness typified in male femininity that is continually framed as sin.

75 Edwin Hawkins and Shirley Miller, "Oh Happy Day," *Celebration of Joy* (compilation), I AM Records, 2015, streaming audio.

76 Yvette Flunder and Walter Hawkins, "Thank You," *Love Alive IV*, Malaco Records MAL 6007, 1990, compact disc.

77 Yvette Flunder, "Church Interlude II: Healing Oppression Sickness," in *Queer Christianities: Lived Religion in Transgressive Forms*, ed. Kathleen T. Talvacchia and Mark Larrimore (New York: New York University Press, 2014), 116, http://ebookcentral.proquest .com/lib/washington/detail.action?docID=1831854.

78 Yvette Flunder, Walter Hawkins, and Shirley Miller, *Full and Complete*, CD, Love Alive IV (Malaco Records – MAL 6007, 1990).

79 Crawley, *Blackpentecostal Breath*, 31.

80 Sunshine, personal interview.

81 Avery Sunshine and Jodine Dorce, "Meet & Greet with Avery Sunshine!!" April 13, 2011, http://grownfolksmusic.com/blog/interview-meet-greet-avery-sunshine.

82 Sunshine and Dorce.

83 Sunshine and Dorce.

84 James H. Cone, *The Spirituals and the Blues: An Interpretation* (Maryknoll, NY: Orbis Books, 1972), 98.

85 Cone, 100.

86 Alan Young, *Woke Me Up This Morning: Black Gospel Singers and the Gospel Life*, American Made Music Series (Jackson: University Press of Mississippi, 1997), 108.

87 Horace Clarence Boyer, *The Golden Age of Gospel* (Urbana: University of Illinois Press, 2000), 85.

88 Davis, *Blues Legacies and Black Feminism: Gertrude "Ma" Rainey, Bessie Smith, and Billie Holiday*, 121.

89 Martin Baumgaertner, dir., *Finally Karen Live!*, Detroit: Island Black Music, 1997, videocassette (VHS).

90 Young, *Woke Me Up This Morning*, 120.

91 Whitney Houston, "Whitney Houston: Down and Dirty," *Rolling Stone*, June 10, 1993, par. 10.

92 Davis, *Blues Legacies and Black Feminism*, 125 (italics in original).

93 Sunshine, interview with the author, Nov. 4, 2012; Sunshine, "A Conversation with Avery Sunshine."

94 Sunshine, interview with the author.

95 Sunshine.

96 Koko Taylor, "I'm a Woman." *The Earthshaker*, Alligator Records, AL4711, 1978, vinyl LP 12″, 33 1/3 rpm.

97 Jones, *Blues People*, 60.

98 Jones, 62.

99 The Clark Sound is used to describe the use of scale-stretching runs, melismas, ad-libs, and growls typified by the Clark Sisters and their mother, Dr. Mattie Moss Clark.

100 Karen Clark Sheard and Kierra "Kiki" Sheard, "You Loved Me," *The Heavens Are Telling*, Elektra Records, 2003.

101 Jill Scott, "He Loves Me (Lyzel in E Flat)" *Jill Scott: Words and Sounds Vol. 1*, Hidden Beach, 2000.

102 I use this phrase after Elsa Barkley-Brown's thoughts on "playing" with the body in public discussed in this interview. There, the concept of playing with oneself in public is described in the way that Michelle Obama adorns and fashions her body using clothing and mannerisms that speak to a certain claim to bodily agency. The sexual overtone of "playing with oneself" is intentional here as the reading of Black women's bodies as being in permanent excess always includes the specter of oversexualization. This is what I find useful in witnessing/listening to Ferrell's performance. Her vocalizations are in excess, and that is precisely what makes them transformative and evocative. Elsa Barkley-Brown, William R. Glass, and Agnieszka Graff, "Race, Sexuality, and African American Women Representing the Nation: An Interview with Elsa Barkley-Brown," *The Americanist. Warsaw Journal for the Study of the United States* 26 (2011): 24.

103 Sunshine, interview with the author.

104 Sunshine and Dorce, "Meet & Greet with Avery Sunshine!!"

105 Avery Sunshine, interview by Kanaal Nodap, June 2011, Avery Sunshine, "Ramona Debreaux Interview with Soulful Avery Sunshine, " September 9, 2011.

106 Sunshine, interview with the author.

107 Sunshine.

108 Avery*Sunshine, "I Need You Now."

109 Aretha Franklin, "Chain of Fools."

110 Thompson, *Flash of the Spirit*, 9.

111 Sunshine, interview with the author.

112 T. V. Reed, *The Art of Protest: Culture and Activism from the Civil Rights Movement to the Streets of Seattle* (Minneapolis : University of Minnesota Press, 2005), 1.

113 Sharpe, *In the Wake*, 112.

114 Crawley, *Blackpentecostal Breath*, 38.

115 Pellett, Gail, dir., *The Songs Are Free*.

116 *The Songs Are Free.*

CHAPTER 4

Epigraph: From the poem "In 2006 I Had an Ordeal with Medicine," Bettina Judd, *patient*. (New York: Black Lawrence Press, 2014), 1.

1 Renée Ater, "Race, Gender, and Nation: Rethinking the Sculpture of Meta Warrick Fuller" (PhD diss, University of Maryland, College Park, 2000), 148, http://search.proquest .com/docview/230893034/.

2 Patrick Moynihan, "Chapter IV. The Tangle of Pathology," in *The Negro Family: The Case for National Action*, Office of Policy Planning and Research, United States Department of Labor, March 1965, accessed January 11, 2020, https://www.dol.gov/general/aboutdol /history/webid-moynihan/moynchapter4.

3 Alexis Pauline Gumbs, "M/Other Ourselves: A Black Queer Feminist Geneaology for Radical Mothering," 16.

4 Dorothy Roberts, *Killing the Black Body: Race, Reproduction, and the Meaning of Liberty* (New York: Vintage, 1998), 3.

5 Dorothy Roberts addresses these interconnected issues of the legal sanctions on Black reproduction and the control of Black children in *Killing the Black Body*.

6 Nicole R. Fleetwood, *Troubling Vision: Performance, Visuality, and Blackness* (Chicago: University of Chicago Press, 2011), 120.

7 As discussed in the introduction of this book, Meta Fuller thought the statue, *A Silent Protest in Memory of Mary Turner*, to be too incendiary for public viewing.

8 Gumbs, "M/Other Ourselves," 17.

9 Robin D. G. Kelley, *Yo' Mama's Disfunktional! Fighting the Culture Wars in Urban America* (Boston: Beacon Press, 2001), 2.

10 For the record, my mama's name is Juanita.

11 Collins, *Black Feminist Thought*, 69.

12 Angela Davis, "Reflections on the Black Woman's Role in the Community of Slaves," *Black Scholar* 3, no. 4 (1971): 4.

13 Davis, 5.

14 Barbara Ransby and Tracye Matthews, "Black Popular Culture and the Transcendence of Patriarchal Illusions," *Race & Class* 35, no. 1 (1993): 60.

15 Cathy J. Cohen, "Punks, Bulldaggers, and Welfare Queens: The Radical Potential of Queer Politics?," *GLQ: A Journal of Lesbian and Gay Studies* 3, no. 4 (May 1, 1997): 453, https://doi.org/10.1215/10642684-3-4-437.

16 Michele Wallace, *Dark Designs and Visual Culture* (Durham, NC: Duke University Press, 2004), 285.

17 Melissa V. Harris-Perry, *Sister Citizen: Shame, Stereotypes, and Black Women in America* (New Haven, CT: Yale University Press, 2011), 115.

18 bell hooks, *Rock My Soul: Black People and Self-Esteem* (New York: Washington Square Press, 2003), 37.

19 Frantz Fanon, *Black Skin, White Masks*, 116.

20 Nicole Fleetwood cites Fanon's "look a negro" moment as one that is foundational to studies of Black visual culture. She states that, "Fanon provides brilliant insight into the terror and trauma of being marked visually as black in the public sphere. Fanon considers the power of that defining moment, the definition itself, and the public declaration to gaze upon blackness." Fleetwood, *Troubling Vision*, 22.

21 Silvan S. Tomkins, *Shame and Its Sisters: A Silvan Tomkins Reader*, ed. Irving E. Alexander and Eve Kosofsky Sedgwick (Durham, NC: Duke University Press, 1995), 36.

22 Musser, *Sensational Flesh*, 54.

23 Hortense J. Spillers, "Mama's Baby, Papa's Maybe: An American Grammar Book," *Diacritics* 17, no. 2 (1987): 80, https://doi.org/10.2307/464747.

24 Musser, *Sensational Flesh*, 107.

25 Snorton, *Black on Both Sides*, 104.

26 William Edward Burghardt Du Bois, *The Souls of Black Folk: Essays and Sketches* (Chicago: A. C. McClurg & Company, 1903), 2.

27 Musser, *Sensational Flesh*, 102.

28 Ahmed, *The Cultural Politics of Emotion*, 105; "Shame, n.," in *OED Online* (Oxford University Press), accessed January 17, 2020, http://www.oed.com/view/Entry/177406.

29 Tomkins, *Shame and Its Sisters*, 37.

30 Fanon, *Black Skin, White Masks*, 110.

31 Du Bois, *The Souls of Black Folk*, 2.

32 Kimberly Nichele Brown, *Writing the Black Revolutionary Diva: Women's Subjectivity and the Decolonizing Text* (Bloomington: Indiana University Press, 2010), 34.

33 Brown, 59.

34 Renée Cox, interview with the author, March 2012.

35 Collins, *Black Feminist Thought*, 114.

36 Deborah B. Gould, *Moving Politics: Emotion and ACT UP's Fight against AIDS* (Chicago: University of Chicago Press, 2009), 89, http://ebookcentral.proquest.com/lib/washington /detail.action?docID=471870.

37 Sylvia Wynter, "On How We Mistook the Map for the Territory, and Reimprisoned Ourselves in Our Unbearable Wrongness of Being, of *Désêtre*: Black Studies Toward the Human Project," in *I Am Because We Are: Readings in Africana Philosophy*, ed. Fred L. Hord and Jonathan Scott Lee (Amherst: University of Massachusetts Press, 2016), 277.

38 Sylvia Wynter, "Rethinking 'Aesthetics': Notes towards a Deciphering Practice," in *Ex-Iles: Essays on Caribbean Cinema* (Trenton, NJ: Africa World, 1992), 258.

39 Sianne Ngai, *Ugly Feelings* (Cambridge, MA: Harvard University Press, 2005), 10.

40 Ahmed, *The Cultural Politics of Emotion*, 103.

41 Quoted by Silvan Tomkins, *Shame and Its Sisters*, 135.

42 Tomkins, 135.

43 James Percelay et al., *Snaps: The Original "Yo' Mama" Joke Book* (New York: HarperCollins, 1994), 44.

44 Spillers, "Mama's Baby, Papa's Maybe," 80.

45 I am thinking here of the poem by the Black gay spoken word poetry ensemble Adodi Muse in which they use the apostrophic 'shamed. *Ain't Got Sense Enuf to Be 'Shamed*, accessed February 11, 2020, https://music.apple.com/md/album/aint-got-sense-enuf -to-be-shamed/573920896.

46 Tiffany Lethabo King, "Black 'Feminisms' and Pessimism: Abolishing Moynihan's Negro Family," *Theory & Event* 21, no. 1 (January 2018): 80.

47 Fleetwood, *Troubling Vision*, 112.

48 For the sake of brevity I only discuss the novel here. However, I do think a rich discussion is to be had regarding Lee Daniel's film adaptation of the book *Precious*. The powerful portrayal of the titular character by actress Gabourey Sidibe brings to fore many of the affective cultural anxieties about Black teen pregnancy, HIV, fatness, and poverty in an urban setting. In particular, the conflation of the actress with the character she portrays, the use of the character's name as a reference for fat Black women, and the public discourse that cast the film as poverty porn are all points of inquiry that speak to the anxieties that the image of Precious evokes. An outline of these criticisms can be found in Mara Gay's article in *The Atlantic*. Gabourey Sidibe herself has also discussed the impact of the role on people's vision of her as an actress in her memoir. Mara Gay, "Problems With 'Precious,'" *The Atlantic*, November 7, 2009, https://www.theatlantic.com/culture/archive/2009/11 /problems-with-precious/347636/; Gabourey Sidibe, *This Is Just My Face: Try Not to Stare* (Boston: Houghton Mifflin Harcourt, 2017).

49 Sapphire, *Push*, 111.

50 Musser, *Sensational Flesh*, 2.

51 Musser, 1.

52 Sapphire, *Push*, 112.

53 Hine, "Rape and the Inner Lives of Black Women in the Middle West," 915.

54 Lisa Gail Collins, *The Art of History: African American Women Artists Engage the Past* (New Brunswick, NJ: Rutgers University Press, 2002), 99.

55 Daphne Brooks, *Bodies in Dissent: Spectacular Performances of Race and Freedom, 1850–1910* (Durham, NC: Duke University Press, 2006), 4.

56 L. H. Stallings, "Sapphire's PUSH for Erotic Literacy and Black Girl Sexual Agency," in *Sapphire's Literary Breakthrough: Erotic Literacies, Feminist Pedagogies, Environmental Justice Perspectives*, ed. Elizazbeth McNeil et al. (New York: Palgrave Macmillan, 2012), 122.

57 Kimberly Wallace-Sanders, *Mammy: A Century of Race, Gender, and Southern Memory* (Ann Arbor: University of Michigan Press, 2008), 3.

58 Wallace, *Dark Designs and Visual Culture*, 280.

59 Michael D. Harris, *Colored Pictures: Race and Visual Representation* (Chapel Hill: University of North Carolina Press, 2003), 107; Lisa E. Farrington, *Creating Their Own Image: The History of African-American Women Artists* (Oxford University Press, 2005), 132.

60 Renee Cox, *Yo Mama Goes to the Hamptons*, 1994, 30 × 40 inches, archival digital inkjet print on cotton rag, artist's website, https://www.reneecox.org/yo-mama.

61 Jo-Ann Morgan, "Mammy the Huckster: Selling the Old South for the New Century," *American Art* 9, no. 1 (1995): 103.

62 Harris, *Colored Pictures*, 117.

63 Renée Cox, *The Liberation of Lady J. and U.B.*, accessed June 4, 2021, http://jstor.org/stable/10.2307/community.14253010.

64 Wallace-Sanders, *Mammy*, 125.

65 Wallace-Sanders, 127.

66 I'd be curious to know what her thoughts are now that the brand, under the parent company PepsiCo, has decided to erase Aunt Jemima altogether and to be known as the Pearl Milling Company. Jacqueline Diaz, "Aunt Jemima No More: Pancake Brand Renamed Pearl Milling Company," National Public Radio, February 10, 2021, https://www.npr.org/2021/02/10/966166648/aunt-jemima-no-more-pancake-brand-renamed-pearl-milling-company.

67 Andrea Shaw Nevins, *The Embodiment of Disobedience: Fat Black Women's Unruly Political Bodies* (Lanham, MD: Lexington Books, 2006), 2.

68 Wallace, *Dark Designs and Visual Culture*, 280.

69 Collins, *Black Feminist Thought*, 84; Elizabeth Alexander, " 'Coming Out Blackened and Whole' Fragmentation and Reintegration in Audre Lorde's *Zami* and *The Cancer Journals*," in *Skin Deep, Spirit Strong: The Black Female Body in American Culture*, ed. Kimberly Wallace-Sanders (Ann Arbor: University of Michigan Press, 2002), 222.

70 Lorraine O'Grady, "Olympia's Maid: Reclaiming Black Female Subjectivity," in *The Feminism and Visual Culture Reader*, ed. Amelia Jones, 174; Morgan, "Mammy the Huckster," 99.

71 Sabrina Strings, *Fearing the Black Body: The Racial Origins of Fat Phobia* (New York: New York University Press, 2019), 211.

72 Andrea Liss, "Black Bodies in Evidence: Maternal Visibility in Renée Cox's Family Portraits," in *The Familial Gaze*, ed. Marianne Hirsch (Hanover, CT: University Press of New England, 1999), 284.

73 Wynter, "Rethinking 'Aesthetics': Notes towards a Deciphering Practice," 269.

74 Terry Gips, "Joyce J. Scott's Mammy/Nanny Series," *Feminist Studies* 22, no. 2 (1996): 313, https://doi.org/10.2307/3178415.

75 Snorton, *Black on Both Sides*, 120.

76 Sheri Parks, *Fierce Angels: The Strong Black Woman in American Life and Culture* (New York: One World / Ballantine, 2010), 33.

77 Parks, 200.

78 Examples of this discourse can be found in the following articles. Feminista Jones, "Black Women Saved Democracy Yet Again. Where's Our Moment of Gratitude?"; Keisha N. Blain, "This Election, Black Women Are Leading the Way—Again"; Doreen St. Félix, "How the Alabama Senate Election Sanctified Black Women Voters"; and Julie Scelfo, "Will Black Women Save Us . . . Again?"

79 Parks, *Fierce Angels*, 202.

80 Zadie Smith, "Through the Portal: Locating the Magnificent," in *Deana Lawson*, by Deana Lawson (New York: Aperture, 2018), 8.

81 Combahee River Collective, "A Black Feminist Statement," 212.

82 Cox, interview with the author.

83 This hair-grooming practice presses the shorter hairs around the temple and forehead to the skull, which straightens those hairs and places them more uniformly in the groomed style of the rest of the crown.

84 The first one described is the official image available in her *Aperture* catalog, the second described is the first iteration of the photograph published in her *Contact Sheet* (Light Work, 2009) and has not been shown by request of the artist. Deana Lawson, *Deana Lawson* (New York: Aperture, 2018).

85 Fr. Michael Scanlan, *The San Damiano Cross: An Explanation* (Steubenville, Ohio: University of Steubenville Press, 1983), 4.

86 Lance B. Richey, "Neoplatonism and Nature in the Canticle of Creatures," *The AFCU Journal: A Franciscan Perspective on Higher Education* 9, no. 1 (January 2019): 48.

87 Sarah Smith, "Towards a Poetics of Bafflement: The Politics of Elsewhere in Contemporary Black Diaspora Visual Practice (1990–Present)" (PhD diss, University of Toronto, 2016), 63, http://search.proquest.com/docview/1889845065/?pq-origsite=primo.

88 Lawson, "In Conversation with Deana Lawson," interview by Sabine Mirlesse. Censoring per the source.

89 Lawson, "In Conversation with Deana Lawson."

90 Deana Lawson, "The Direct Gaze: Deana Lawson in Conversation with Arthur Jafa," in *Deana Lawson* (New York: Aperture, 2018), 96.

91 Franklin Sirmans, "Deana Lawson," *Contact Sheet* 152 (2009): 16.

92 Smith, "Towards a Poetics of Bafflement," 8.

93 Smith, 72.

94 Spillers, "Mama's Baby, Papa's Maybe," 68.

95 King, "Black 'Feminisms' and Pessimism: Abolishing Moynihan's Negro Family," 84.

CHAPTER 5

1 Patricia Spears Jones, "Sapphire," *Black Scholar* 38, no. 2/3 (2008): 42.

2 Audre Lorde, "The Uses of Anger: Women Responding to Racism," in *Sister Outsider: Essays and Speeches*, (Berkeley, CA: Crossing Press, 1984), 127.

3 The specificity of the term "Angry Black Woman" makes it a concept by which Black women are uniquely affected. I use the term "misogynoir," coined by Moya Bailey, to highlight the specificity of the trope as both anti-Black and misogynist in its overtones. See Moya Bailey, "Race, Class, Region, and Gender in Early Emory School of Medicine Yearbooks" (PhD diss., Emory University, 2013), 26.

4 J. Celeste Walley-Jean's research on Black women's anger revealed that Black women are "actually *less* likely to experience angry feelings even when faced with situations in which they are criticized, disrespected, or evaluated negatively." J. Celeste Walley-Jean, "Debunking the Myth of the 'Angry Black Woman': An Exploration of Anger in Young African American Women," *Black Women, Gender + Families* 3, no. 2 (2009): 68–86.

5 Donnetrice C. Allison, introduction to *Black Women's Portrayals on Reality Television: The New Sapphire*, ed. Donnetrice C. Allison (Lanham, MD: Lexington Books, 2016), x.

6 Sheri Parks, *Fierce Angels: The Strong Black Woman in American Life and Culture* (New York: One World / Ballantine, 2010), 110.

7 Collins, *Black Feminist Thought*, 76, 7.

8 This contrapuntal ghazal is inspired by the paradox form found in Tyehimba Jess's book *Olio*, in which the lament that typifies the ghazal is internal to each side of the contrapuntal, here the repetition of the words "angry" and "being." It can be read across lines, which blurs the distinct voice of each side of the poem in any direction, reproducing the paradoxical relationship between being and anger. As a paradox, its multidirectional voice allows the poem to be unending, as it can also be read from the bottom upwards. See the "Bert Williams/George Walker Paradox" in Tyehimba Jess, *Olio* (Seattle: Wave Books, 2016).

9 Mae Henderson, "Speaking in Tongues: Dialects, Dialogics, and the Black Woman Writer's Literary Tradition," in *Speaking in Tongues and Dancing Diaspora: Black Women Writing and Performing* (Oxford: Oxford University Press, 2014), 60. Henderson proposes a model for analyzing Black women's literature that takes into account the ways that Black women writers' discourse is structured by race and gender, simultaneously. The result is a form of speech that addresses both internal and external dialogues.

10 Sylvia Wynter, "The Ceremony Found: Towards the Autopoetic Turn/Overturn, Its Autonomy of Human Agency and Extraterritoriality of (Self-)Cognition," in *Black Knowledges/Black Struggles* (Liverpool, Eng.: Liverpool University Press, 2015), 245, http://www.jstor.org/stable/j.ctt1gn6bfp.12. Wynter uses Aime Césaire to describe how "only poetry" can give an approximate notion of a new order of knowledge she proposes.

11 L. H. Stallings, *Funk the Erotic*, 60; Smitherman, *Talkin and Testifyin*, 135.

12 Julia S. Jordan-Zachary, "Beyond the Side Eye: Black Women's Ancestral Anger as a Liberatory Practice," *Journal of Black Sexuality and Relationships* 4, no. 1 (2017): 68.

13 I use African American Vernacular English (AAVE) here to better make use of the activating components of the term *human*. According to Smitherman the AAVE use of the verb "to be," for example, marks habitual or continuing conditions when the word "be" is used and stressed. Smitherman, *Talkin and Testifyin*, 19.

14 Smitherman, 135.

15 Staples, "The Myth of the Black Macho," 25. It should also be noted that Staples responded with a rejoinder to his article in the Black Sexism Debate issue of *The Black Scholar*. Robert Staples, "A Rejoinder: Black Feminism and the Cult of Masculinity: The Danger Within," *Black Scholar* 10, no. 8/9 (1979): 63–67.

16 Audre Lorde, "The Great American Disease," *Black Scholar* 10, no. 8/9 (1979): 17.

17 Lorde, "The Uses of Anger," 124.

18 Lorde, 133.

19 Audre Lorde, "Eye to Eye: Black Women, Hatred, and Anger," in *Sister Outsider: Essays and Speeches* (Berkeley, CA: Crossing Press, 1984), 171.

20 Rebecca Wanzo, *The Suffering Will Not Be Televised: African American Women and Sentimental Political Storytelling* (Albany: State University of New York Press, 2009), 5.

21 Marilyn Yarbrough and Crystal Bennett, "Cassandra and the 'Sistahs': The Peculiar Treatment of African American Women in the Myth of Women as Liars," *Journal of Gender, Race, and Justice* 3 (2000), 645.

22 Yarbrough and Bennett, 649. Even now, while writing this, I am afraid to mention Tawana Brawley's name next to Anita Hill's. My internalized mistrust of Black women's speech is so ingrained, and the disposability of Black women's speech so intrinsic to such matters.

23 Sheri Parks, *Fierce Angels: The Strong Black Woman in American Life and Culture*, 110.

24 Audre Lorde, *Sister Outsider*, 129.

25 Darlene Clark Hine, "Rape and the Inner Lives of Black Women in the Middle West," *Signs* 14, no. 4 (1989): 912–20.

26 Sylvia Wynter, "The Ceremony Must Be Found: After Humanism," 36. Wynter describes "nigger chaos" as the totalizing otherness in which Black folks have no language worth studying, no culture, and therefore no relationship to reason, which differentiates natural man from human.

27 Hortense J. Spillers, "Mama's Baby, Papa's Maybe," 69.

28 For more on white male anger and its effects see Michael S Kimmel, *Angry White Men: American Masculinity at the End of an Era* (New York: Nation Books, 2013); and Ruth Frankenberg, *Displacing Whiteness: Essays in Social and Cultural Criticism* (Durham, NC: Duke University Press, 1997).

29 Smitherman, *Talkin and Testifyin*, 20.

30 Elaine Richardson, *African American Literacies* (Abingdon, Eng.: Taylor and Francis, 2002), 77.

31 Sharpe, *In the Wake*, 117.

32 LaShonda Barnett, ed., *I Got Thunder: Black Women Songwriters on Their Craft* (New York: Thunder's Mouth Press, 2007), 154.

33 Nina Simone, *I Put a Spell on You: The Autobiography of Nina Simone* (New York: Da Capo Press, 2003), 90.

34 In the live 1964 recording of the song, she tells her audience that the song is a show tune for a show that hasn't been written, "yet." Nina Simone, track 7 on *In Concert*, 1964.

35 Simone, *I Put a Spell on You*, 90.

36 Simone, 91.

37 Simone, 90.

38 Richard Lischer, *The Preacher King: Martin Luther King Jr. and the Word That Moved America* (New York: Oxford University Press, 1997), 35; James H. Cone, *A Black Theology of Liberation: Twentieth Anniversary Edition* (Maryknoll, NY: Orbis Books, 1990), 55.

39 Judd, "In 2006 I Had an Ordeal with Medicine," *patient.*, 1.

40 Judd, *patient.*, 12.

41 Terri Kapsalis, "Mastering the Female Pelvis: Race and the Tools of Reproduction," in *Skin Deep, Spirit Strong: The Black Female Body in American Culture*, ed. Kimberly Wallace-Sanders (Ann Arbor: University of Michigan Press, 2002), 265.

42 Benjamin Reiss, *The Showman and the Slave: Race, Death, and Memory in Barnum's America* (Cambridge, MA: Harvard University Press, 2001), 212.

43 Judd, *patient.*, 48.

44 Reiss, *The Showman and the Slave*, 164.

45 Rebecca Skloot, *The Immortal Life of Henrietta Lacks* (New York: Broadway Books, 2011).

46 Skloot, 48.

47 Dorothy Roberts recounts the widespread practice of performing unnecessary hysterectomies on Black women at teaching hospitals in the US South. Dorothy E. Roberts, *Killing the Black Body: Race, Reproduction, and the Meaning of Liberty* (New York: Vintage, 1999), 91.

48 Marilyn Nelson, *Fortune's Bones: The Manumission Requiem* (Asheville, NC: Front Street, Inc., 2004).

49 From "Haunted by the Living, I Talk to the Dead," Judd, *patient.*, 63.

50 Julia S. Jordan-Zachary takes up Viviane Saleh-Hanna's concept of Black feminist hauntology to argue for Black women's ancestral anger as Black feminist work to heal trauma. Jordan-Zachary, "Beyond the Side Eye: Black Women's Ancestral Anger as a Liberatory Practice," 63.

51 Viviane Saleh-Hanna, "Black Feminist Hauntology. Rememory the Ghosts of Abolition?," *Champ Pénal/Penal Field* 12 (March 23, 2015), https://doi.org/10.4000/champpenal.9168 par. 6.

52 Lorde, "Eye to Eye: Black Women, Hatred, and Anger," 152.

53 Lorde, 146.

54 The title "On or about July 10, 2015" is from the lawsuit filed by Sandra Bland's family against Waller County (*Geneva Reed-Veal, mother of Sandra Bland, deceased, v. Brian Encinia, Texas Department of Public Safety, Elsa Magnus, Oscar Prudente, Waller County Sheriff's Office; Complaint at law*). A version of this poem was previously published as Bettina Judd, "On or about July 10, 2015," *The Offing*, March 24, 2016, https://theoffingmag .com/here-you-are/on-or-about-july-10-20151/.

55 Scholars of law and rhetoric as well as commentators have also analyzed this encounter for the ways that Encinia used coded language to enact powers beyond his authority. For example, Lowrey-Kinberg and Buker discuss how Bland's lawful asking of questions was deemed inappropriate behavior for a police officer who wishes to assert power. I examine a small excerpt of their conversation here as instructive for the writing prompt of the poem that begins this section. For more on this topic, see Belén V. Lowrey-Kinberg and Grace Sullivan Buker, "'I'm Giving You a Lawful Order': Dialogic Legitimacy in Sandra Bland's Traffic Stop," *Law & Society Review* 51, no. 2 (June 1, 2017), and K. K. Rebecca Lai et al., "Assessing the Legality of Sandra Bland's Arrest," *New York Times*, July 20, 2015. Panama Jackson also offers an insightful and beautifully written close reading of the interaction between Encinia and Bland. Panama Jackson, "The Moment That Ended Sandra Bland's Life," *The Root*, July 22, 2015, https://www.theroot.com/the-moment-that-ended-sandra -blands-life-1822521368.

56 Ryan Grim, "The Transcript of Sandra Bland's Arrest Is as Revealing as the Video," *Huffington Post*, July 23, 2015, sec. Politics, http://www.huffingtonpost.com/entry/sandra -bland-arrest-transcript. See also *Geneva Reed-Veal, mother of Sandra Bland, deceased, v. Brian Encinia, Texas Department of Public Safety, Elsa Magnus, Oscar Prudente, Waller County Sheriff's Office; Complaint at law* (Case No. 4:15-cv-02232; wrongful death lawsuit), Legislative Reference Library of Texas, "Related Court Documents," August 4, 2015, http://www.lrl.state.tx.us/currentissues/clips/casePage.cfm?pageID=8&reportID=28329.

57 Harry Houk, a CNN contributor and former NYPD detective, stated that Bland was "arrogant" and "uncooperative" and that her behavior was the cause of her arrest. Blue Telusma, "Ex-Cop on CNN Says Sandra Bland Died Because She Was 'Arrogant from the Beginning.'"

58 Du Bois, *The Souls of Black Folk*, 1.

59 Lowrey-Kinberg and Buker describe the encounter as follows: "Encinia establishes that he has the right to govern how the interaction unfolds." Lowrey-Kinberg and Sullivan Buker, "I'm Giving You a Lawful Order," 392.

60 Blue Telusma, "Ex-Cop on CNN Says Sandra Bland Died Because She Was 'Arrogant from the Beginning.'"

61 Claudia Rankine aptly writes this lyric, "*Because white men can't police their imaginations, black men are dying,*" in *Citizen*. Rankine, *Citizen: An American Lyric*, 135.

62 bell hooks, *Killing Rage: Ending Racism* (New York: Macmillan, 1996), 19.

63 "Sandra Bland Voice Mail from Jail Expresses Disbelief," *Chicago Tribune*, July 23, 2015, https://www.chicagotribune.com/nation-world/ct-sandra-bland-20150723-story.html.

64 Crawley, *Blackpentecostal Breath*, 1.

THE END

1 Tiffany Lethabo King, *The Black Shoals: Offshore Formations of Black and Native Studies* (Durham, NC: Duke University Press, 2019), 2.

2 King, 4.

3 King, 49.

4 King, 49.

5 Jacqueline Jones Lamon, "Rockaway," in *What Water Knows* (Evanston, IL: TriQuarterly Books, 2021), 47.

6 Aracelis Girmay, "Inside the sea, there is more," in *The Black Maria* (Rochester, NY: BOA Editions, Ltd., 2016), 40.

7 Aracelis Girmay, "The Black Maria," in *The Black Maria* (Rochester, NY: BOA Editions, Ltd., 2016), 93.

8 Girmay, 94.

9 Adjua Gargi Nzinga Greaves, "We Live on Earth Where Sex Is Fuel, 2012," in *Letters to the Future: Black Women/Radical Writing*, ed. Erica Hunt and Dawn Lundy Martin (Tucson, AZ: Kore Press, 2018), 78.

10 Greaves, 79.

11 The line "Water is another country" comes from Dionne Brand, *A Map to the Door of No Return: Notes to Belonging* (Toronto: Doubleday Canada, 2001), 56.

12 Gumbs, *M Archive*, 107.

13 Alexis Pauline Gumbs, *Undrowned: Black Feminist Lessons from Marine Mammals* (Chico, CA: AK Press, 2020), 7.

14 Da Silva, "Toward a Black Feminist Poethics," 84.

15 Tourmaline, "Alternate Endings, Radical Beginnings Video & Artist Statement: Tourmaline," *Visual AIDS* (blog), accessed June 25, 2021, https://visualaids.org/blog/aerb-tourmaline-statement.

16 Tourmaline.

17 Lucille Clifton, "Atlantic Is a Sea of Bones," in *Next* (Brockport, NY: BOA Editions, Ltd., 1987), 26.

18 Dionne Brand, *A Map to the Door of No Return: Notes to Belonging* (Toronto: Doubleday Canada, 2001), 224.

Sources

Adodi Muse: A Gay Negro Ensemble. *Ain't Got Sense Enuf to Be 'Shamed*, 2004, streaming audio. Accessed February 11, 2020. https://music.apple.com/md/album/aint-got-sense -enuf-to-be-shamed/573920896.

Ahmed, Sara. *The Cultural Politics of Emotion*. New York: Routledge, 2013.

Alexander, Elizabeth. "'Coming Out Blackened and Whole': Fragmentation and Reintegration in Audre Lorde's *Zami* and *The Cancer Journals*." In Wallace-Sanders, ed., *Skin Deep, Spirit Strong*, 218–36.

Alexander, M. Jacqui. *Pedagogies of Crossing: Meditations on Feminism, Sexual Politics, Memory, and the Sacred*. Durham, NC: Duke University Press, 2005.

Allison, Donnetrice C. Introduction to *Black Women's Portrayals on Reality Television: The New Sapphire*, edited by Donnetrice C. Allison, ix–xxix. Lanham, MD: Lexington Books, 2016. http://ebookcentral.proquest.com/lib/washington/detail.action?docID=4398701.

Anzaldúa, Gloria. *Borderlands/La Frontera: The New Mestiza*. San Francisco: Aunt Lute Books, 1987.

Anzaldúa, Gloria, and Cherríe Moraga. *This Bridge Called My Back: Writings by Radical Women of Color*. Albany: State University of New York Press, 2015.

Ater, Renée. "Race, Gender, and Nation: Rethinking the Sculpture of Meta Warrick Fuller." PhD diss., University of Maryland, College Park, 2000. http://search.proquest.com /docview/230893034/?pq-origsite=primo.

Ater, Renée. *Remaking Race and History: The Sculpture of Meta Warrick Fuller*. Berkeley: University of California Press, 2011.

Austin, Tiffany, Sequoia Maner, Emily Ruth Rutter, and darlene anita scott. *Revisiting the Elegy in the Black Lives Matter Era*. New York: Routledge, 2019.

Bailey, Moya. "Race, Class, Region, and Gender in Early Emory School of Medicine Yearbooks." PhD diss., Emory University, 2013. https://search.proquest.com/docview /1466659791/abstract/1301BC1DA7F14B68PQ/1.

Baraka, Amiri. *See* Jones, LeRoi.

Barkley-Brown, Elsa, William R. Glass, and Agnieszka Graff. "Race, Sexuality, and African American Women Representing the Nation: An Interview with Elsa Barkley-Brown." *The Americanist. Warsaw Journal for the Study of the United States* 26 (2011): 17–36.

Barnett, LaShonda K., ed. *I Got Thunder: Black Women Songwriters on Their Craft*. New York: Thunder's Mouth Press, 2007.

Baumgaertner, Martin, dir. *Finally Karen Live!* Detroit: Island Black Music, 1997. Videocassette (VHS), 75 min.

Bingham, Remica. "Finding the Myth in the Human and the Human in the Myth: Midrash and Mythos in the Work of Lucille Clifton." *Langston Hughes Review* 22 (Fall 2008): 27–35.

Blain, Keisha N. "This Election, Black Women Are Leading the Way—Again," *The Nation*, November 2, 2020. https://www.thenation.com/article/politics/black-women-voting -rights/.

Boone, Eva Grace. "Little Sally Walker." *Field Recordings Vol. 4: Mississippi & Alabama (1934–1942)*, 1998, streaming audio. Music Online: American Music database. https://search.alexanderstreet.com/view/work/bibliographic_entity%7Crecorded_cd %7C74522.

Boyer, Horace Clarence. *The Golden Age of Gospel*. Urbana: University of Illinois Press, 2000.

Brand, Dionne. *A Map to the Door of No Return: Notes to Belonging*. Toronto: Doubleday Canada, 2001.

Brevard, Lisa Pertillar. "'Will the Circle Be Unbroken': African-American Women's Spirituality in Sacred Song Traditions." In *My Soul Is a Witness: African-American Women's Spirituality; A Sourcebook*, edited by Gloria Wade-Gayles, 32–47. Boston: Beacon Press, 1995.

Brooks, Daphne A. *Bodies in Dissent: Spectacular Performances of Race and Freedom, 1850–1910*. Durham, NC: Duke University Press, 2006.

Brooks, Daphne A. *Liner Notes for the Revolution: The Intellectual Life of Black Feminist Sound*. Cambridge, MA: Belknap Press of Harvard University Press, 2021.

Brown, Claude. "The Language of Soul." In *Mother Wit from the Laughing Barrel: Readings in the Interpretation of Afro-American Folklore*, edited by Alan Dundes, 230–37. Englewood Cliffs, NJ: Prentice-Hall, 1973.

Brown, Ellen. "Writing Is Third Career for Morrison." *Cincinnati Enquirer*, September 27, 1981, sec. F-11.

Brown, Jericho. *The Tradition*. Port Townsend, WA: Copper Canyon Press, 2019.

Brown, Kimberly Nichele. *Writing the Black Revolutionary Diva: Women's Subjectivity and the Decolonizing Text*. Bloomington: Indiana University Press, 2010.

Burrell, Kim. "She Said: Exclusive Interview with Kim Burrell." Interview by Troy Lilly, *GospelPundit* (blog), May 20, 2011. https://web.archive.org/web/20150724114344/http://www.gospelpundit.com/2011/05/she-said-exclusive-interview-with-kim-burrell/.

Burrell, Kim. "Love's Holiday." *The Love Album*. Shanachie, 2011. Streaming audio.

Campt, Tina M. *Listening to Images*. Durham, NC: Duke University Press, 2017.

Carby, Hazel V. "It Jus Be's Dat Way Sometime: The Sexual Politics of Women's Blues." *Radical America* 20, no. 4 (1987): 9–22.

Cheng, Anne Anlin. *The Melancholy of Race: Psychoanalysis, Assimilation, and Hidden Grief*. New York: Oxford University Press, 2001.

Christian, Barbara. "The Race for Theory." *Cultural Critique*, no. 6 (1987): 51–63. https://doi.org/10.2307/1354255.

Clark, Ella E. *Indian Legends of the Pacific Northwest*. Berkeley: University of California Press, 2003. https://doi.org/10.1525/9780520350960.

Clark Sheard, Karen and Kierra "Kiki" Sheard. "You Loved Me." *The Heavens Are Telling*. Elektra Records, 2003.

Clifton, Lucille. "Between Starshine and Clay: An Interview with Lucille Clifton by Remica Bingham." *Writers Chronicle* 43, no. 4 (February 2011): 8–12.

Clifton, Lucille. *The Book of Light*. Port Townsend, WA: Copper Canyon Press, 1993.

Clifton, Lucille. *Good News About the Earth: New Poems*. New York, Random House, 1972.

Clifton, Lucille. "Her Last Interview, with Chard DeNiord." *American Poetry Review* 39, no. 3 (May/June 2010): 5–13.

Clifton, Lucille. "I'd Like Not to Be a Stranger in the World: A Conversation/Interview with Lucille Clifton." Interview by Michael S. Glaser. *Antioch Review* 58, no. 3 (Summer 2000): 310–28.

Clifton, Lucille. "An Interview with Lucille Clifton." Interview by Charles H. Rowell. *Callaloo* 22, no. 1 (Winter 1999): 56–72.

Clifton, Lucille. *Mercy*. Rochester, NY: BOA Editions, Ltd., 2004.

Clifton, Lucille. *Next: New Poems*. Brockport, NY: BOA Editions, Ltd., 1987.

Clifton, Lucille. *Quilting: Poems, 1987–1990*. Rochester, NY: BOA Editions, Ltd., 1991.

Clifton, Lucille. "Spirit Writing, 1977." Stuart A. Rose Manuscript, Archives, and Rare Book Library, Emory University, box 30, folder 1.

Clifton, Lucille. *The Terrible Stories*. Rochester, NY: BOA Editions, Ltd., 1996.

Clinton, George, and Ben Greenman. *Brothas Be, Yo Like George, Ain't That Funkin' Kinda Hard on You?: A Memoir*. New York: Simon and Schuster, 2017.

Clough, Patricia Ticineto. Introduction to *The Affective Turn: Theorizing the Social*, edited by Jean O'Malley Halley and Patricia Ticineto Clough, 1–33. Durham, NC: Duke University Press, 2007.

Cohen, Cathy J. "Punks, Bulldaggers, and Welfare Queens: The Radical Potential of Queer Politics?" *GLQ: A Journal of Lesbian and Gay Studies* 3, no. 4 (May 1, 1997): 437–65. https://doi.org/10.1215/10642684-3-4-437.

Collins, Lisa Gail. *The Art of History: African American Women Artists Engage the Past.* New Brunswick, NJ: Rutgers University Press, 2002.

Collins, Lisa Gail. "'The Evidence of the Process.'" *Transition*, no. 109 (2012): 45–61. https://doi.org/10.2979/transition.109.45.

Collins, Patricia Hill. *Black Feminist Thought: Knowledge, Consciousness, and the Politics of Empowerment.* New York: Routledge, 2008.

Collins, Patricia Hill. "Comment on Hekman's 'Truth and Method: Feminist Standpoint Theory Revisited': Where's the Power?" *Signs* 22, no. 2 (1997): 375–81.

Combahee River Collective. "A Black Feminist Statement." In Anzaldúa and Moraga, *This Bridge Called My Back: Writings by Radical Women of Color*, 210–18.

Cone, James H. *A Black Theology of Liberation: Twentieth Anniversary Edition.* Maryknoll, NY: Orbis Books, 1990.

Cone, James H. *God of the Oppressed.* New York: Seabury Press, 1975.

Cone, James H. *The Spirituals and the Blues: An Interpretation.* Maryknoll, NY: Orbis Books, 1972.

Cox, Renee. Personal interview by Bettina Judd, March 2012.

Cox, Renee. *The Liberation of Lady J. and U.B.* 1998. Cibachrome photograph by Larry Qualls, 48 × 60 inches. Accessed August 23, 2022. http://jstor.org/stable/10.2307/community.14253010.

Cox, Renee. *Yo Mama Goes to the Hamptons.* 1994. Archival digital ink jet print on cotton rag, 30 × 40 inches. Artist's website. https://www.reneecox.org/yo-mama.

Crawley, Ashon T. *Blackpentecostal Breath: The Aesthetics of Possibility.* New York: Fordham University Press, 2016.

Cummings, Moriba. "Oh, Word? Kim Burrell Disrespectfully Slams 'Perverted' Homosexuals in Sermon." *Celebrity News and Media.* BET (blog), December 31, 2016. https://www.bet.com/article/j85pv8/kim-burrell-disrespectfully-slams-homosexuals-in-sermon.

Dall, Christine, dir. *Wild Women Don't Have the Blues.* DVD. California Newsreel, 2007, 58 min.

da Silva, Denise Ferreira. "Toward a Black Feminist Poethics: The Quest(ion) of Blackness Toward the End of the World." *Black Scholar* 44, no. 2 (2014): 81–97.

Davis, Angela Y. *Blues Legacies and Black Feminism: Gertrude "Ma" Rainey, Bessie Smith, and Billie Holiday.* New York: Pantheon Books, 1998.

Davis, Angela Y. *Freedom Is a Constant Struggle: Ferguson, Palestine, and the Foundations of a Movement.* Chicago: Haymarket Books, 2016.

Davis, Angela Y. "Reflections on the Black Woman's Role in the Community of Slaves." *Black Scholar* 3, no. 4 (1971): 2–15.

Dearmont, Diane. "Automatic Writing: A History from Mesmer to Breton." PhD diss., University of Washington, 2004. http://search.proquest.com.proxy.wm.edu/docview/305106649/abstract.

DeCarava, Roy. *Edna Smith.* 1955. Black-and-white photograph. Accessed August 23, 2022. https://www.moma.org/collection/works/50486 or https://www.phillips.com/detail/roy-decarava/NY040317/38.

Diaz, Jacqueline. "Aunt Jemima No More: Pancake Brand Renamed Pearl Milling Company." National Public Radio, February 10, 2021. https://www.npr.org/2021/02/10/966166648/aunt-jemima-no-more-pancake-brand-renamed-pearl-milling-company.

Douglas, Kelly Brown. "Black and Blues: God-Talk/ Body-Talk for the Black Church." In *Sexuality and the Sacred, Second Edition: Sources for Theological Reflection*, edited by Marvin Mahan Ellison and Kelly Brown Douglas, 44–66. Louisville, KY: Westminster John Knox Press, 2010.

Douglas, Kelly Brown. *The Black Christ.* Maryknoll, NY: Orbis Books, 1993.

Dove, Rita. "Rita Dove: An Interview." Interview with Grace Cavalieri. *The American Poetry Review* 24, no. 2 (1995): 11–15.

Du Bois, William Edward Burghardt. *The Souls of Black Folk: Essays and Sketches.* Chicago: A. C. McClurg & Company, 1903.

Evans, David. "Blues: Chronological Overview." In *African American Music: An Introduction*, edited by Portia K. Maultsby and Mellonee V. Burnim, 79–96. New York: Routledge, 2006.

Fanon, Frantz. *Black Skin, White Masks.* New York: Grove Press, 1967.

Farrington, Lisa E. *Creating Their Own Image: The History of African-American Women Artists.* New York: Oxford University Press, 2005.

Finney, Nikky. *Head Off & Split: Poems.* Evanston, IL: Northwestern University Press, 2011.

Finney, Nikky. *The World Is Round*. Atlanta, GA: InnerLight Publishing, 2003.

Fleetwood, Nicole R. *Troubling Vision: Performance, Visuality, and Blackness*. Chicago: University of Chicago Press, 2011.

Flunder, Yvette. "Church Interlude II: Healing Oppression Sickness." In *Queer Christianities: Lived Religion in Transgressive Forms*, edited by Kathleen T. Talvacchia and Mark Larrimore, 115–24. New York: New York University Press, 2014.

Forché, Carolyn. *The Angel of History*. New York: HarperCollins, 1994.

Frankenberg, Ruth. *Displacing Whiteness : Essays in Social and Cultural Criticism*. Durham, NC: Duke University Press, 1997.

Franklin, Aretha. *Amazing Grace*. Atlantic SD-2-906, 1972, vinyl LP 12˝, 33 1/3 rpm.

Franklin, Aretha. *Aretha: Live at Fillmore West*. Atlantic, SD 7205, 1971, vinyl LP 12˝33 1/3 rpm.

Franklin, Aretha, and David Ritz. *From These Roots*. New York: Crown, 1999.

Franklin, Aretha. *Aretha Franklin—Full Concert—03/06/71—Fillmore West (OFFICIAL)*, 2014. https://www.youtube.com/watch?v=bzOKVInJ8vc.

Franklin, Aretha. *Aretha Franklin—Full Concert—03/07/71—Fillmore West (OFFICIAL)*, 2014. https://www.youtube.com/watch?v=Vyx34kgHGng.

Franklin, Aretha. *Lady Soul*. Rhino Records R2 71933, 1968 (remastered), compact disc.

Galassi, Peter. *Roy DeCarava: A Retrospective*. New York: Museum of Modern Art, 1996.

Galloway, Brent Douglas. *Phonology, Morphology, and Classified Word List for the Samish Dialect of Straits Salish*. Ottawa: University of Ottawa Press, 1990. http://muse.jhu.edu /book/65590.

Garland, Phyl. *The Sound of Soul*. Chicago: Henry Regnery Company, 1969.

Gay, Mara. "Problems with 'Precious.' " *The Atlantic*, November 7, 2009. https://www .theatlantic.com/culture/archive/2009/11/problems-with-precious/347636/.

Geneva Reed-Veal, mother of Sandra Bland, deceased, v. Brian Encinia, Texas Department of Public Safety, Elsa Magnus, Oscar Prudente, Waller County Sheriff's Office; Complaint at law (Case No. 4:15-cv-02232; wrongful death lawsuit). Legislative Reference Library of Texas. "Related Court Documents," August 4, 2015. http://www.lrl.state.tx.us /currentissues/clips/casePage.cfm?pageID=8&reportID=28329.

Gips, Terry. "Joyce J. Scott's Mammy/Nanny Series." *Feminist Studies* 22, no. 2 (1996): 311–20. https://doi.org/10.2307/3178415.

Girmay, Aracelis. *The Black Maria*. Rochester, NY: BOA Editions, Ltd., 2016.

Gordon, Avery. *Ghostly Matters: Haunting and the Sociological Imagination*. Minneapolis: University of Minnesota Press, 1997.

Gould, Deborah B. *Moving Politics: Emotion and ACT UP's Fight against AIDS*. Chicago: University of Chicago Press, 2009.

Greaves, Adjua Gargi Nzinga. "We Live on Earth Where Sex Is Fuel, 2012." In *Letters to the Future: Black Women/Radical Writing*, edited by Erica Hunt and Dawn Lundy Martin, 78–79. Tuscon, AZ: Kore Press, 2018.

Green, Kai M., and Treva Ellison. "Tranifest." *TSQ: Transgender Studies Quarterly* 1, no. 1/2 (May 1, 2014): 222–25. https://doi.org/10.1215/23289252-2400082.

Griffin, Farah Jasmine. "That the Mothers May Soar and the Daughters May Know Their Names: A Retrospective of Black Feminist Literary Criticism." *Signs* 32, no. 2 (2007): 483–507. https://doi.org/10.1086/508377.

Griffin, Farah Jasmine. "When Malindy Sings: A Meditation on Black Women's Vocality." In *Uptown Conversation: The New Jazz Studies*, edited by Robert G. O'Meally, Brent Hayes Edwards, and Farah Jasmine Griffin, 102–25. New York: Columbia University Press, 2004. http://www.degruyter.com/doi/book/10.7312/omea12350.

Griggs, Dan (Media Revolution), dir. *Lannan Foundation: Lucille Clifton*. VHS. Los Angeles, 1996. 60 min.

Grim, Ryan. "The Transcript of Sandra Bland's Arrest Is as Revealing as the Video." *Huffington Post*, July 23, 2015, sec. Politics. http://www.huffingtonpost.com/entry /sandra-bland-arrest-transcript_us_55b03a88e4b0a9b94853b1f1.

Gumbs, Alexis Pauline. *M Archive: After the End of the World*. Durham, NC: Duke University Press, 2018.

Gumbs, Alexis Pauline. "M/Other Ourselves: A Black Queer Feminist Genealogy for Radical Mothering." In *Revolutionary Mothering: Love on the Front Lines*, edited by Mai'a Williams, Alexis Pauline Gumbs, and China Martens, 14–28. Oakland, CA: PM Press, 2016.

Gumbs, Alexis Pauline. *Undrowned: Black Feminist Lessons from Marine Mammals*. Chico, CA: AK Press, 2020.

Haba, James, David Grubin, and Bill D. Moyers. *The Language of Life: A Festival of Poets*. New York: Doubleday, 1995.

Hadley, Fredara. "Remarks on Black Feminine Genius." *Aretha Franklin's Amazing Grace: From Watts to Detroit: A Two-Day Symposium Celebrating the Life of the Queen of Soul*. University of California Los Angeles, March 24 and 25, 2019. https://youtu.be /HV7X3rTXFfI.

Hammonds, Evelynn. "Black (w)Holes and the Geometry of Black Female Sexuality." *Differences* 6, no. 2/3 (Summer 1994): 126–45.

Handy, D. Antoinette. *Black Women in American Bands and Orchestras*. Lanham, MD: Scarecrow Press, 1998.

Hansberry, Lorraine. *To Be Young, Gifted, and Black: A Portrait of Lorraine Hansberry in Her Own Words*. Edited by Robert Nemiroff. New York: Signet, 1970.

Hansen, Kenneth C. *The Maiden of Deception Pass: A Spirit in Cedar*. Anacortes, WA: Samish Experience Productions, 1983.

Harding, Sandra. "Comment on Hekman's 'Truth and Method: Feminist Standpoint Theory Revisited': Whose Standpoint Needs the Regimes of Truth and Reality?" *Signs* 22, no. 2 (1997): 382–91.

Harris, Michael D. *Colored Pictures: Race and Visual Representation*. Chapel Hill, NC: University of North Carolina Press, 2003.

Harris-Perry, Melissa V. *Sister Citizen: Shame, Stereotypes, and Black Women in America*. New Haven, CT: Yale University Press, 2011.

Hartman, Saidiya. *Lose Your Mother: A Journey Along the Atlantic Slave Route*. New York: Macmillan, 2008.

Hartman, Saidiya. "The Time of Slavery." *South Atlantic Quarterly* 101, no. 4 (2002): 757–77.

Hartman, Saidiya. *Wayward Lives, Beautiful Experiments: Intimate Histories of Social Upheaval*. New York: W. W. Norton, 2019.

Hawkins, Edwin, and Shirley Miller. "Oh Happy Day." *Celebration of Joy* (compilation). I AM Records, 2015, streaming audio.

Hawkins, Walter. *Love Alive IV*. Malaco Records MAL 6007, 1990, compact disc. Featuring Yvette Flunder on "Thank You" and Yvette Flunder and Shirley Miller on "Full and Complete."

Henderson, Mae. "Speaking in Tongues: Dialects, Dialogics, and the Black Woman Writer's Literary Tradition." In *Speaking in Tongues and Dancing Diaspora: Black Women Writing and Performing*, 59–75. New York: Oxford University Press, 2014.

Hine, Darlene Clark. "Rape and the Inner Lives of Black Women in the Middle West." *Signs* 14, no. 4 (1989): 912–20.

Holladay, Hilary. *Wild Blessings: The Poetry of Lucille Clifton*. Baton Rouge: Louisiana State University Press, 2004.

Holland, Sharon Patricia. *Raising the Dead: Readings of Death and (Black) Subjectivity*. Durham, NC: Duke University Press, 2000.

Holloway, Karla FC. *Passed On: African American Mourning Stories, A Memorial*. Durham, NC: Duke University Press, 2003.

hooks, bell. *Killing Rage: Ending Racism*. New York: Macmillan, 1996.

hooks, bell. *Rock My Soul: Black People and Self-Esteem*. New York: Washington Square Press, 2003.

hooks, bell. *Teaching to Transgress: Education as the Practice of Freedom*. New York: Routledge, 1994.

Houston, Marsha, and Olga Idriss Davis. *Centering Ourselves: African American Feminist and Womanist Studies of Discourse*. Cresskill, NJ: Hampton Press, 2002.

Houston, Whitney. "Whitney Houston: Down and Dirty." Interview by Anthony DeCurtis. *Rolling Stone*, June 10, 1993.

Hull, Gloria T. *Soul Talk: The New Spirituality of African American Women*. Rochester, VT: Inner Traditions, 2001.

Hunt, Erica, and Dawn Lundy Martin, eds. *Letters to the Future: Black Women/Radical Writing*. Tucson, AZ: Kore Press, 2018.

"In the News: COGIC Music Dept. Issues Statement about Kim Burrell." *GospelPundit* (blog), February 18, 2010. https://web.archive.org/web/20160803005216/http://www .gospelpundit.com/2010/02/in-the-news-cogic-music-dept-issues-statement-about-kim -burrell/.

Jackson, Panama. "The Moment That Ended Sandra Bland's Life." *The Root*, July 22, 2015. https://www.theroot.com/the-moment-that-ended-sandra-blands-life-1822521368.

Jacobs, Harriet Ann. *Incidents in the Life of a Slave Girl*. New York: Skyhorse Publishing, 1861.

Jess, Tyehimba. *Olio*. Seattle: Wave Books, 2016.

Johnson, James Weldon. *God's Trombones: Seven Negro Sermons in Verse*. Electronic edition. Chapel Hill: University of North Carolina at Chapel Hill Libraries, 2004.

Johnson, E. Patrick. "Feeling the Spirit in the Dark: Expanding Notions of the Sacred in the African-American Gay Community." *Callaloo* 21, no. 2 (1998): 399–416.

Jones, Feminista. "Black Women Saved Democracy Yet Again: Where's Our Moment of Gratitude?" *Philadelphia Inquirer*, November 10, 2020, Opinion. https://www.inquirer.com/opinion/commentary/joe-biden-victory-philadelphia-pennsylvania-black-women-voters-20201110.html.

Jones, LeRoi. *Blues People: Negro Music in White America*. New York: Harper Perennial, 1999.

Jones, Patricia Spears. "Sapphire." *Black Scholar* 38, no. 2/3 (2008): 42–43.

Jones, William R. *Is God a White Racist? A Preamble to Black Theology*. Boston: Beacon Press, 1998.

Jordan, June. "Some of Us Did Not Die." In *Some of Us Did Not Die: New and Selected Essays*, 8–16. New York: Basic Books, 2003.

Jordan-Zachary, Julia S. "Beyond the Side Eye: Black Women's Ancestral Anger as a Liberatory Practice." *Journal of Black Sexuality and Relationships* 4, no. 1 (2017): 61–81.

Judd, Bettina. "GLOSSOLALIA: Lucille Clifton's Creative Technologies of Becoming." In *Black Bodies and Transhuman Realities: Scientifically Modifying the Black Body in Posthuman Literature and Culture*, edited by Melvin G. Hill, 133–49. Lanham, MD: Lexington Books, 2019.

Judd, Bettina. "On or about July 10, 2015." *The Offing*, March 24, 2016. https://theoffingmag.com/here-you-are/on-or-about-july-10-20151/.

Judd, Bettina. *patient*. New York: Black Lawrence Press, 2014.

Junior, Nyasha. "The Mark of Cain and White Violence." *Journal of Biblical Literature* 139, no. 4 (2020): 661–73. http://dx.doi.org/10.15699/jbl.1394.2020.2.

Kapsalis, Terri. "Mastering the Female Pelvis: Race and the Tools of Reproduction." In Wallace-Sanders, ed., *Skin Deep, Spirit Strong*, 263–300.

Karsen Lou, and Tracy Rector, dirs. *Maiden of Deception Pass: Guardian of Her Samish People*. Video, 26 min., 48 secs. Longhouse Media, 2015. https://vimeo.com/130576433.

Kelley, Robin D. G. *Yo' Mama's Disfunktional!: Fighting the Culture Wars in Urban America*. Boston: Beacon Press, 2001.

Kimmel, Michael S. *Angry White Men: American Masculinity at the End of an Era*. New York: Nation Books, 2013.

King, Debra Walker. *African Americans and the Culture of Pain*. Charlottesville: University of Virginia Press, 2008.

King, Tiffany Lethabo. "Black 'Feminisms' and Pessimism: Abolishing Moynihan's Negro Family." *Theory & Event* 21, no. 1 (January 2018): 68–87.

King, Tiffany Lethabo. *The Black Shoals: Offshore Formations of Black and Native Studies*. Durham, NC: Duke University Press, 2019.

Kirk-Duggan, Cheryl A. *Exorcizing Evil: A Womanist Perspective on the Spirituals*. Vol. 14, Bishop Henry McNeal Turner/Sojourner Truth Series in Black Religion. Maryknoll, NY: Orbis Books, 1997.

Lai, K. K. Rebecca, Haeyoun Park, Larry Buchanan, and Wilson Andrews. "Assessing the Legality of Sandra Bland's Arrest." *New York Times*, July 20, 2015, sec. U.S. https://www.nytimes.com/interactive/2015/07/20/us/sandra-bland-arrest-death-videos-maps.html.

Lamon, Jacqueline Jones. *What Water Knows*. Evanston, IL: TriQuarterly Books, 2021.

Lawson, Deana. *Deana Lawson*. New York: Aperture, 2018.

Lawson, Deana. "In Conversation with Deana Lawson." Interview by Sabine Mirlesse. *Whitehot Magazine of Contemporary Art*, November 2011. https://whitehotmagazine.com/articles/in-conversation-with-deana-lawson/2403.

Lischer, Richard. *The Preacher King: Martin Luther King Jr. and the Word That Moved America*. New York: Oxford University Press, 1997.

Liss, Andrea. "Black Bodies in Evidence: Maternal Visibility in Renée Cox's Family Portraits." In *The Familial Gaze*, edited by Marianne Hirsch, 276–92. Lebanon, NH: University Press of New England, 1999.

Long, Charles H. *Significations: Signs, Symbols, and Images in the Interpretation of Religion*. Philadelphia: Fortress Press, 1986.

Lorde, Audre. "The Great American Disease." *Black Scholar* 10, no. 8/9 (1979): 17–20.

Lorde, Audre. *The Collected Poems of Audre Lorde*. W. W. Norton, 2000.

Lorde, Audre. *Sister Outsider: Essays and Speeches*. Berkeley, CA: Crossing Press, 1984.

Lordi, Emily J. *Black Resonance: Iconic Women Singers and African American Literature*. New Brunswick, NJ: Rutgers University Press, 2013.

Lordi, Emily J. *The Meaning of Soul: Black Music and Resilience since the 1960s*. Durham, NC: Duke University Press, 2020.

Lowrey-Kinberg, Belén V., and Grace Sullivan Buker. "'I'm Giving You a Lawful Order': Dialogic Legitimacy in Sandra Bland's Traffic Stop." *Law & Society Review* 51, no. 2 (June 1, 2017): 379–412. https://doi.org/10.1111/lasr.12265.

Mae, Nettie, Alenda Turner, and Sid Hemphill's Band. "Little Sally Walker." *Afro-American Folk Music from Tate and Panola Counties, Mississippi*. Rounder Records, 2000.

Mahon, Maureen. *Black Diamond Queens: African American Women and Rock and Roll*. Durham, NC: Duke University Press, 2020. https://doi.org/10.1215/9781478012771.

Maparyan, Layli. *The Womanist Idea*. New York: Routledge, 2012.

McDowell, Deborah. *"The Changing Same": Black Women's Literature, Criticism, and Theory*. Bloomington: Indiana University Press, 1995.

McKittrick, Katherine. "Mathematics Black Life." *Black Scholar* 44, no. 2 (2014): 16–28.

Million, Dian. "Felt Theory: An Indigenous Feminist Approach to Affect and History." *Wicazo Sa Review* 24, no. 2 (October 8, 2009): 53–76. https://doi.org/10.1353/wic.0.0043.

Morgan, Jo-Ann. "Mammy the Huckster: Selling the Old South for the New Century." *American Art* 9, no. 1 (1995): 87–109.

Morrison, Toni. *Beloved*. New York: Knopf, 2007.

Morrison, Toni. *The Bluest Eye*. New York: Knopf, 1993.

Morrison, Toni. *Song of Solomon*. New York: Vintage International, 2004.

Morrison, Toni. *Sula*. Knopf, 2007.

Moynihan, Patrick. "Chapter IV: The Tangle of Pathology," in *The Negro Family: The Case for National Action*, Office of Policy Planning and Research, United States Department of Labor, March 1965. Accessed January 11, 2020. https://www.dol.gov/general/aboutdol/history/webid-moynihan/moynchapter4.

Murphy, Eddie, dir. *Harlem Nights*. Paramount, 2002.

Musser, Amber Jamilla. *Sensational Flesh: Race, Power, and Masochism*. New York: New York University Press, 2014.

Nash, Jennifer C. *The Black Body in Ecstasy: Reading Race, Reading Pornography*. Durham, NC: Duke University Press, 2014.

Ngai, Sianne. *Ugly Feelings*. Cambridge, MA: Harvard University Press, 2005.

Nietzsche, Friedrich Wilhelm. *The Joyful Wisdom ("La Gaya Scienza")*. In *The Complete Works of Friedrich Nietzsche*, vol. 10. Edited by Oscar Levy. Translated by Paul V. Cohn and Thomas Common. Edinburgh: T. N. Foulis, 1910. [Project Gutenberg, 2016.]

O'Grady, Lorraine. "Olympia's Maid: Reclaiming Black Female Subjectivity." In *The Feminism and Visual Culture Reader*, edited by Amelia Jones, 174–87. New York: Routledge, 2002.

Ogundipe, Ayodele. "Esu Elegbara, the Yoruba God of Chance and Uncertainty: A Study in Yoruba Mythology. (Volumes I and II)." PhD diss., Indiana University, 1978.

Otero, Solimar, and Toyin Falola. *Yemoja: Gender, Sexuality, and Creativity in the Latina/o and Afro-Atlantic Diasporas*. Albany: State University of New York Press, 2013.

Paris, Rae. *The Forgetting Tree: A Rememory*. Detroit: Wayne State University Press, 2017.

Parks, Sheri. *Fierce Angels: The Strong Black Woman in American Life and Culture*. New York: One World / Ballantine, 2010.

Pavlic, Ed. Keynote address to *Aretha Franklin's Amazing Grace: From Watts to Detroit: A Two-Day Symposium Celebrating the Life of the Queen of Soul*. University of California Los Angeles, March 24 and 25, 2019. https://youtu.be/HV7X3rTXFfI.

Pellett, Gail, dir. *The Songs Are Free: Bernice Johnson Reagon and African American Music*. With Bill D. Moyers, Sweet Honey in the Rock, and Freedom Singers. Public Affairs Television, aired on PBS, 1991. Distributed by Films for the Humanities and Sciences, Princeton, NJ, 1997.

Percelay, James, Monteria Ivey, Stephan Dwek, and Quincy Jones. *Snaps: The Original "Yo' Mama" Joke Book*. New York: HarperCollins, 1994.

Perkins, Margo. "The Church of Aretha." In *My Soul Is a Witness: African-American Women's Spirituality; A Sourcebook*, edited by Gloria Jean Wade-Gayles, 128–30. Boston: Beacon Press, 1995.

Pinn, Anthony B. *Why, Lord? Suffering and Evil in Black Theology*. New York: Continuum, 1995.

Pryse, Marjorie. "Introduction: Zora Neale Hurston, Alice Walker, and the 'Ancient Power' of Black Women." In *Conjuring: Black Women, Fiction, and Literary Tradition*, edited by Marjorie Pryse and Hortense Spillers, 1–24. Bloomington: Indiana University Press, 1985.

Quashie, Kevin. *The Sovereignty of Quiet: Beyond Resistance in Black Culture*. New Brunswick, NJ: Rutgers University Press, 2012.

Quashie, Kevin. "To Be (a) One: Notes on Coupling and Black Female Audacity." *Differences: A Journal of Feminist Cultural Studies* 29, no. 2 (2018): 68–95. https://doi.org/10.1215/10407391-6999774.

Rankine, Claudia. *Citizen: An American Lyric*. Minneapolis: Graywolf, 2014.

Rankine, Claudia. "'The Condition of Black Life Is One of Mourning.'" *New York Times*, June 22, 2015. https://www.nytimes.com/2015/06/22/magazine/the-condition-of-black-life-is-one-of-mourning.html.

Ransby, Barbara, and Tracye Matthews. "Black Popular Culture and the Transcendence of Patriarchal Illusions." *Race & Class* 35, no. 1 (1993): 57–68.

Reed, T. V. *The Art of Protest: Culture and Activism from the Civil Rights Movement to the Streets of Seattle*. Minneapolis: University of Minnesota Press, 2005.

Reiss, Benjamin. *The Showman and the Slave: Race, Death, and Memory in Barnum's America*. Cambridge, MA: Harvard University Press, 2001.

Richardson, Elaine. *African American Literacies*. Abingdon, Eng.: Taylor and Francis, 2002.

Richey, Lance B. "Neoplatonism and Nature in the Canticle of Creatures." *The AFCU Journal: A Franciscan Perspective on Higher Education* 9, no. 1 (January 2019): 43–61.

Roberts, Dorothy. *Killing the Black Body: Race, Reproduction, and the Meaning of Liberty*. New York: Vintage, 1998.

Robinson-Martin, Trineice. "Developing a Pedagogy for Gospel Singing: Understanding the Cultural Aesthetics and Performance Components of a Vocal Performance in Gospel Music." PhD diss., Columbia University, 2010. http://search.proquest.com/docview/756254736/.

Saleh-Hanna, Viviane. "Black Feminist Hauntology: Rememory the Ghosts of Abolition?" *Champ Pénal/Penal Field* 12 (March 23, 2015). https://doi.org/10.4000/champpenal.9168.

"Sandra Bland Voice Mail from Jail Expresses Disbelief." *Chicago Tribune*, July 23, 2015. https://www.chicagotribune.com/nation-world/ct-sandra-bland-20150723-story.html.

Sapphire. *Push*. New York: Vintage Books, 1997.

Scanlan, Fr. Michael. *The San Damiano Cross: An Explanation*. Steubenville, OH: University of Steubenville Press, 1983.

Scelfo, Julie. "Will Black Women Save Us . . . Again?" *Boston Globe*, April 26, 2019. https://www.bostonglobe.com/ideas/2019/04/26/will-black-women-save-again/nIayQS9Gyzz9z6jmFqpGSI/story.html.

Scott, Jill. "He Loves Me (Lyzel in E Flat)." *Jill Scott: Words and Sounds Vol. 1*. Hidden Beach, 2000.

Senior, Olive. "Yemoja: Mother of Waters." *Conjunctions* 27 (1996): 57–60.

Sexton, Jared. "Afro-Pessimism: The Unclear Word." *Rhizomes: Cultural Studies in Emerging Knowledge* 29 (2016). http://www.rhizomes.net/issue29/sexton.html.

Shange, Ntozake. *The Lizard Series*. 67/100 of a limited-edition, self-published chapbook, 2007.

Sharpe, Christina. *In the Wake: On Blackness and Being*. Durham, NC: Duke University Press, 2016.

Shaw, Andrea Elizabeth. *The Embodiment of Disobedience: Fat Black Women's Unruly Political Bodies*. Lanham, MD: Lexington Books, 2006.

Shaye, Amaryah. "Kim Burrell and the Power and Pleasure of Authority: On Sexuality and Transformative Justice in the Black Church." *Women in Theology* (blog), January 9, 2017. https://womenintheology.org/2017/01/09/kim-burrell-and-the-power-and-pleasure-of-authority-on-sexuality-and-transformative-justice-in-the-black-church/.

Sidibe, Gabourey. *This Is Just My Face: Try Not to Stare*. Boston: Houghton Mifflin Harcourt, 2017.

Simone, Nina. *I Put a Spell on You: The Autobiography of Nina Simone*. New York: Da Capo Press, 2003.

Simone, Nina. *In Concert*. The Verve Music Group, 1964, streaming audio.

Simone, Nina. *Said*. RCA Victor LSP-4065, 1968, compact disc.

Sirmans, Franklin. "Deana Lawson." *Contact Sheet* 152 (2009): 16–21.

Skloot, Rebecca. *The Immortal Life of Henrietta Lacks*. New York: Broadway Books, 2011.

Smith, Barbara. *The Truth That Never Hurts*. New Brunswick, NJ: Rutgers University Press, 1999.

Smith, Sarah. "Towards a Poetics of Bafflement: The Politics of Elsewhere in Contemporary Black Diaspora Visual Practice (1990–Present)." PhD diss., University of Toronto, 2016. http://search.proquest.com/docview/1889845065/.

Smith, Zadie. "Through the Portal: Locating the Magnificent." In Lawson, *Deana Lawson*, 5–9.

Smitherman, Geneva. *Black Talk: Words and Phrases from the Hood to the Amen Corner*. Boston: Houghton Mifflin, 2000.

Smitherman, Geneva. *Talkin and Testifyin: The Language of Black America*. Detroit: Wayne State University Press, 1986.

Snorton, C. Riley. *Black on Both Sides: A Racial History of Trans Identity*. Minneapolis: University of Minnesota Press, 2017.

Snorton, C. Riley. *Nobody Is Supposed to Know: Black Sexuality on the Down Low*. Minneapolis: University of Minnesota Press, 2014.

Spillers, Hortense J. "A Hateful Passion, a Lost Love." *Feminist Studies* 9, no. 2 (1983): 293–323. https://doi.org/10.2307/3177494.

Spillers, Hortense J. "Interstices: A Small Drama of Words." In *Black, White, and in Color: Essays on American Literature and Culture*, 152–75. Chicago: University of Chicago Press, 2003.

Spillers, Hortense J. "Mama's Baby, Papa's Maybe: An American Grammar Book." *Diacritics* 17, no. 2 (1987): 65–81. https://doi.org/10.2307/464747.

Stallings, L. H. *Funk the Erotic: Transaesthetics and Black Sexual Cultures*. Urbana, Chicago: University of Illinois Press, 2015.

Stallings, L. H. *Mutha' Is Half a Word: Intersections of Folklore, Vernacular, Myth, and Queerness in Black Female Culture*. Black Performance and Cultural Criticism. Columbus: Ohio State University Press, 2007.

Stallings, L. H. "Sapphire's PUSH for Erotic Literacy and Black Girl Sexual Agency." In *Sapphire's Literary Breakthrough: Erotic Literacies, Feminist Pedagogies, Environmental Justice Perspectives*, edited by Elizazbeth McNeil, Neal A. Lester, DoVeanna S. Fulton, and Lynette D. Myles, 113–39. New York: Palgrave Macmillan, 2012.

Staples, Robert. "A Rejoinder: Black Feminism and the Cult of Masculinity: The Danger Within." *Black Scholar* 10, no. 8/9 (1979): 63–67. https://doi.org/10.1080/00064246.1979.11644173.

Staples, Robert. "The Myth of Black Macho: A Response to Angry Black Feminists." *Black Scholar* 10, no. 6/7 (1979): 24–33.

St. Félix, Doreen. "How the Alabama Senate Election Sanctified Black Women Voters." *New Yorker*, December 14, 2017. https://www.newyorker.com/news/daily-comment/how-the-alabama-senate-election-sanctified-black-women-voters.

Strings, Sabrina. *Fearing the Black Body: The Racial Origins of Fat Phobia*. New York: New York University Press, 2019.

Sullivan, Graeme. *Art Practice as Research: Inquiry in Visual Arts*. 2nd ed. Thousand Oaks, CA: Sage Publications, 2010.

Sunshine, Avery. "A Conversation with Avery Sunshine." Interview by Tamara Harris, *Kick Mag*, August 13, 2010. http://www.kickmag.net/2010/08/13/a-conversation-with-avery-sunshine/.

Sunshine, Avery. *Avery*Sunshine*. Big Shine Music, 2010, compact disc.

Sunshine, Avery. Interview by Kanaal Nodap. YouTube Video, June 2011. http://www.youtube.com/watch?v=Z2vaHAYA4WI.

Sunshine, Avery. Personal interview by Bettina Judd. Skype, November 4, 2012.

Sunshine, Avery. "Ramona Debreaux Interview with Soulful Avery Sunshine." Youtube Video, September 9, 2011. http://www.youtube.com/watch?v=DyJFANmP85c.

Sunshine, Avery, and Jodine Dorce. "Meet & Greet with Avery Sunshine!!" April 13, 2011. http://grownfolksmusic.com/blog/interview-meet-greet-avery-sunshine.

Sweet Honey in the Rock. *Good News*. Flying Fish FF245, 1981, vinyl LP 12", 33 1/3 rpm.

Taylor, Koko. "I'm a Woman." *The Earthshaker*. Alligator Records AL4711, 1978, vinyl LP 12", 33 1/3 rpm.

Telusma, Blue. "Ex-Cop on CNN Says Sandra Bland Died Because She Was 'Arrogant from the Beginning.' " *theGrio*. Accessed August 2, 2017. http://thegrio.com/2015/07/22/ex-cop-on-cnn-says-sandra-bland-died-because-she-was-arrogant-from-the-beginning/.

Thomas, Rufus. "Little Sally Walker." Stax 45-167, 1965, vinyl 7", 45 rpm.

Thompson, Robert Farris. *Flash of the Spirit: African & Afro-American Art & Philosophy*. New York: Knopf, 2010.

Till-Mobley, Mamie, and Christopher Benson. *Death of Innocence: The Story of the Hate Crime That Changed America*. New York: Random House, 2011.

Tomkins, Silvan S. *Shame and Its Sisters: A Silvan Tomkins Reader*. Edited by Irving E. Alexander and Eve Kosofsky Sedgwick. Durham, NC: Duke University Press, 1995.

Toro-Pérez, Germán. "On the Difference Between Artistic Research and Artistic Practice." In *Art and Artistic Research: Music, Visual Art, Design, Literature, Dance*, edited by Corina Caduff, Fiona Siegenthaler, and Tan Wälchli, 30–39. Zurich: Scheidegger & Spiess, 2010.

Tourmaline. "Alternate Endings, Radical Beginnings Video & Artist Statement: Tourmaline." *Visual AIDS* (blog). Accessed June 25, 2021. https://visualaids.org/blog/aerb-tourmaline-statement.

Wade-Gayles, Gloria Jean, ed. *My Soul Is a Witness: African-American Women's Spirituality; A Sourcebook*. Boston: Beacon Press, 1995.

Walker, Alice. *In Search of Our Mother's Gardens: Womanist Prose*. San Diego, CA: Harcourt Brace Jovanovich, 1983.

Walker, Alice. *Possessing the Secret of Joy*. New York: Harcourt Brace Jovanovich, 1992.

Wallace, Michele. *Dark Designs and Visual Culture*. Durham, NC: Duke University Press, 2004.

Wallace-Sanders, Kimberly. *Mammy: A Century of Race, Gender, and Southern Memory*. Ann Arbor: University of Michigan Press, 2008.

Wallace-Sanders, Kimberly, ed. *Skin Deep, Spirit Strong: The Black Female Body in American Culture*. Ann Arbor: University of Michigan Press, 2002.

Walley-Jean, J. Celeste. "Debunking the Myth of the 'Angry Black Woman': An Exploration of Anger in Young African American Women." *Black Women, Gender + Families* 3, no. 2 (2009): 68–86.

Wanzo, Rebecca. *The Suffering Will Not Be Televised: African American Women and Sentimental Political Storytelling*. Albany: State University of New York Press, 2009.

Warren, Calvin. "Calling into Being: Tranifestation, Black Trans, and the Problem of Ontology." *TSQ: Transgender Studies Quarterly* 4, no. 2 (May 2017): 266–74. https://doi.org/10.1215/23289252-3815057.

Washington, Mary Helen. *Invented Lives: Narratives of Black Women, 1860–1960*. New York: Doubleday, 1987.

Weheliye, Alexander G. "Feenin: Posthuman Voices in Contemporary Black Popular Music," *Social Text* 20, no. 2 (June 1, 2002): 21–47. https://doi.org/10.1215/01642472-20-2_71-21.

Weheliye, Alexander G. *Habeas Viscus: Racializing Assemblages, Biopolitics, and Black Feminist Theories of the Human*. Durham, NC: Duke University Press, 2014.

Weheliye, Alexander G. *Phonographies: Grooves in Sonic Afro-Modernity*. Durham, NC: Duke University Press, 2005. https://doi.org/10.2307/j.ctv125jh4w.

Wiley, Dennis. "Spirit in the Dark: Sexuality and Spirituality in the Black Church." In *Walk Together Children: Black and Womanist Theologies, Church, and Theological Education*, edited by Dwight N. Hopkins and Linda E. Thomas, 210–27. Eugene, OR: Cascade Books, 2010.

Williams, Delores S. "Black Women's Surrogacy Experience and the Christian Notion of Redemption." In *After Patriarchy: Feminist Transformations of the World Religions*, edited by Paula M. Cooey, William R. Eakin, and Jay B. McDaniel, 1–14. Maryknoll, NY: Orbis Books, 1991.

Williams, Raymond. "Structures of Feeling." In *Marxism and Literature*. Oxford: Oxford University Press, 1977.

Williams, Rhaisa Kameelah. "Toward a Theorization of Black Maternal Grief as Analytic." *Transforming Anthropology* 24, no. 1 (2016): 17–30. https://doi.org/10.1111/traa.12057.

Williamson, Terrion L. *Scandalize My Name: Black Feminist Practice and the Making of Black Social Life*. New York: Fordham University Press, 2016.

Willis, Susan. "Eruptions of Funk: Historicizing Toni Morrison." *African American Review* 50, no. 4 (Winter 2017): 683–91.

Woubshet, Dagmawi. *The Calendar of Loss: Race, Sexuality, and Mourning in the Early Era of AIDS*. Baltimore: Johns Hopkins University Press, 2015.

Wynter, Sylvia. "The Ceremony Found: Towards the Autopoetic Turn/Overturn, Its Autonomy of Human Agency and Extraterritoriality of (Self-)Cognition." In *Black Knowledges/Black Struggles: Essays in Critical Epistemology*, 184–252. Liverpool, Eng.: Liverpool University Press, 2015. http://www.jstor.org/stable/j.ctt1gn6bfp.12.

Wynter, Sylvia. "The Ceremony Must Be Found: After Humanism." *Boundary 2* 12/13 [vol. 12, no. 3 and vol. 13, no. 1] (Spring–Autumn 1984): 19–70. https://doi.org/10.2307/302808.

Wynter, Sylvia. "On How We Mistook the Map for the Territory, and Reimprisoned Ourselves in Our Unbearable Wrongness of Being, of *Désêtre*: Black Studies toward the Human Project." In *I Am Because We Are: Readings in Africana Philosophy*, edited by Fred L. Hord and Jonathan Scott Lee, 267–80. Amherst: University of Massachusetts Press, 2016.

Wynter, Sylvia. "Rethinking 'Aesthetics': Notes towards a Deciphering Practice." In *Ex-Iles: Essays on Caribbean Cinema*, 237–79. Trenton, NJ: Africa World, 1992.

Yarbrough, Marilyn, and Crystal Bennett. "Cassandra and the 'Sistahs': The Peculiar Treatment of African American Women in the Myth of Women as Liars," *Journal of Gender, Race, and Justice* 3 (2000), 625–58.

Young, Alan. *Woke Me Up This Morning: Black Gospel Singers and the Gospel Life*. Jackson: University Press of Mississippi, 1997.

Index

Adodi Muse, 203n45

affective sedulity, 6, 11, 12, 57; anger and, 29; in Clifton, 28

affective turn (and theory), 6–7

Ahmed, Sarah, 133, 187n39

Alexander, M. Jacqui, 10–11, 16, 59, 195n93

Allen, Richard, 164

anger (and angry Black woman trope), 13, 29, 155–76, 205n3

anointing. *See under* singing

Anzaldúa, Gloria, 27, 192n21

apocalypse, 29, 85, 90, 181–82, 194n89, 195n93

Armstrong, Amaryah Shaye, 112, 199n72

àshe, 109–10, 122

atheology, 28, 70–77, 90

Augustine, 83

Aunt Jemima. *See* Black motherhood: mammy figure

Austin, Tiffany, 63

automatic writing, 75–77, 192n26

Avery*Sunshine. *See* Sunshine, Avery*

Bambara, Toni Cade, 30

Baraka, Amiri, 58, 98, 117–18

Barkley-Brown, Elisa, 201n102

Barnett, LaShonda, 164

Barnum, P. T., 167

Barthes, Roland, 19

Bennett, Christina, 160

Bergson, Henri, 6

biblical citations, 70, 79–80, 84, 87, 108, 196n127

Black academic language, 19, 20–21, 26

Black church, 74, 101–2, 104, 107–18

Black English, 9, 10–11, 136, 186n23; African American Vernacular English (AAVE), 162, 206n13; Black American Language (BAL), 162

Black female sexuality, 13–17, 29–30, 91, 106, 146, 152, 158, 181, 186n33; "funky erotixxx" concept, 16, 28, 186n34; "playing with oneself" concept, 201n102; shame and, 135. *See also* sacred sexuality

Black feminist oceanographics, 29, 177–84

Black grief, 12, 27–28, 33–34, 57–67; grievance vs., 61

Black liberation theology. *See under* theology

Black motherhood: autobiographical remarks on, 21–22, 155–56, 159; images and stereotypes of, 12–13, 127–54; mammy figure, 128, 129, 131, 139–47; matriarchy thesis on, 29, 127–28, 130–31, 134, 136; reproductive decisions in, 128, 131; shame and, 16, 28, 129, 131–38, 148, 179; strong Black woman archetype in, 146–47, 157, 160

"blackpain" (Deborah Walker King's concept of), 15

Black queer poetics, 14, 29, 30

Black resistance, 60–61

Black trans individuals, 63

Black women musicians, 18, 110

Black women singers. *See* singing; *and individual singers*

Black women's literacies, 162

Bland, Sandra, 29, 159, 163, 170–75, 208n57

blues genre, 28, 58, 100, 102, 108, 110–11; Baraka on, 117–18; "blues body," 110

Boyer, Horace C., 115

Brand, Dionne, 29, 181, 184

Brawley, Tawana, 160, 206n22

Bridgeforth, Sharon, 27, 188n74

Brockington, Blake, 63

Brooks, Daphne, 18, 96, 97, 98, 107, 137–38

Brooks, Gwendolyn, 98

Brown, Claude, 10

Brown, Jericho, 63

Brown, Kimberly Nichele, 133–34

Brown, Mike, 60

Burrell, Kim, 96, 111–13, 199n74

Bynum, Juanita, 199n70

capitalism, 34, 90, 105, 159

Carby, Hazel, 110

Carroll, Charles, 155, 156

Césaire, Aime, 206n10

223